The Entanglements of Nathaniel Hawthorne

Studies in American Literature and Culture:
Literary Criticism in Perspective

Scott Peeples, Series Editor
(*Charleston, South Carolina*)

About *Literary Criticism in Perspective*

Books in the series *Literary Criticism in Perspective* trace literary scholarship and criticism on major and neglected writers alike, or on a single major work, a group of writers, a literary school or movement. In so doing the authors — authorities on the topic in question who are also well-versed in the principles and history of literary criticism — address a readership consisting of scholars, students of literature at the graduate and undergraduate level, and the general reader. One of the primary purposes of the series is to illuminate the nature of literary criticism itself, to gauge the influence of social and historic currents on aesthetic judgments once thought objective and normative.

The Entanglements of Nathaniel Hawthorne

Haunted Minds and Ambiguous Approaches

Samuel Chase Coale

 CAMDEN HOUSE
Rochester, New York

First published 2011
by Camden House

Camden House is an imprint of Boydell & Brewer Inc.
668 Mt. Hope Avenue, Rochester, NY 14620, USA
www.camden-house.com
and of Boydell & Brewer Limited
PO Box 9, Woodbridge, Suffolk IP12 3DF, UK
www.boydellandbrewer.com

ISBN-13: 978-1-57113-363-2
ISBN-10: 1-57113-363-1

Library of Congress Cataloging-in-Publication Data

Coale, Samuel.
    The entanglements of Nathaniel Hawthorne: haunted minds and
ambiguous approaches / Samuel Chase Coale.
    p. cm. — (Studies in American literature and culture: Literary
    criticism in perspective)
Includes bibliographical references and index.
ISBN-13: 978–1–57113–363–2 (hardcover : acid-free paper)
ISBN-10: 1–57113–363–1 (hardcover : acid-free paper)
    1. Hawthorne, Nathaniel, 1804–1864 — Criticism and
interpretation. I. Title.

PS1888.C57 2011
813'.3—dc22

                                                    2011008210

This publication is printed on acid-free paper.
Printed and bound in Great Britain by
CPI Antony Rowe, Chippenham, Wiltshire

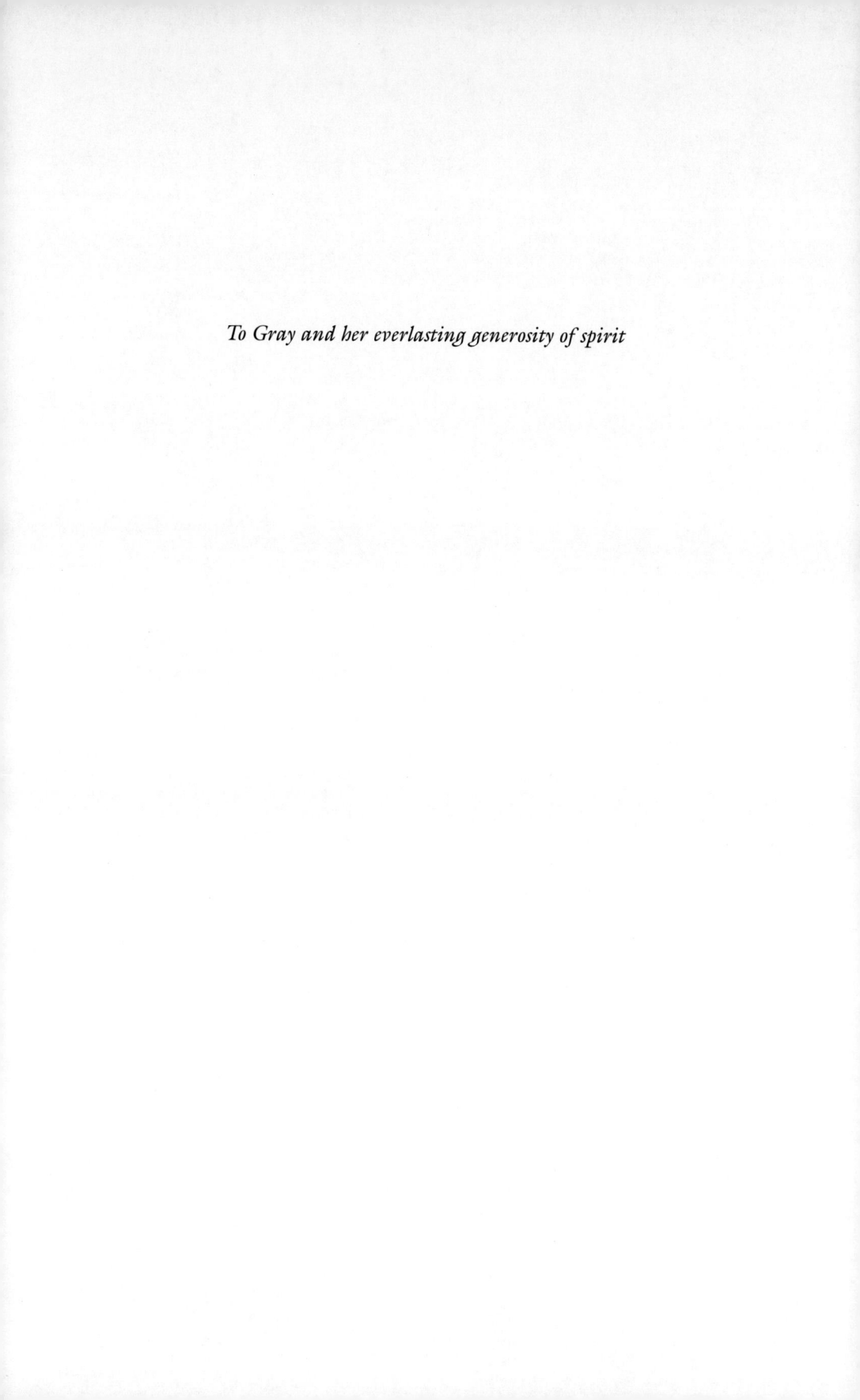

To Gray and her everlasting generosity of spirit

Contents

Acknowledgments

IN A BOOK OF THIS NATURE so many people have been so helpful that it's very difficult to narrow it down and all too easy to miss someone's advice and contribution. But we all must start somewhere. Hawthorne casts a very long shadow on our literature and our culture, and so much criticism has been spawned in that dusky place that I was afraid at times I'd wander into it and get lost forever.

That vast and lengthy shadow I first discovered in high school with Ernest Spieler, at Trinity College with Paul Smith, and re-discovered at Brown University with the sharp-eyed and often unsettling help of my adviser, Hyatt H. Waggoner. Barton St. Armand, my roommate in graduate school, contributed much from the depth of his scholarly knowledge. Articles and books emerged from the shadow over time, including *In Hawthorne's Shadow: American Romance from Melville to Mailer* (1985) and *Mesmerism and Hawthorne: Mediums of American Romance* (1998). It seems to be my curse to tackle Hawthorne almost every decade.

A Mellon Summer Research Stipend in the summer of 2007 allowed me to select three students from Wheaton College to help unearth, vet, and critique every possible article and book that they could find on Hawthorne from the 1830s onward: Tim Johnson '07, Reginald Bates '08, and William Levenson '09. They dug deep into the shelves and archives at the John Hay Library at Brown and the Peabody Essex Museum in Salem. Our spirited lunches and work sessions continued throughout that summer and produced a veritable mountain of material.

To all the many Hawthorne scholars from all over the world, from Magnus Ullen in Sweden to Boulos Sarru in Lebanon, from Julio Jeha in Brazil to Yuji Kato in Japan, and to several American scholars, such as Millicent Bell, Jason Courtmanche, Monika M. Elbert, David Greven, John T. Idol, Buford Jones, Richard Kopley, Richard H. Millington, Thomas Mitchell, Leland S. Person, Arthur Riss, Pierre A. Walker, Brenda Wineapple, and many many others, thank you for suggesting material and approaches, for steering me in directions I might never have discovered on my own. Thank you, too, for all the fine papers and discussions I have enjoyed at several Hawthorne conferences, including Boston in 2000, Salem in 2004, Oxford in 2006, Bowdoin in 2008, and Concord in 2010, and the ones yet to appear in Florence in 2012. A special note to the newly established Hawthorne Drinking Society, which launched discussions far into the night, some of them incredibly incisive and helpful. Thank you Courtmanche, Greven, and Ullen as well as Millington and James Hewitson. I raise a glass often to salute you.

I would like to thank Scott Peeples, who wrote the critically acclaimed *The Afterlife of Edgar Allan Poe,* and who, as editor of the Literary Criticism in Perspective series, commissioned this book, for advising me on how to construct the initial manuscript, overwhelmed as I was by the sheer burden of material. He never ceased to suggest, re-shape, cajole, instruct, and inspire, all with grace and wit — and patience.

I owe enormous thanks to my editor, Jim Walker, a meticulous, compassionate, and incredibly patient individual who waded through pages of notes and chapters, always finding the most direct way for me to say exactly what I thought I had said in the first place — and hadn't. The careful editing belongs to him. Any errors, alas, belong to me.

The last word must go to Gray and our son Sam. He would call from a production site in Los Angeles every once in awhile, sigh deeply, and exclaim, "Did you know that — [pause, a hush] — Hawthorne has died?" This became a running family joke, and there were times when we thought he never had. I was hoping to finish this book before Gray's death from cancer, but she was there every step of the way, at times more hopeful than I, always supportive as a critical sounding board and cheerleader. I miss her terribly and could not have come through without her. It's her shadow that will continue to light my spirit and my hopes.

S. C. C.
Providence, Rhode Island
March 2011

Abbreviations

Bosco/Murphy Ronald A. Bosco and Jillmarie Murphy, eds. *Hawthorne in His Own Time.* Iowa City: University of Iowa Press, 2007.

Crowley J. Donald Crowley, ed. *Hawthorne: The Critical Heritage.* London: Routledge and Kegan Paul, 1970.

Idol/Jones John T. Idol and Buford Jones, Jr., eds. *Nathaniel Hawthorne: The Contemporary Reviews.* Cambridge: Cambridge University Press, 1994.

CE *The Centenary Editions of the Works of Nathaniel Hawthorne,* ed. William Chavat et al., 23 volumes. Columbus: Ohio State University Press, 1962–97.

Introduction: Entanglements

WHEN THE OPPORTUNITY AROSE to write about Hawthorne once again, how could I refuse? I had critically wrestled with his work in *In Hawthorne's Shadow: American Romance from Melville to Mailer* (1985) and *Mesmerism and Hawthorne: Mediums of American Romance* (1998). While the first book traces the thematic influences and images of Hawthorne's Manichean vision on the many writers who came after him, and the second explores the effects of mesmerism on his fiction, not just thematically but structurally in terms of how he described the American romance, in this book I have produced a critical overview of critics who have written about Hawthorne and his work from as far back as the 1830s up to 2010.

This new book is meant to be a survey of Hawthorne's critics, an introduction to their work, which offers many perspectives, and will explore their strengths and weaknesses, providing an overall view of the development of Hawthorne criticism over the span of more than a hundred and fifty years. The book, therefore, attempts not to produce some new perspective on Hawthorne's fiction, although I will suggest a new way of regarding it, but to investigate and scrutinize the field of Hawthorne studies from the mid-nineteenth-century up to the present day. Its organization depends both on chronological and topical points of view, with individual chapters that deal with nineteenth-century, twentieth-century and early-twenty-first century biographies and criticism as well as the developing critical assumptions that underlie them.

The first chapter, "The Legacy of *The Scarlet Letter*: Hawthorne in Contemporary Culture," examines the letter as icon and how it operates in popular culture in newspaper articles, cartoons, and contemporary editorials; how high schools — where students have usually been introduced to the novel — have generally presented the book; and how theatre, film, and opera have appropriated Hester Prynne's story to show or re-tell it from various points of view. I will also mention several contemporary authors who have acknowledged the influence that *The Scarlet Letter* has had on their own work.

Chapters 2 through 7 are chronological and move from Hawthorne's popular nineteenth-century image as a morbid genius — I hope to convey how that image took hold in terms of its Romantic roots and Hawthorne's own prefaces and asides — through the biographical and critical veils of both the nineteenth century and the beginning of the twenty-first, and what critical assumptions have underscored such approaches as exhibited by the New Criticism, psychoanalytical criticism, deconstruction, feminism, and the New Historicism. Chapter 6 deals specifically with the strategies that Hawthorne uses in creating his romances and makes the critical case that he knew exactly what he was up to every step of the way.

There are two concepts of entanglement that are fundamental to the focus of this book, the first one more theoretical and complex than the second. As defined by the physicist, Louisa Gilder, in her description of quantum theory, entanglement is "a condition of two or more bits of matter or light behaving, though separately, as if intimately connected" (337). The second involves the more conventional idea of being "caught up in things" as are Hawthorne's critics with the man and his work.

Quantum theory suggests that everything in the subatomic world participates in a complex "web of interactions" (Oerter 90) in which particles, once they have encountered one another, become entangled with one another. Once this occurs, "the entanglement persists no matter how far these entities separate . . . in doing so, they lose their separate existence" (Gilder 3). They become forever bound to one another, however far apart they remain in terms of space and distance. They remain "intimately connected" forever and are no longer separate. If something should happen to one, the other will be affected in just the same manner. They remain, as Gilder suggests, no longer "*locally causal*, not *fully separable*, or even not *independently real*" (9). They defy our usual laws of cause and effect and become so intertwined with one another that they can no longer act separately, individually or independently.

In terms of Hawthorne's fiction, he may begin several of his short stories and romances as allegories — each character represents a particular point of view or condition that eventually clashes with its opposite — but as they develop, the allegorical "separation," the dualistic structure of his vision, becomes more intertwined, interpenetrating and "intimately connected." In fact the outlines of an initial rigid dualism or polarity — Dimmesdale vs. Chillingworth, Coverdale vs. Hollingsworth, Hester vs. Puritan Boston, female vs. male, etc. — begin to merge and become entangled with one another, so that the result is far more complicated and labyrinthine than the original allegorical signs at first glance would suggest. Each helps create the other. Each proves to be far more complicitous in the actions of the text than may at first appear. Each is entangled with the other, unable in many cases to exist without the other, each inhabited and "infected" by the other. No ultimate harmony is ever reached but rather a kind of negative dialectic, an unfathomable experience and sense of mystery that lies beyond human understanding and comprehension and remains disturbingly intact.

For example at first it may appear that Hester Prynne is purely the victim of the patriarchal Calvinist society in which she is confined, but as the romance develops, we find that many Calvinist-influenced ideas and concepts have infiltrated her own personality as well. Dimmesdale readily appears to be the victim of Chillingworth's psychological probings and, perhaps, chemical poisons, but their relationship is one in which each is so entangled with the other, so "intimately connected," that they almost cannot exist separately. Allegory becomes complicity, antagonists and adversaries become mutual supporters of one another, polarities produce or become part of a dynamic dialectic, each necessarily entangled with the other. As Hawthorne writes about the emotions, love and horror, in "Rappaccini's Daughter":

> It was not love, although [Beatrice's] rich beauty was a madness to [Giovanni]; nor horror, even while he fancied her spirit to be imbued with the same baneful essence that seemed to pervade her physical frame; but a wild offspring of both love and horror that had each parent in it, and burned and shivered like the other. [986–87]

Love and horror are here entangled, "intimately connected." As Hawthorne goes on to suggest, "Blessed are all simple emotions, be they dark or bright! It is the lurid intermixture of the two that produces the illuminating blaze of the infernal regions." Here we see him "re-allegorizing" the original opposed emotions: their "intermixture" is both "lurid" and "infernal." The resulting entanglement, however allegorized at this particular moment — the allegory does not so much sustain itself as it displaces and often reverses itself from moment to moment — remains mysteriously complex, intriguing, frightening and unsettling.

Hawthorne's characters and often the narrator find themselves confused and mesmerized. As Hawthorne goes on to describe the situation in "Rappaccini's Daughter," "Whatever had looked ugly, was now beautiful; or, if incapable of such a change, it stole away and hid itself among those shapeless half-ideas, which throng the dim region beyond the daylight of our perfect consciousness" [994]. Here is where we enter into the entangled vision of Hawthorne's American romance.

The second and more common concept of entanglement, of things tangled up together, is a way to address Hawthorne's critics' involvement with the author and his fiction. Certain critical positions become sacrosanct and solidified over time, and each critic must wrestle with past images and ideas. For instance the image of Hawthorne in the nineteenth century as a "morbid genius" was so entrenched — morbid because of his dark themes, genius because of the Augustan elegance of his style and Americans' need to celebrate their own writer-genius of fiction at a time when British fiction dominated the literary marketplace — that few managed to escape from its persistent shadow. The Freudian psychological point of view in the twentieth century attempted to explain where that "morbidity" came from as critics, exploring Hawthorne's literary strategies as a romancer, tried to overcome its pervasive power by focusing on his structural and stylistic choices. The psychological "props" of New Critical myths and patterns, while not entirely undermined, gave way to the feminist, New Historicist and cultural-studies perspectives that have taken up Hawthorne's fiction since the 1960s. Each critic necessarily becomes involved with previous criticism and in attempting to refine or reject it may find herself or himself entangled in a "lurid intermixture" of past assumptions and present questionings of them.

Each biography and critical approach, I hope to show, depends upon what has preceded it, either in terms of consciously blazing a new critical trail and trying to disregard that past or building upon it and looking at it from different directions in terms of political possibilities and cultural values. This "lesser" entanglement underscores this book, even though I have tried to assess each critical perspective as clearly and directly as I can in its own terms, while at the same time pointing out its limitations and omissions.

The quantum idea of entanglement provides an effective framework and approach to Hawthorne's fiction in terms of Hawthorne's own view of his subject matter and the structure of his stories and romances. It also provides a framework for the way in which critics attempt to define and analyze them. This is an ongoing, "entangled" process, and this book cannot rest on any definitive approach since these approaches continue to form, re-group, splinter and divide. The "lurid intermixture" of characters and their actions lies at the heart of Hawthorne's vision and represents the elusive, shadowy core of his romances that critics will continue to shed light upon as best they can. As Hawthorne's son Julian wrote in 1884, "The true revelation will be made only to those who have in themselves somewhat of the same mystery they seek to fathom" (375).

1: The Legacy of *The Scarlet Letter:* Hawthorne in Contemporary Culture

O N JUNE 22, 2006, AN ILLUSTRATED INVITATION arrived via email. It showed two women, one with a high starched collar and white bow, the other in the foreground, a nun, her face shrouded in a nun's habit in all of its whiteness with the black wimple curtaining it. The invitation read:

> Public Ceremony
> 2:30 PM on June 26, 2006
>   at
> The Old Manse
> 269 Monument Street
> Concord, Massachusetts
> Followed by
> Reception & Refreshments
> Graveside Visitation after 3 PM
> Sleepy Hollow Cemetery — Author's Ridge
> Hosted by
> The Dominican Sisters of Hawthorne
> And
> The Help of the Good People of Concord

Preceding pages offered oval portraits of Sophia, Una, and Nathaniel Hawthorne to honor the memory of Sophia, Hawthorne's wife, and Una, their older daughter, "on the historic day of their re-interment alongside Nathaniel Hawthorne." Their original graves in Kensal Green Cemetery, the oldest English cemetery still in operation in London, had fallen into disrepair over the years when a hawthorn tree, oddly enough, had fallen and damaged the original cemetery markers, knocking over Una's headstone. Sophia had been buried there in 1871 at sixty-two. Una had followed in 1877 at thirty-three. The Dominican nuns, a Catholic order established by Rose Hawthorne, Sophia and Nathaniel's younger daughter, to care for dying cancer patients in what was one of the first hospices of its kind, had taken care of the graves and had tried for many years to raise funds to move the remains to Concord. In 2003, Rose Hawthorne had been proposed as a candidate for sainthood. In December 2000, the Sisters had celebrated the centennial of the founding of their order with a Mass of Thanksgiving at St. Patrick's Cathedral in New York City.

For Hawthorne scholars and readers, of course, the occasion prompted much interest, but the surprise was the interest of the national press. In the *Boston Globe* on June 1, Raja Mishra and Sally Heaney reported in an article entitled "Hawthornes to be Reunited: Wife's Remains to be Returned from UK" that a great-granddaughter, Joan Deming Ensor, ninety-three, from Redding, Connecticut, had gladly given her consent for the reinterment. She told reporters from National Public Radio that family lore always insisted upon the "eternal love" affair between Sophia and Hawthorne (NPR 27 June 2006). At the ceremony there were readings from Nathaniel's, Sophia's, and Una's journals. Brenda Wineapple, whose biography of Hawthorne appeared in 2003, spoke of "a terrific marriage . . . [they were] well-suited to each other" and described Hawthorne's letters to Sophia as passionate. Robert Derry, the park ranger who oversees the Hawthorne house, "The Wayside," in Concord, was quoted in the *Globe* article as saying, "At least on a romantic and philosophical level, it is nice that they were in love right to the end," even though Derry described Hawthorne as a writer of "searing Puritan-influenced moralism and melancholy tales" (2).

On June 26 *USA Today* picked up the story in Ken Maguire's "Hawthorne Joined by Kin in Final Plot." Maguire described about forty descendents gathered at the gravesite after a modern casket containing the remains was carried on a horse-drawn 1860 wooden hearse, which traced the original path of Hawthorne's funeral procession. The hearse was believed to be the same one that had carried Hawthorne's body to the cemetery in 1864, the *New York Times* reported on June 27. Relatives followed behind on foot to the private family ceremony and placed flowers and objects in the open coffin before it was resealed. Maguire quoted Philip McFarland, author of *Hawthorne in Concord*, as commenting, "It was a great love story."

"Historic Literary Couple Are Reunited After 142-Year Separation," proclaimed the headline of the *Times* in its article by Katie Zezima, in which Imogen Howe, sixty-seven, a great-great-granddaughter of the Hawthornes, was quoted as stating, "It's very emotional." The Sisters, reported Zezima, had managed to raise $15,000.00 to transport and bury the remains. National Public Radio's "All Things Considered" also reported on the event on June 27 in a piece by Nancy Cohen. Alison Hawthorne Deming, fifty-nine, a professor of creative writing at the University of Arizona, another great-great-granddaughter, described the whole affair as healing "a sad disconnect." According to NPR, Deming addressed a crowd of three hundred that included seven generations above and below the ground. Megan Marshall, author of *The Peabody Sisters* (2005), mentioned the fact that Sophia had exhibited her paintings at the Boston Athenaeum, a rare accomplishment for a woman in her day.

And finally in an article in *The Catholic News Service* on June 29, "Hawthorne Dominicans Bring Remains of Founder's Mother, Sister Home" by Claudia McDonnell, Mother Anne Marie Holden, the superior general of the motherhouse and headquarters at Rosary Hill, explained, "It was the right thing to do."[1]

Why all the fuss? Why all the coverage? It speaks, of course, to Hawthorne's iconic status in American literature and culture. Think of how many people have suffered through *The Scarlet Letter* in high school (though I loved its darkness and sense of fate, akin to *Macbeth* in its inevitable outcome). Think of how many have trooped through the House of the Seven Gables in Salem, bewitched by its hidden staircase. In popular culture Hawthorne remains an icon, painted in dark colors as dark as those with which he painted the puritans, for the most part, in his fiction.

The Scarlet Letter as Cultural Icon

The scarlet letter as a symbol of shaming, punishment, and scorn has virtually always been a popular icon in our culture since it appeared as the title of Hawthorne's first romance in 1850. Even those who have never read the book know what that red letter suggests. Leland S. Person, in his traveling slide show of Hawthorne's infamous icon, showed the February 22, 1999, issue of *Time* magazine with its "framed portrait of President Bill Clinton with a scarlet letter on his chest. A year earlier, Monica Lewinski's attorney, William Ginsburg had complained, 'How mortifying all this is . . . Monica has been branded with a scarlet letter, an A for adultery. Now will she be branded with an I for indictment, a C for conviction and a J for jail'"? Person cited other instances: "SCARLET LETTERS," exclaimed a headline in the *St. Louis Post-Dispatch* on February 8, 1997, in order to pique interest in a story about an Illinois farmer whose property was posted with a sign identifying him as a "violent felon" (30).

The infamous letter also surfaces during political campaigns. Why were "Giuliani and other Republican worthies not being forced by their devout Christian supporters to wear Hester Prynne's scarlet 'A,'" asked David Rosen in his article on the political website *Counterpunch*, "The Scarlet Hypocrites: Republicans, Christians and the All-American Politics of Adultery" on November 17, 2007. Rosen went on to discuss various adulterers such as John McCain, Tom DeLay, Newt Gingrich, Andrew Jackson, Grover Cleveland, and Warren G. Harding, concluding that "Adultery is an all-American sin." In 2004 twenty-four states, as Rosen explained, still outlawed adultery, ten have anti-fornication statutes prohibiting sex before marriage, and in Massachusetts, Michigan, Oklahoma, and Idaho, it is still listed as a felony.

Sex and the scarlet letter complement one another in other ways as well. According to Katharine Mieszkowski in *Broadsheet* on November 6, 2006, a Delaware judge "ordered gardener Russell Teeter, 69, to wear a T-shirt to work that says 'I am a registered sex offender.'" He had exposed himself to a ten-year-old girl. The attorney general hoped jail and the T-shirt would "teach him to keep his zipper up," but Teeter's defense attorney compared the shirt "to a 'modern-day scarlet letter' . . . a form of public shaming." Added Mieszkowski, "A grown man exposing himself to a child is not really comparable to Nathaniel Hawthorne's heroine's crime of adultery."

Dana Canedy reported in the *New York Times* on May 31, 2003, that Governor Jeb Bush of Florida had repealed "the state's 'Scarlet Letter' law [which had taken effect in October, 2001] that required single women planning to put their infants up for adoption to first publish their sexual histories in a newspaper if they did not know the identity of the father." The law required women to disclose "their names, ages, height, hair and eye color, race and weight. . . ." They also were required "to provide details of the dates and places of sexual encounters that might have produced the child. Women were required to run the advertisements once a week for a month in the community where the child may have been conceived." Instead the new law established a "'father registry' through which men who believe they may be the fathers must provide the name, address and physical description of the mother and the date and place where conception took place to protect their parental rights." Howard Simon, executive director of the American Civil Liberties Union of Florida, commented, "Only a male-dominated legislature could possibly pass a law that facilitates adoptions by requiring public humiliation of women" (web). Hester Prynne may have gotten off easy.

The letter is never far away from popular culture. On June 16, 2007, *The New York Times* published an editorial, "The Scarlet Letter," castigating Senator Lindsey Graham of South Carolina for having been so "burned by the uproar of the hard right" over the issue of immigration that he "feels the need to act tough, lest he be saddled . . . with the scarlet letter A, for amnesty." In "Branded With the 'Scarlet U': From Manhattan Commutes to Morning School Drop-off Rituals: It's Not Easy Adjusting to Unemployed Life," which appeared in *Newsweek* on March 3, 2009 (*My Turn*, 22), John Blomfield describes his suffering as a result of losing his job, worrying about bills and people's perceptions of him: "To make things simpler and clearer for everyone, I'm thinking of stitching a big scarlet 'U' [for "Unemployed"] on my clothing." In Richard M. Magee's article, "Food Puritanism and Food Pornography: The Gourmet Semiotics of Martha and Nigella," in *Americana* in the fall of 2007,

Martha Stewart's ankle bracelet, which she had to wear after being con-
victed of insider trading, is referred to as the scarlet letter "unfettered
from its legal meanings," and Stewart "evokes all of the images of the
stern, critical, fault-finding Puritan of the popular imagination" (3).
Magee continues: "In Stewart's attempts to maintain appearances despite
turmoil we can perhaps see echoes of Hawthorne's puritans: Reverend
Dimmesdale's outwardly placid and holy state contrasting with his inner
recognition of sin" (4).

A cartoon by P. Byrnes in *The New Yorker* of June 8 and 15, 2009,
shows a Puritan mother and her baby daughter strolling through a
New England village with a church and thatched-roof hut in the background, a cooking pot hung over an open fire. The mother wears a fancy
letter "A." Her daughter wears a smaller "B." And after the scandal
broke, in late 2009, about late-night television host David Letterman's
sleeping with members of his staff, he was referred to as "The Scarlet
Letterman."

Why does the scarlet letter appear so often in popular culture? One of
the reasons may be that since everyone has had to read Hawthorne's novel
in high school, they are very familiar with the emblem, which strikes them
as cruel and unusual punishment in the case of Hester Prynne. At the same
time, one who suggests without sarcasm that someone deserves the scarlet
"A" is usually seen as puritanical and overzealous. The letter epitomizes
not only punishment but punishment above and beyond an acceptable
level, a public shaming that in contemporary times is seen as revealing
more about the accuser than it does about the accused.

The Scarlet Letter in High School

In a 1999 article in *The Journal of Popular Culture,* Bruce Daniels pointed
out that American literary specialists in 1997 ranked Hawthorne as the first
among American writers and that twenty-nine editions of *The Scarlet Letter*
were still in print. *The Scarlet Letter* remains, therefore, a perennial, widely
used text in high school, and it is taught across the board in public, private,
and Catholic schools as part of the foundation of students' literary experience. Most Americans, therefore, first come in contact with Hawthorne
because of this book and several of his short stories that are taught in
American literature courses.

On the web and elsewhere one can find several examples, though by
no means comprehensive, of how *The Scarlet Letter* is actually being taught
in high schools and how and why so many students today dislike it, as
indicated below. These selective examples reveal some of the problems
with — and challenges posed by — Hawthorne's "blasted allegories" on
the high-school level.

First of all we should remember what most scholarly critics have recognized over the years: Hawthorne's fiction destabilizes and deconstructs the polarized visions of its characters, thus undermining their allegorical vision of the world, however much Hawthorne himself often employs polarization and allegory in constructing his works. Many high-school teachers seem to be re-allegorizing Hawthorne's work, setting up "units" of instruction in terms of polarized issues and simplistic symbols, the very antithesis of Hawthorne's accomplishment. Such an allegorical approach necessarily flattens the fiction in the very manner in which many of Hawthorne's male characters approach the world and the "other." The men in his fiction such as Chillingworth, Hollingsworth, Young Goodman Brown, Giovanni Guasconti, and others tend to view the world in polarized terms — good and evil, love and hate, male and female, beautiful and monstrous — a vision that Hawthorne subtly undermines and deconstructs within his narratives, thereby pointing out the danger of such a dualistic and rigidly either/or point of view. His fiction exposes the entangled nature of all of these characters: their repressed self-doubts, their ambiguous self-justifications, the psychological compulsions and obsessions that underlie their stark and severe judgments of others. Entanglement conceived of and mistaken for blunt allegory distorts Hawthorne's intended ambiguity, and his questioning of black and white distinctions is lost.

There seem to be several prevalent approaches to teaching *The Scarlet Letter* at the high-school level. Many teachers have worked to link Hester's "outcast" state to present-day adolescent angst and anxiety. In this manner the teacher continues to uphold and express a polarized and dualistic vision, setting the outcast over and against the general conventions of society and its members, a duality that Hawthorne often complicates and undermines. Teachers have also taken a "cultural studies" approach in their discussion of class, gender, race, and social status in relation to Hawthorne's work. The allegorical approach, mentioned above, is deeply ingrained in all of these approaches, and as I have suggested, ultimately misrepresents the dramatic process of Hawthorne's fiction.

In my unscientific web survey, many high-school students found the style tedious and, for that reason, the book boring, yet many reacted to it more deeply. For example, Tracey, raised in a very "Puritanical . . . legalistic . . . two-dimensional [way]," was stunned by the book: "It changed me . . . I really think that after reading it, I began to separate, mentally, from some of the views held in my family. Still maintaining faith, but making room in my heart for people to be human, flawed. That was so HUGE for me." Once out of school, far beyond the classroom, those who read the book again loved it. Dona expressed sentiments similar to those of several others: "Even better than when I loved it as a sophomore in high school. Hawthorne serves up shame, hypocrisy and redemption with stylistic prose and pithy psychological insights."

Reader and blogger Sheila O'Malley of *The Sheila Variations* weblog objected to the "hi-falutin' language . . . the bleakness, the foreignness of that world, [but the teacher] helped us through it. He helped us crack the code of symbols, and that's all I really remember of the book." While the idea of cracking codes may be necessary to help students grapple with a strange text, it reminds me of the old way of killing a book entirely by dismissing much of it as a shell inside which we must search for the peanut in order to extract it. The shell becomes dispensable, an obstacle to the "meaning" of or theme within the text. Rather than surveying the drama of it, the process of going through it, we scrape out the insides, allegorically tag every "symbol" — another way of killing them — and delight in a tidy pile of signs and statements. O'Malley continues: "In 2001, I launched my 'let's go back and read all those books from high school' project. I started with *The Scarlet Letter*. And, naturally, was amazed by the book." For her the episodes and descriptions, "all of that combine [*sic*] to create an IMAGE of a world. . . . We are not meant to be IN that world . . . we look at it, in wonder and compassion . . . but we are meant to maintain our distance from it."

Adaptations of *The Scarlet Letter* in Popular Culture

The Scarlet Letter continues to be dramatized and staged in popular culture. At least three composers have recently created operas based on the novel. The one I saw, "*The Scarlet Letter*: A New Rock Musical" by Mark Governor, premiered in Boston in June, 2000. Prepared to dislike it, I was instead delighted by the swinging chorus of witches, the often wrenching arias, and the overall energy of the piece, enthusiastically presented. The singers included a feisty, likeable Faye DeBonis as Hester, a snarling, villainous Jason Simon as Chillingworth, and a doomed, self-absorbed, handsome Gene Dante as Dimmesdale, all members of the Fiddlehead Theatre Company. The opera's broad strokes still captured the emotional fervor of Hawthorne's romance, as if shedding its Augustan carapace.

In the Donald W. Reynolds Theater at the University of Central Arkansas in 2008, another opera based on Hawthorne's novel premiered, this one by Lori Laitman. The poet David Mason wrote the libretto: "*The Scarlet Letter* is better suited to opera than any novel I have ever read," Mason offered. "Its dramatic structure has particular clarity and resonance . . . an exciting story about . . . the tragic possibility of America . . . my primary goal has been to use spare, often lyrical verse as a way of revealing character and heightening drama . . ."

The Academy of Vocal Arts in Philadelphia presented another operatic version in November 2010. Philadelphia composer Margaret Garwood created the neo-romantic score, which was sung in English with English supertitles. The production, conducted by Richard A. Raub, directed by Dorothy Danner, and featuring the AVA Opera Orchestra, took place at the Merriam Theater on South Broad Street.

Several film directors have also tackled *The Scarlet Letter*, which accounts for the dozen film versions within the last hundred years. Early versions included two silent films, one in 1917 that featured Colleen Moore and another in 1926 with Lillian Gish. Having seen scenes from the latter, I remember the sweet, girlish Gish running to hide behind bushes with her underwear splayed and hung out to dry on one of the bushes. The film opens with a canary in a cage, an obvious visual metaphor for Hester's incarceration in the cruel Calvinist compound. In 1934 Colleen Moore again played Hester in a sound version of the tale. Franklin J. Schaffner directed a Studio One version on television in 1951, as well as a televised version of *The Marble Faun* in 1950.

Probably the most famous and most successful filmed production remains the rather studied and slow-moving PBS mini-series from 1979 that starred Meg Foster with her opalescent eyes as Hester, John Heard as Dimmesdale, and Kevin Conway as Chillingworth. It took Rick Hauser four and a half years to conceive and produce the adaptation for WGBH in Boston. It won an Emmy for videotaping, but, however authentic looking, meticulously staged, and authentically costumed, it moves more like a pageant, as if the aura of a "classic" demanded that it be treated with reverence like some sacred text. It is still available on tape and DVD and has been shown in hundreds of classrooms. The production was faithful to the book, if somber and stately in its execution.

Only the Lillian Gish film in 1926 was a success at the box office, whereas the Demi Moore version, which cost over $60 million to make, lost $50 million and was spectacularly savaged by critics. While borrowing the images of caged birds from the 1926 version, Moore's film included an infamous nude bathing scene and concluded with Hester and Dimmesdale's rescue by Indians. One of the responses to the film can be seen in a *New Yorker* cartoon of Moore standing next to Captain Ahab with a huge white whale strung up next to him. The caption reads: "The Demi Moore version of *Moby-Dick*." Caryn James's *New York Times* review, "Passion, Nudity, Puritans and, Oh, Yes, That Scarlet Letter 'A,'" from October 13, 1995, begins by describing Hester and Dimmesdale's (Gary Oldman's) passionate kiss, from which they break away: "'Nay! We could be hanged for this,' she realizes. Hanging, in this case, is no deterrent. Hester and Arthur . . . as if they were in 'The Red Shoe Diaries' instead of 'The Scarlet Letter,' are soon rolling around the barn in a pile of grain."

The review gets deliciously worse. Shouldn't the film have been called "Puritans in Lust" and labeled a comedy? "There is plenty of room for interpretation in Hawthorne's novel, but a movie version should never be this goofy [or] so trashy and nonsensical." Hester first discovers a naked man swimming in the woods and later realizes that he is the minister. A new character has been added, "a loyal black servant referred to as 'poor, mute Mituba'" (a reference to Tituba, the servant involved in the Salem witch trials, whose appearance provides a greater role for people of color, whom Hawthorne treated marginally, if at all, in the romance), and while Hester and Dimmesdale are fornicating in the grain — "Her hand clutches the grain! She's in ecstasy!" — we see Mituba in Hester's bathing tub "and a little red bird that fills the screen often, for no apparent reason." The filmmakers "throw in witch hunts and Indian attacks" to relieve the dullness that follows — Hester "makes Arthur promise to shut up (no point in both of them suffering)" — and loony Chillingworth (Robert Duvall) "who has been set free by his Indian captors because he has become too weird for them, [is seen] dancing around the campfire with a dead deer on his head." The movie was rated R with the following promotional description: "When intimacy is forbidden and passion is sin, love is the most defiant crime of all."

The *Washington Post's* Desson Howe began to worry when the opening credits announced that the film had been "freely adapted" from Hawthorne's romance; that it had been "revisited . . . to speak directly to our own age . . . to warm up this humorless town, Joan Plowright is rolled out as the colony's token liberal, a sort of wisecracking Good Witch of the North, who chortles at hypocrisy." Director Roland Jaffe suggests that Hawthorne would have included a more upbeat ending — the rescue by Indians of Demi and Gary — "if he wasn't so repressed." Howe responds: "Picture a reincarnated, aghast Hawthorne, standing poolside and listening to a semi-naked producer telling him, 'Nate — can I call ya Nate? — this is a fun culture now. Work with me on this!' Then picture yourself trudging out of the theater with a letter 'D' (for 'disappointment') firmly pinned to your chest."

While some feminist scholars, such as Jamie Barlowe, supported the film's opening up of the story through its representation of characters who are excluded and marginalized in Hawthorne's work — Native Americans, African Americans — others like Bruce Daniels and Sacvan Bercovitch exposed some of the real problems with and assumptions behind the film.

Daniels delights in the details of "baying hounds, Nazi-like militia, native tom-toms, Laura Ashley clothes, sidesaddles from Victoria England, nineteenth-century buggies, and wonderful scenes of two lovers galloping over the countryside." The film's greatest fault, according to him, is that it removes all ambiguities from Hawthorne's text, creates characters who are all too obviously good or bad, and "it pillories an entire people and feeds a long-standing animosity toward Puritanism that scholars have been trying to overcome for most of the twentieth century." Hawthorne respected the complexities of such a society and did not conjure them up as some simplistic "external fascist power." It is the savage, one-dimensional, not to mention stereotypical, image of these Calvinist colonists that Daniels objected to most.

Bercovitch in "The Scarlet Letter: A Twice-Told Tale" offered a similar argument, attacking the film's simplistic myth of the individual versus the oppressive society that imprisons all individuals and kills all natural desire. Such a myth undercuts Hawthorne's more tragic vision of the entanglement of self and society; neither is free from the other; each is a cultural artifact in relation to the other: "Liberation for Hawthorne is a reciprocal process rather than a flight from bondage." Society carries with it duties and obligations within which individuals are necessarily enmeshed in complicated issues, which the film evades entirely: "The trouble with Hawthorne's lovers is that their love had a consecration *of its own*, whereas, in his view, we all love, for better and worse, in a relational sphere, the realm of non-transcendence called history and community." All the characters are hypocrites, concealing their sins, "and hypocrisy is above all a social act."

The simple extremes in the film — sexual liberation versus repressive society — avoid Hawthorne's complexities entirely: "There's really no serious issue between Demi Moore and the world. She simply has to choose what's right for herself," Bercovitch explained. Hawthorne, on the other hand, grapples with the interpenetration of self and society, "a cultural aesthetic" that must be "designed to curb and rechannel the high individualism and simmering violence of antebellum America." Moore's Hester recognizes no self-restraint, whereas for Bercovitch Hester is aware of her own culpability and appreciates the need for such constraints. The battle between self-reliance and social progress, between personal rights and civic duties, constitutes a very American phenomenon, all of which remain "entwined, interlocked . . . The virtues of process that Hawthorne celebrates require the sacrifice of individuality" (13), and therein lies American possibility and tragedy.

A satirical film that gets its central conceit from *The Scarlet Letter, Easy A,* opened on September 17, 2010, to generally good reviews (as if Demi Moore's wasn't satirical!). Emma Stone, as Olive Penderghast, who is studying *The Scarlet Letter* in her high-school English class, makes a pretense of having sex with boys, beginning with a gay friend, to enhance their sexual reputations. "At the height of her notoriety she sews a capital A (A for what? — it's not clear) on her clothes and parades around the school in skimpy, suggestive outfits," wrote Stephen Holden in his review in the *New York Times.* She's gleefully assaulted by "a circle of pious Jesus freaks who have vowed celibacy and picket for Olive's expulsion." In the *Providence Journal* on the same day, Michael Janusonis titled his review "*The Scarlet Letter* Goes to High School," where, of course, it's always been for years, and explains, "Author Nathaniel Hawthorne's poor Hester Prynne, condemned by her Puritan neighbors and sent to jail in 1640s Boston for an adulterous affair that left her with an out-of-wedlock child, seems an unlikely inspiration for a fizzy social comedy set at a sunny California high school. And yet it's carried off wonderfully in the smart, funny 'Easy A.'" Janusonis acknowledges in his headline that the film is "A Sly Send-Up of *Scarlet Letter*" and adds drily, "What, one wonders, would Hester Prynne have done?"

In 1994 a staged version of Phyllis Nagy's adaptation of *The Scarlet Letter* was trashed by a critic in Denver in a review entitled "Dead Letter," in which he found it "utterly banal . . . inert . . . [doomed by] the vagaries of twentieth-century psychological doublespeak . . . the moral of which has been surgically removed . . . Why anyone would want to update Hawthorne is a mystery to me — and one I don't care to solve." When I saw a fine production of Nagy's adaptation, directed by Judith Swift, at the Gamm Theatre in Pawtucket, Rhode Island, in May 2009, it had its problems but was also intriguing and at times emotionally involving. Nagy creates Pearl as the narrator-observer (Casey Seymour Kim in Swift's production) who comments on the other characters, though they, of course, are unable to hear her, at times reverting to childish uncertainty, at others calling out hurtful truths that skewer the adults around her. The device worked well, playing on Pearl's demonic, giddy, and perceptive ways of regarding the strange world she finds herself in. Jeanine Kane's Hester holds her head high, wounded but self-possessed, angular and forceful in terms of her focused presence and smoldering anger or disappointment. Steve Kidd's Dimmesdale had been directed to appear wounded and in pain from the beginning, as he lurched and moaned and grabbed at his heart, bordering on over-the-top mania. He was so agonized that he made Alan K. Hawridge's disheveled and crafty Chillingworth almost delightfully human by comparison, sipping liquor, speaking lasciviously of lust and its pleas- ures, stalking his prey. In one scene he forces Hester to grovel, to crawl to him and lick his boots, the most emotionally gripping encounter of the entire production.

Swift, a theater scholar and director at the University of Rhode Island, kept things moving, but it was hard to overcome the puritan- inspired posturings of Hester and Dimmesdale, ever aware of their dam- aged roles in the Calvinist cosmos. Dimmesdale kept complaining of his feminine traits and his dislike of children as if constantly confessing to some unseen god and seemed too weak and weary to command much attention at all. He was sufficiently dim and sexless, but when Hester commanded him, after removing her cap in the forest, to "Take me," should he really have been so lame as to respond, "Where?" Making Mistress Hibbins a well-ripened strumpet-like creature was a master- stroke, dramatizing the Calvinist obsession with sin and/as sexuality, but the huge red "A" on Dimmesdale's torso at his death on the scaffold reduced Hawthorne's entanglements to a single choice and the sour possibility of Dimmesdale's earnest redemption.

In an interview with Bryan Rourke in the *Providence Journal* before the premiere, Swift explained what for her was the play's essence: "What's fascinating in the play is the role of passion and the way in which we repress it. In our society that is very much something we do all the time." In the production Hester wears her badge of dishonor honorably, recognizing that it is her duty to do so, thus complicating the passion that got her in trouble to begin with, but in the interview Swift noted, "We're still obsessed with sex scandals . . . Human nature is such that it doesn't always match up with the rules."

Literary Influences of Hawthorne's Fiction

In *Newsweek* in 2007 author Gay Talese listed *The Scarlet Letter* as the first among his five most important books: "Religious hypocrisy in America — it's all there, and amazingly relevant" (16). In 2009, Paul Auster also revealed in *Newsweek* that Hawthorne's novel is the first of the five books on his list of the most important: "This is where American literature begins" (17).

Along with Richard Brodhead, Emily Miller Budick, and others, I have tried to trace Hawthorne's influence on writers who have followed in his wake. In my 1985 book, *In Hawthorne's Shadow: American Romance from Melville to Mailer*, I discuss the Manichean worldview of many of his characters, which at times Hawthorne shares. Such a cosmic vision, in which the universe is equally and rigidly divided between God and Satan, who continually battle one another, shows up in the fiction of Joyce Carol Oates, Joan Didion, John Updike, John Gardner, John Cheever, and others.

The red letter itself and the opening scene in the romance can be clearly seen to have influenced, for example, Harold Frederic's *The Damnation of Theron Ware* (1896) and Stephen Crane's *The Red Badge of Courage* (1895). The list lengthens in terms of plot, characters, narrative strategies, and atmosphere in such works as William Faulkner's *Absalom, Absalom!* (1936); John Updike's trilogy — *A Month of Sundays* (1975; Dimmesdale's repentance), *Roger's Version* (1986; Chillingworth as computer scientist), and *S* (1988; Hester in a commune); Tim O'Brien's *In the Lake of the Woods* (1994) in terms of his open-ended narrative strategy and reference to "Wakefield"; many of Philip Roth's works such as *The Ghost Writer* (1979) and his references to Hawthorne's assault on the Puritans' "persecuting spirit" in *The Human Stain* (2000); Rick Moody's memoir, *The Black Veil* (2002), in which he tries to trace his ancestry back to the

Joseph Moody whom Hawthorne mentions in his footnote to "The Minister's Black Veil"; Paul Auster's *The Book of Illusions* (2002), including his recent *Man in the Dark* (2008), where a character is writing a biography of Rose Hawthorne.

Other writers influenced by Hawthorne's fiction include Carson McCullers, Toni Morrison, and Flannery O'Connor, and the title of the Indian American Pulitzer Prize-winning author Jhumpa Lahiri's 2008 book of stories, *Unaccustomed Earth*, is a phrase borrowed from a passage in Hawthorne's "The Custom-House" that serves as the epigraph to her book: "Human nature will not flourish, any more than a potato, if planted and replanted, for too long a series of generations, in the same worn-out soil. My children have had other birthplaces, and, so far as their fortunes may be within my control, shall strike their roots into unaccustomed earth." Playwrights have also adapted his fiction to their dramas, such as Robert Lowell in *The Old Glory* (1965) and others in such provocative works as Suzan Lori Parks's *The Red Letter Play*, which includes *In the Blood* (1998) and *Fuckin' A* (2001).

The Indian-born American writer Baharti Mukherjee provides a historical and cultural background for *The Scarlet Letter* that is lush and elaborate, complete with Indian ancestors, in her splendid *The Holder of the World* (1993). "Who can blame Nathaniel Hawthorne for shying away from the real story of the brave Salem mother and her illegitimate daughter?," the narrator asks at the conclusion of the novel (284), suggesting that he ignored or suppressed the "real" ancestry and legacy of Hester Prynne.

Hawthorne's novel persists in baffling and tantalizing readers and scholars as well as other writers as it continues to be rewritten and reinterpreted in American literature and culture. It remains a staple in high-school American literature courses, the letter itself has achieved a lasting power as a pop-icon in contemporary culture, and critics continue writing books about Hawthorne's influence on other writers from the late nineteenth century to the twenty-first.

Hawthorne's Scholarly Legacy

Two developments of the last fifty years have had strong positive effects on the already-thriving field of Hawthorne scholarship. First, Hawthorne scholarship was significantly enhanced when Ohio State University Press, with the meticulous assistance of editors William Charvat, Roy Harvey Pearce, Claude M. Simpson, Fredson Bowers, and Matthew J. Bruccoli, on March 15, 1964, launched the Centenary Edition of Hawthorne's complete works, which now runs to twenty-three volumes with additional editing by Thomas Woodson and Neal Smith. It has become the first complete edition since the thirteen Riverside volumes published in the 1880s.

Second, in 1974 C. E. Frazer Clark, Jr., the prolific collector of Hawthorne volumes, whose *Nathaniel Hawthorne: A Descriptive Bibliography* (1978) has become the standard reference guide for primary sources and editions, along with David B. Kesterson, an established Hawthorne scholar, launched the Nathaniel Hawthorne Society, which has been active ever since in keeping analyses and explorations of Hawthorne's fiction alive and well in various annual conferences around the country and the world. Its original founders included Darrel Abel, Roger Asselineau, Nina Baym, Matthew Bruccoli, J. Donald Crowley, Edward H. Davidson, Richard H. Fogle, Rita Gollin, Manning Hawthorne, John L. Idol, Jr., Buford Jones, Jerome Klinkowitz, Terence Martin, John P. McWilliams, Jr., Arthur Monke, George Monteiro, Norman Holmes Pearson, Barton Levi St. Armand, Arlin Turner, and Hyatt Waggoner. In 1976 the society held its first conference at Bowdoin College, an occasion that was also notable for Waggoner's presentation of his discovery of *The Lost Notebook: 1835–1841*.[2]

Later Hawthorne Society Conferences have continued to feature his work, his life, and his cultural and historical importance as a writer. The 150th anniversary of the publication of *The Scarlet Letter* was celebrated at the conference in Boston in 2000. In 2004 at the conference in Salem on the bicentennial of his birth, several artists, such as Maxine Kingston, Bobbie Ann Mason, Ned Rorem, Elizabeth Spencer, and Richard Wilbur paid tribute to Hawthorne in the conference's program. The topic, "Transatlanticism in American Literature: Emerson, Hawthorne, Poe," produced a splendid and well-attended conference at the Rothermere American Institute in Oxford in 2006, as did "Starting Over at Bowdoin" in 2008. In 2010 the society held a conference in Concord, "Hawthorne in Concord: Eden and Beyond," and will hold another in 2012 in Florence.

The analysis and appreciation of *The Scarlet Letter*, as well as Hawthorne's other major romances and tales, continue in academe at all levels from the undergraduate to the graduate and beyond in terms of articles in journals and presentations at conferences, and these, of course, are very different from popular culture's use of the letter itself. The over-wrought high-school lesson plans and the disastrous Demi Moore film have many things in common, among them the attempt to make the novel more "relevant" by focusing on outcasts and marginalized groups and the reduction of a complex narrative to a simplistic conflict between an individual trying to be liberated and an authoritarian society. It is fascinating to see how such a popular concoction as film incorporates images that betray the original tale, not that this does not happen often enough to other works of literature when they are filmed, and how academics recoil from what they see as the cheap exploitation of a classic text.

Hawthorne still manages to attract the popular media, as we have seen in the reburial of his wife and oldest daughter next to him in Concord in 2006. However macabre the ceremony, it was attended by academics and journalists alike, each delighted to comment on the scene and underscore Hawthorne's continuing presence in our culture, more perhaps in this case for the "letter" of his popularity than for his spirit.

The letter is alive and well. Its legacy thrives and expands. With this in mind, it is time to take a look at Hawthorne's reputation during his life-time and after his death in the nineteenth century. Why was he touted as America's greatest writer from the very beginning? From there we will move on to Hawthorne's biographers as they have grappled with this elu-sive soul over the years and then move on to the critical battles over the romance and the novel, among other things, during the time the New Criticism held sway from the 1930s well into the 1960s, then to the cul-tural and social convulsions that generated such new critical perspectives as feminist, Marxist, deconstructionist, race-based, and New Historicist cul-tural studies, all of which are thriving in contemporary scholarship. Entanglements will surely follow, but let us try to cut our way through the darkest wood and see what we can unearth.

Notes

[1] As McDonnell found out, all novices of the order must make the pilgrimage to Hawthorne's grave, and the sisters once tried, unsuccessfully, to finance a film about Rose's life. It is certainly a dramatic story; as McDonnell's article recounts: Rose, having married a man who turned out to be an alcoholic and having lost her son at the age of four, separated from her husband — with the Catholic Church's permission — and with her companion, Alice Huber, joined the Dominican order in December 1900. The next year they began the Servants of Relief for Incurable Cancer, Rose became known as Mother Alphonsa and moved to the Rosary Hill Home in Hawthorne, New York. (The village had been renamed in honor of her father.) She died there in 1926. Today the Servants of Relief have grown to seven hospices in six states, the sisters accept no remuneration from their patients, and they each administer bedside care as part of their calling.

[2] Barbara S. Mouffe had discovered the notebook in one of two small trunks that, after her mother's death in 1976, had been shipped to her home, appropriately enough, on Hawthorn Avenue in Boulder, Colorado. It had belonged to her great grandfather, William James Reynolds, who was born in Salem in 1814.

2: Hawthorne as Nineteenth-Century Morbid Genius

DESPITE RADICAL CHANGES in American culture and society since Hawthorne's day, he has managed to remain at the top of the list of American literature's classic writers. In fact over the years he has never been displaced. Through psychological criticism and the study of symbols, myth criticism and deconstruction, linguistic, Marxist and feminist analysis, he has managed to stay in place in the American canon. Jane Tompkins tried in 1985 to undermine his position or at least expose it as the result of a cabal led by the champions of Dead White Males and New England elitists to keep him in the forefront of the concept of a newly emerging American literature in the 1850s and beyond:

> The prominence of Hawthorne's texts in the post–Civil War era is a natural consequence of his relation to the mechanisms that produced literary and cultural opinion. Hawthorne's initial connections with the Boston literati — his acquaintance with Longfellow at college, his residence next door to Alcott and a half mile from Emerson (his son and Emerson's nephew roomed together at Harvard), his marrying a Peabody, becoming fast friends with Ticknor and Lowell, being published by the indefatigable Fields, socializing with Duyckinck and Whipple — these circumstances positioned Hawthorne's literary production so that it became the property of a dynastic cultural elite which came to identify itself with him . . . In short, the friends and associates who outlived Hawthorne kept his fiction up-to-date by writing about it, and then their friends took over. (29–30)

Many have tried to discredit him because of his suspect, conservative, status-quo political perspective, which we will examine. One feminist critic, Louise DeSalvo, even suggested in 1987 that he literally supported the murdering of women once and for all. Hawthorne, however, for all his recognizable faults, remains intact as one of our most important classic American writers.

It is true that Hawthorne was enshrined early on in the American literary pantheon — some suggest by the 1840s — and remained in place, unlike Melville, Whitman, Dickinson, Poe, and Thoreau, who were discovered or re-discovered later, as even Emerson was. "The reputation of Mr. Hawthorne is sufficiently established and widely known, to procure for any stories of his production a large and eager circle of readers," proclaimed the anonymous reviewer in "Notices of New Books" in the *United States Magazine and Democratic Review* (where several of Hawthorne's sketches and tales had been published) in May 1851. "He occupies the first rank among the imaginative writers of his day, and his productions are not excelled here or elsewhere" (Idol/Jones 164).

How did this happen? Why did critics generally applaud him so early? What did they see in him? Can we isolate that early Hawthorne in the 1840s, 1850s, and 1860s? Can we trace how his reputation solidified after his death in 1864? Were the seeds of future critical approaches sown within that early critical approval, or can we find only a repetitious and dated critical vocabulary that embalmed him altogether?

One thing that critics agreed upon virtually unanimously was Hawthorne's style, however much they fought about his "morbid" subjects and the content of his dark tales. As early as 1828, an anonymous reviewer in the *Boston Daily Advertiser* referred to "the elegance of language which frequently occurs in [*Fanshawe*]" (Idol/Jones 5), a view that would be picked up again and again by other reviewers. What was described in 1828 as a language that was "simple, chaste and appropriate" (Idol/ Jones 6) became in Richard Henry Stoddard's view in 1853, a celebration of "the simplicity, purity, and beauty of his style" (Crowley 288). In 1837 Thomas Green Fessenden praised "a sedate, quiet dignity displayed in his diction" (Idol/Jones 20), and Horatio Bridge in the same year found Hawthorne's style remarkable for its "grace and delicacy; in which qualities, as well as in purity and classical finish, it will compare advantageously with that of the best living English writers" (Idol/Jones 21). Evert A. Duyckinck in 1841 welcomed this style as ever "pure, serene, cheerful" (Idol/Jones 418) and in 1842 proclaimed it "very pure . . . and it is the vehicle for sentiment as unpolluted" (Idol/Jones 59). Anne W. Abbott, reviewing *The Scarlet Letter* in 1850, wrote of Hawthorne's "genuine poetry . . . His style may be compared to a sheet of transparent water . . . while in its clear yet mysterious depths we espy rarer and stranger things, which we must dive for, if we would examine" (Idol/Jones 129, 131). Diving would also become Herman Melville's metaphor for trying to fathom the depths of Hawthorne's vision, while others would linger at the threshold of his style, assume that its purity and grace reflected his view of the world and, particularly in the nineteenth century, praise the reflection in contrast to the dark waters below.

No wonder that Hawthorne's most popular tales in his lifetime, excluding the romances, were "Little Annie's Ramble" and "A Rill from the Town Pump," essayistic and sentimental fictions that Longfellow loved and celebrated in his constant public support of Hawthorne's work, and "Sunday at Home and "Sights from a Steeple," which Elizabeth Palmer Peabody, Hawthorne's sister-in-law, also loved because of Hawthorne's sentimental editorializing, along with "Little Annie's Ramble," valued most highly because they suggested to her Wordsworth's romanticizing of everyday life.

Yet others probed more incisively. In that anonymous 1828 review of *Fanshawe*, the writer made mention of "the throwing in of light and shade to give effect to the picture" (Idol/Jones 5). He saw this, however, as a means of "filling up" the novel in place of a decent plot. In an unsigned review in the *Westminster Review* of October 1852, the writer characterized Hawthorne's main tendency as "toward isolation — for the ruling faculty is analytic. It is ever hunting out the anomalous; it discovers more points of repulsion than of attraction; and the creatures of its fancy are all morbid beings — all 'wandering stars,' plunging into the abyss of despair" (Crowley 260). Elizabeth Palmer Peabody in "Twice-told Tales," published in the *New-Yorker* in March 1838, had recognized "the objective power of the mind" (Idol/Jones 31) in "Little Annie's Ramble," but she apparently didn't ramble any further, leaving it to later critics in the latter half of the twentieth century to delve into this aspect of Hawthorne's writings.

That anonymous reviewer of 1828 helped set the stage for future Hawthorne criticism that attempted to reconcile the "morbidity" of his themes with the elegant and formal "purity" of his style. Critics, as we will see, tried to reconcile the limpid calm of the language and the dark implications of some of the tales or avoided them altogether. How did Hawthorne manage to achieve both? A reviewer in the *North British Review* of November 1853 thought the answer lay in Hawthorne's ability to make the supernatural "credible by refining away the line of demarcation between the natural and the supernatural . . . The 'supernatural' is only interesting beyond other things so long as it continues to vibrate between the credible and the incredible" (Crowley 300, 301).

Hawthorne was also often seen through the eyes of more famous critics, writers themselves, for example, Poe and Melville. While admiring "Sights from a Steeple," "Sunday at Home," "Little Annie's Ramble," and "A Rill from the Town Pump," Poe in 1842 viewed them as essays, not tales. He found the style, as most did, "subdued, quiet, thoughtful, soothing and calm," akin to Washington Irving's restraint, but also hinted at a certain "somewhat repressed" quality in it as well. Poe found "The Rill from the Town Pump," Hawthorne's most famous fiction at the time, his least meritorious. He preferred to discuss "The Hollow of the Three Hills," "The Minister's Black Veil," and "Wakefield." He admired the total effect in which "every word tells" in "The Hollow," using it to boost his own critical theory about the unity of effect that should be achieved in any written piece but particularly in fiction and poetry (Idol/Jones 67). He praised the analysis of motive in "Wakefield" and set the minister's self-declared moral in "The Minister's Black Veil" in conflict with its actual and insinuated meaning. The style might be pure, but the vision was anything

but. It might be too melancholy and mystical, itself repressed in the process of hiding more "uneasy" visions.

After having praised Hawthorne's originality and genius in 1842,
Poe declared in 1847 that Hawthorne wasn't original at all, that in fact
he relied too heavily on allegory and that lesser kind of writing produced
by "a charmingly obvious fancy . . . best exemplified . . . in Addison,
Irving and *Hawthorne*" (Idol/Jones 100). Samuel Taylor Coleridge had
derided fancy in contrast to the truer imagination; Poe decided that the
"strain of allegory . . . completely overwhelms the greater number of his
subjects . . . In defence of allegory . . . there is scarcely one respectable
word to be said . . . if allegory ever establishes a fact, it is by dint of
overturning a fiction . . . it must always interfere with that unity of effect
which, to the artist, is worth all the allegory in the world" (Idol/Jones
101). For Poe visible design and/or a moral destroyed a writer's work.
It got in the way of the effect of more mysterious possibilities, intimated
not proclaimed. Thus for Poe, Hawthorne "is peculiar and *not* original
. . . He is infinitely too fond of allegory, and can never hope for
popularity so long as he persists in it. Let him . . . come out from the
Old Manse, cut Mr. Alcott, hang (if possible) the editor of *The Dial*"
(Idol/Jones, 104). Poe's rant wrongly relates Hawthorne to the more
optimistic and hopeful transcendentalists of Concord and obscures its
target.

It is Herman Melville on the other hand who almost single-handedly
conjured up the dark Hawthorne that modernists, New Critics, deconstructionists, and more contemporary critics would come to acknowledge
and appreciate. In his sexually explicit and dizzyingly rapturous review of
Mosses from an Old Manse in 1850, in which he poses as a Southerner, he
waxes rhapsodic about the blackness of Hawthorne's vision, obviously in
the process of creating his own and longing for a soul mate. For him
Hawthorne's intellect plumbs the depths "shrouded in a blackness, ten
times black. . . . It is that blackness in Hawthorne . . . that so fixes and
fascinates me . . . this blackness it is that furnishes the infinite obscure of
his background . . . those short, quick probings at the very axis of reality
. . . Nathaniel Hawthorne is a man as yet almost utterly mistaken among
men" (Idol/Jones 108–9). Melville continues in a famously lubricious
passage:

> But already I feel that this Hawthorne has dropped germanous seeds
> into my soul. He expands and deepens down . . . and further and
> further, shoots his strong New England roots into the hot soil of my
> Southern soul. . . "Young Goodman Brown" . . . is deep as Dante . . .
> when Spenser was alive, he was thought of very much as Hawthorne
> is now, — was generally accounted just such a "gentle" harmless man
> . . . In all men, hiddenly reside certain wondrous, occult properties
> . . . (Idol/Jones 112, 113, 115)

Yet even Melville wasn't entirely certain of his black vision. Hawthorne's style again confounded a disciple: "This darkness but gives effect to the ever-moving dawn . . . Whether Hawthorne has simply availed himself of this mystical blackness as a means to the wondrous effects he makes it to produce in his lights and shades; or whether there really lurks in him, perhaps unknown to himself, a touch of Puritanic gloom — this, I cannot altogether tell . . . it appeals to that Calvinistic sense of Innate Depravity and Original Sin . . . Nor need you fix upon that blackness in him, if it suit you not" (Idol/Jones 107, 109). Did a blackness lurk beneath the style that was as transparent as water? Or was it merely a picturesque technique to bring out the lights and shadows first discovered by that anonymous reviewer of *Fanshawe* in 1828?

Much came to a head in the triumph of *The Scarlet Letter* in 1850. Hawthorne had proclaimed in *Mosses from an Old Manse* that he was finished with writing tales, but no one quite expected the book that has long been proclaimed the first great American novel. For the most part critics loved it, and we can see in many of the reviews a culmination of the several points they had emphasized previously: the focus on morbidity played off against the purity of style, the fascination with Puritan New England and the past as part of Hawthorne's genuine Americanist interests, Hawthorne the brooding solitary soul using allegory to grapple with the Calvinist blackness of his themes, and his curious blend of light and shadow, intimations of the supernatural, and the mixture of masculine and feminine qualities that result in Hester Prynne's primary role.

Edward Percy Whipple in 1850 in *Graham's Magazine* recognized the "tragic power" of *The Scarlet Letter* with readers "watching patiently the movements of morbid hearts when stirred by strange experiences . . . The fault of the book, if fault it have, is the almost morbid intensity with which the characters are realized" (Idol/Jones 124). Caleb Foote acknowledged its "peculiar power" (Idol/Jones 119) and, in the "Book Notices" of the *Portland Transcript,* its "painful distinctness" (Idol/ Jones 121).

The critics who applauded the work praised Hawthorne for discovering a new kind of "psychological romance," a term that Hawthorne himself would not use until his preface to *The Snow Image* in 1851. Duyckinck praised this "new" Hawthorne in a review in the *Literary World* as "less companionable, of sterner Puritan aspect, with the shadow of the past over him, a reviver of witchcrafts and of those dark agencies of evil which lurk in the human soul . . . It has the mystic element, the weird forest influences of the old Puritan discipline and era" (Idol/Jones 122). For him Hawthorne had created "a psychological romance . . . in which the human heart is anatomized," and he went on to mention "The Minister's Black Veil" as an earlier work that had accomplished similar things. Lewis Gaylord Clark in the *Knickerbocker* also described *The Scarlet Letter* as "a psychological romance. It is a tale of remotes, a study of character. . . . the scarlet letter . . . in Hawthorne's hands, skilled to these allegorical, typical semblances, becomes vitalized as the rest. It is the hero of the volume" (Idol/Jones 126).

All praised the style and the presentation. Clark viewed it as similar to "a Flemish painting [with] a few unduly satiric and Hogarthian touches in the portraits" (Idol/Jones 125). Whipple saw Hawthorne as undermining "the whole philosophy on which the French novel rests, by seeing farther and deeper into the essence both of conventional and moral laws . . . In this respect there is hardly a novel in English literature more purely objective . . . [The characters] are developed more in the way of logical analysis than by events. The descriptive portions . . . are in a high degree picturesque and vivid" (Idol/Jones 125). Henry Fothergill Chorley in 1850 liked the "mixture of Puritan reserve and wild imagination" and ranked the novel "on a level with Brockden Brown and the author of *Rip Van Winkle*" (Idol/Jones 126).

George Bailey Loring, also in 1850, suggested that "perhaps [Hawthorne] verges strongly on the supernatural . . . But man's nature is, by birth, *super*natural; and the deep mystery which lies beneath all his actions is far beyond the reach of any mystical vision" (Idol/Jones 133). Loring also admired the labyrinthine moral questions the novel raised: "There is a false delicacy which avoids the contemplation of evil, and which severe experience may destroy. There is a sweeping belief that vice stands at one pole and virtue at the other, which the deep trials of life may eradicate . . . The elements of character upon which vice and virtue hang are so nearly allied" (Idol/Jones 142, 141). In every instance Hester's heroism transcends the other characters' obsessions and raises her above them: "How far behind her in moral and religious excellence was the accredited religious teacher, who was her companion in guilt! We forget that what society calls chastity is often far the reverse" (Idol/Jones 140). Whipple would agree: "The novelist has mastered the whole philosophy of that guilt" (Idol/Jones 124).

Critics also found darker doings in the tale. Chorley recognized that Dimmesdale's "final confession and expiation are merely a relief, not a reconciliation" (Idol/Jones 127). Anne W. Abbott, who preferred Hawthorne's introductory piece "The Custom-House" to the novel itself, saw Dimmesdale as a character portraying "mere suffering, aimless and without effect for purification or blessing to the soul . . . a seven year's agony without penitence . . . he was but a changeling, or an imp in grave apparel, not an erring, and consequently suffering human being" (Idol/Jones 130). Loring, who liked the novel, agreed: "We do not find that out of [Dimmesdale's] sin, came any revelation of virtue . . . We see in him the powerlessness of belief, alone, to furnish true justification through repentance" (Idol/Jones 137).

We must remember that Christianity, however under attack and assaulted by the middle of the nineteenth century, still provided the foundation of conventional social values. Sin and suffering, at least when publicly addressed, should lead to penitence and repentance: that was the trajectory of the Christian vision, the grace that would finally take hold after staggering through the Valley of Darkness. Some critics still held those values dear and castigated *The Scarlet Letter* because it did not reflect the Christian pattern. Anne Abbott admitted that you couldn't put the book down, with its "pain and pleasure strangely mixed . . . [its] intoxication . . . [and its] enchantment," but she liked only "the exhilarating presence of 'Little Pearl,'" who "retains her perfect and vivid human individuality . . . The child is a true child, the only genuine and consistent moral in the book" (Idol/Jones 130, 131). For Abbott Pearl invokes the entire Romantic notion of the wise and innocent child. As for Roger Chillingworth? He is "such a gnome-like phantasm, such an unnatural personification of an abstract idea" (Idol/Jones 129). We already know how Abbott felt about the unredemptive nature of Dimmesdale's suffering: "The closing scene [in which] the pillory platform is made the stage for a triumphant *coup de theatre*, seems to us more than a failure." Ultimately, "no authority can be found, however, which affords any remedy or redress against determined outlaws" (Idol/Jones 130).

In 1851 Arthur Cleveland Coxe took *The Scarlet Letter* to task in what has become an infamous review because of what he revealed of an age still shadowed by Calvinist leanings and dogmatic religious beliefs. For him Hawthorne's romance should be placed in the "Brothel Library" (Idol/Jones 146) where George Sand and Eugene Sue also resided. Hawthorne, he growls, may be "venting something of his spirit against the Puritans," but how can we be certain "whether he is making fun of all religion"? Why has he chosen adultery as his subject? "Is it, in short, because a running undertide of filth has become as requisite to a romance, as death in the fifth act to a tragedy? Is the French era actually begun in our literature?" Of course even Coxe recognized the purity of Hawthorne's style: "*The Scarlet Letter* is delicately immoral," but no matter how delicate, school girls reading the book have "done injury to their young sense of delicacy, by devouring such a dirty story" (Idol/Jones 146, 148, 149, 151).

Orestes Augustus Brownson, who eventually turned to Catholicism as his ultimate refuge after flirting with transcendentalism, blasted *The Scarlet Letter* for its un-Christian maneuverings, condemning mere psychology as undermining the more truly theological moorings and message: "Men are not for us mere psychological phenomena, to be studied, classed, and labeled . . . it is a story that should not have been told. It is a story of crime, of an adulteress . . . not fit subjects for popular literature, and moral health is not promoted by leading the imagination to dwell on them" (Idol/Jones 143). As for the unfortunate Hester? "The adulteress suffers not from remorse, but from regret . . . [She never] really repents of the criminal deed . . . Mr. Hawthorne . . . seeks to excuse Hester Prynne, a married woman." In Brownson's world there is always time for sermons and sodawater: "We are never to forget that sin is sin, and that it is pardonable only through the great mercy of God, on condition of the sincere repentance of the sinner . . . But in the present case neither of the guilty parties [Hester and Dimmesdale] repent of the sin . . . They hug their illicit love; they cherish their sin . . . It is not their conscience that is wounded, but their pride [which is] itself a sin . . . the root of all sin . . . The Christian who reads *The Scarlet Letter* cannot fail to perceive that the author is wholly ignorant of Christian asceticism" (Idol/Jones 144).

Loring brings up an interesting point in his positive review that locates him squarely within the cultural sympathies of the nineteenth century. While he does agree that Hawthorne's view of the Puritans is accurate — "Zest of life was no part of the Puritan's belief. He scorned his own flesh and blood. His appetites were crimes . . . He had no sympathy, no tenderness, for any sinner . . . and love, illegalized, was that burning, scarlet sin" (Idol/Jones 136) — he conjures up a "spot" within every human breast that remains untainted and corrupted by human actions, a very Romantic notion that reflects Wordsworth's vision, "Places have we all within our selves / Where all stand single":

> Between the individual and his God, there remains a spot, larger or smaller, as the soul has been kept unclouded, where no sin can enter, where no mediation can come, where all the discords of life are resolved into the most delicious harmonies, and his whole existence becomes illuminated by a divine intelligence. Sorrow and sin reveal this spot to all men. (Idol/Jones 138)

Here is that unstained, rigorously democratic inner self that the Romantic vision helped create, a place that for Hawthorne remained unfathomable, murky, twisted, and ominous. Loring here reveals a nineteenth-century faith in "the most delicious harmonies" that cannot be shattered or subverted no matter what. It was precisely the kind of image Hawthorne could not abide in *The Scarlet Letter* and elsewhere, and his fiction persistently if erratically set out to undermine it, to problematize the middle-class ideas of autonomous selves and spotless interiors. Not for nothing did he often describe the human heart as a dark place steeped in its own guilt and strange compulsions.

The impact of *The Scarlet Letter* on American fiction and Hawthorne's reputation proved to be so strong and lasting that all his later work was compared to and/or contrasted with it. *The House of the Seven Gables*, published in 1851, carried forth the idea of a Calvinist curse with the sins of the fathers seeming to determine the destinies of the sons, but Hawthorne swaddled this grim shadow in vivid, scintillant, often raucous descriptions and scenes of contemporary Salem that delighted the critics, who again compared his meticulous prose to the realistic brightness of Dutch paintings. He also sided with the triumph of love literally emerging from the shadow of death in the corpse of Judge Jaffrey Pyncheon, thus ending the long-standing, generational confrontation between the Pyncheons and the Maules over the true ownership of the house and the land. The first Pyncheon had seized both as well as the deeds, hidden until the end of the novel, that supposedly turned the ownership of lands in Maine over to the Pyncheons. Holgrave, a Maule, and Phoebe, a Pyncheon, eradicate the curse's power by marrying. This was by far Hawthorne's sunniest book, and while a few critics found the happy ending forced and flimsy, most praised him for his descriptive powers and human sympathies. They liked the aging, aristocratic Hepzibah, the warmly open and genuine Phoebe, the decadent artist Clifford in all his ineffectual musings about beauty, and the stolidly materialistic Jaffrey Pyncheon, whose death rescues them all from his prominent clutches. The romance reads like an exorcism of nightmares, revenge against a commercial and capitalist society with its cold heart and colder cash.

One anonymous critic in 1860 found *The House of the Seven Gables* burdened by "the absence of incident [which] has here reached its utmost; there is literally no action in the whole romance. The only event is the sudden death [of Judge Pyncheon] . . . the descriptive nearly swallows up every other characteristic [with] pages upon pages of unbroken description. . . . There is no self-manifesting quality in the characters. They have all to be introduced, taken to pieces and explained" (Idol/Jones 459). It is as if in trying to overcome the Pyncheon-Maule curse, in attempting to disconnect himself from the unbroken chain of guilt and isolation, Hawthorne brought his fiction to a standstill, but this was a decidedly minor opinion.

Critics split over 1852's *The Blithedale Romance*, either finding it too cynical because of Miles Coverdale's narration or too suddenly disrupted by Zenobia's suicide, an action so seemingly unexpected that it wrenched the novel out of its Romantic path and left it shattered. All the veils in the novel — Priscilla's Veiled Lady, Old Moodie's and Zenobia's names, Old Moodie's eyepatch, Zenobia's legend of Theodore, Coverdale's half-digested speculations as well as his name — seemed as light and inconsequential as air until Zenobia's rigid body was pulled from the river at midnight. Some kind of artistic balance was thrown off by so rude and horrible a death. Some liked Hawthorne's realistic descriptions — Henry James liked this book best among Hawthorne's major works — while others tried to find links between the fictional characters and real-life people, for example between Zenobia and Margaret Fuller: the novel was based on Hawthorne's time in 1841 at the Transcendentalist community at Brook Farm. Still others were put off by the mesmeric machinations of the plot in which each character nursed his or her hidden agenda and tried to co-opt everyone else's. Many were never exactly certain of just who had done what to whom. Hawthorne seemed more calculating than somber, reducing his tapestry to a series of sexual, political, and theatrical power plays.

An anonymous reviewer in *Blackwood's Magazine* in 1855 condescendingly lambasted the novel, as only a British critic at the time could: "How thoroughly worn out and *blasé* must that young world be, which gets up excitements in its languid life, only by means of veiled ladies, mysterious clairvoyants, rapping spirits, or, in a milder fashion, by sherry-cobbler and something cocktails for the men, and lectures on the rights of women for the ladies. We enter this strange existence with a sort of wondering inquiry whether any *events* ever take place there, or if, instead, there is nothing to be done but for everybody to observe everybody else . . . we want more than thoughts and fancies — we want *things*" (Crowley 311, 312).

Things rode roughshod over characters and plot in Hawthorne's final romance. *The Marble Faun* was welcomed and applauded in 1860, eight years after *The Blithedale Romance*, more as a guidebook to Rome, richly stuffed with descriptions and images, than as a completely successful work of fiction. Several reviewers complained that the hidden connections of the plot were more remote than ever, veiled to the point of incomprehensibility, but they marveled at Hawthorne's reach in trying to portray a mythic landscape wherein one's fall from and growth beyond innocence, highlighted by Donatello's murdering Miriam's tormentor, paralleled the Etruscan, Roman, and Christian worlds of Italian history. Others saw the same formula at work: the mysterious, dark-haired, sensual Miriam as the final incarnation of Hester Prynne and Zenobia, dwarfed by the languid corpse of Rome itself; the prissy, self-righteous Hilda as the decayed and dwindled embodiment of Phoebe Pyncheon and Priscilla; the humanly undeveloped and allegorically rigid presence of evil, the model, as a vaguer version of Roger Chillingworth, Judge Pyncheon, and Hollingsworth; and the young man surrounded by doubts, the sculptor Kenyon, as a pale imitation of Holgrave and Coverdale. Calvinist ideas abroad looked frail and preachy when subjected to the labyrinthine history amid the cultural artifacts of Rome. The narrative left huge gaps, more so than in any of Hawthorne's romances, both structurally and thematically, so much so that the public demanded an explanation. Hawthorne gave them one almost as vague as the original text, mentioning Miriam's family connections within the Papal government, which may have led to the discovery of Donatello's murder of the model, and Hilda's imprisonment in the Convent of the Sacre Coeur. And Donatello? He remained in prison whereas as Kenyon explained, Miriam's "crime lay merely in a glance; she did no murder" (467).

By 1860 Hawthorne was firmly established as *the* American author of his day. The campaign to declare him so started as early as the 1840s, but by 1860 he was clearly King of the Hill. An anonymous critic in the *Universal Review* in June, 1860, praised his "accumulation of external detail mingled with deep psychological insight [and] the idea of secret guilt" (Idol/Jones 437, 432). The power of such stories as "The Birthmark" and "Young Goodman Brown" was publicly recognized: "We are brought face to face with the portals into the unseen and inscrutable . . . Every object, every power presents itself to him as striking its roots deep into the subsoil of mystery . . . We are made to feel . . . a haunting presence" (Idol/Jones 452). The critic, an anonymous writer for the *Universal Review*, continues as if aware that he is trying to sum up a career and an achievement: "The sympathy or magnetism among human beings is more subtle and universal than we think; it exists, indeed, among different classes of organized life, and vibrates from one to another [pursuing] the subtle, untraceable, interpenetrating affinities of mind and matter" (Idol/Jones 452, 453). He goes on to speak of "Rappaccini's Daughter," "Roger Malvin's Burial," and "The Minister's Black Veil" as intensely wrought with "the creeping sense of mystery . . . There is nothing we know of in literature at once so tender and so unflinching, so harrowingly painful . . . step by step" (Idol/Jones 457).

James Russell Lowell's review of *The Marble Faun* in the *Atlantic Monthly* of April 1860 summarizes both the critical vocabulary and the critical perspectives used and shaped by critics about Hawthorne in the preceding years. For instance he praises Hawthorne's "genius and originality." The word "genius" was used so many times by critics of Hawthorne's work in previous essays and reviews that it became the catch-all description for Hawthorne, the man and writer, as if the Romantic era had singled out one more celebrated solitary, anguished soul. Both Elizabeth Palmer Peabody in 1838 and Henry T. Tuckerman in June 1851 used the word six times in their articles; Poe used it five times in May 1842; Evert A. Duyckinck employed it three times in May 1841. The noun became a brand name, more touted than analyzed.

Lowell linked Hawthorne's originality to his power "of peculiarity" along with "his morbid tendency." Morbidity became another catchall phrase in which to capture the essence of Hawthorne's vision, especially since the nineteenth century publicly celebrated an overt optimism and healthy-minded perspective, which became one of the main underpinnings of Victorian criticism. Poe found him original and then just peculiar. Caleb Foote and Edward Percy Whipple in 1850 linked the peculiar with the morbid and the weird. An anonymous essayist writing about "Contemporary Literature of America" in the *Westminster Review* of October 1852 saw morbidity as pervasive in all of Hawthorne's fiction: "His moral faculty is morbid as well as weak; all his characters partake of the same infirmity . . .

He lives in the region and shadow of death, and never sees the deep glow of moral health anywhere" (Crowley 261). The anonymous writer of "'Sir Nathaniel': Hawthorne and the Delineation of the Abnormal" in June 1853 — the title reveals the writer's perspective — bemoaned the fact that "with special ability to depict exceptional modes of human nature, is conjoined special temptation to linger amid what is morbid, and to court intimacy with whatever deviates from the dull standard of conventionalism, and give to distortion and oddity the preference over 'harmonic union'" (Crowley 293). Does this mean that "harmonic union" exposes "the dull standard of conventionalism" or that the anonymous writer seeks unity at all costs; that everything else must be distortion, oddity, and deviation? By 1860 Hawthorne reigned as a peculiar, original, weird, and morbid genius, a Romantic stock character, a creature caged.

Lowell goes on in his review to mention Hawthorne's "world of moral realities [and] a certain remoteness in his writings," which a British critic, yet another anonymous writer, in 1868 described as "the withdrawal of the whole scene [in fiction] from the atmosphere of actual life" (Idol/Jones 450). How was one to contextualize or "normalize" such work?

Lowell declared that Hawthorne was undoubtedly a "son of New England and the Puritans," a more cultural perspective also recognized by Melville as his "touch of Puritan gloom" (Crowley 116), by Duyckinck — "It has the mystic element, the weird forest influences of the old Puritan discipline and era" (Crowley 156) — and by Richard Holt Hutton in 1864: "He was really the ghost of New England [with] a mind steeped in the metaphysical and moral lore of New England endowed with much of the cold simplicity of the Puritan nature" (Crowley 407, 411). So the weird and the peculiar, in which the genius Hawthorne is steeped, are really as much a part of our cultural, regional, and national heritage of Calvinism as they are of Hawthorne's fiction. Of course, Hawthorne worships the dark side of such a faith: "He has imbibed a deep personal antipathy to the Puritanic ideal of character . . . His brain has been subtly infected by the Puritanic perception of Law, without being warmed by the Puritanic faith in Grace," pronounced Whipple in the *Atlantic Monthly* of May 1860 (Crowley 345). On the other hand Hawthorne found, according to Oliver Wendell Holmes in his essay, "Hawthorne," of July 1864, "such wealth of poetry to our New England home, and invested the stern outlines of Puritan character with the colors of romance" (Bosco/Murphy 127).

One of the best overviews of Hawthorne's fiction was Hutton's "Hawthorne and the Calvinist Imagination" in the *National Review* of October 1860. He makes a very strong case for Hawthorne's writing romances — not novels — that conjure up one major idea or focus per book: "They are ideal situations expanded by minute study and trains of closely related thought into the dimensions of novels. A very small group of figures is presented to the reader in some marked ideal relation" (Crowley 369). These figures are then observed analytically from several different angles and perspectives, each a product of the major focus of the given novel: "the analysis of the deranging effect of the sin of adultery on the intrinsically fine characters" in *The Scarlet Letter*; the transmission of "the malign influences of evil action" in *The House of the Seven Gables*; "the deranging effect of an absorbing philanthropic idea on a powerful mind" in *The Blithedale Romance*; and the illustration of "the intellectually and morally awakening power of a sudden impulsive sin, committed by a simple, joyous, instinctive, 'natural' man" in *The Marble Faun"* (Crowley 371, 372). The secret of Hawthorne's power as a writer thus "lies in the great art with which he reduplicates and reflects and re-reflects the main idea of the tale from the countless faces of his imagination, until the reader's mind is absolutely saturated and haunted by it" (Crowley 372). Hutton's thesis sounds incredibly contemporary. Hawthorne's power lies in his ability "to be haunted, and in his turn to haunt the reader, with his conceptions, far more than in their intrinsic force" (Crowley 373).

Hutton also discovers a design that may begin allegorically — the good woman, the evil scientist, the innocent young man — but gradually deepens and expands beyond the lineaments of the allegorical: "The more certainly do the allegorical shadows of its first outline gather solidity of form and variety of color, and gradually substantiate themselves into real living men . . . If written down in that faint early form, the tale seems allegorical. But if allowed to lie by in the imagination, it deepens into a real dramatic situation" (Crowley 374). Hawthorne "must have an ideal centre and an ideal bond for his characters, or they would fall asunder into loose unconnected atoms. He has either no power or else no desire to construct what is ordinarily meant by a plot" (Crowley 375).

Hutton also unearths some of the complex psychological depths of Hawthorne's fiction when he describes "the adulterous mixture of emotions . . . not exactly of *discordant* emotions, but of emotions which *ought* to be mutually exclusive, and which combine with the thrill and the shudder of disease. This is almost the antithesis of Allegory" (Crowley 376). He views this as an offshoot of Calvinism, for "Calvinism, with all its noble features, can never keep its eyes off that one fact, as it thinks it, of God's calm foreknowledge of a wide-spread damnation; and this gradually encroaches on the attention till the mind is utterly absorbed in the fascinating terror of the problem how to combine the clashing emotions of love and horror which its image of Him inspires" (Crowley 376–77). He then quotes the famous line from "Rappaccini's Daughter" to prove his point: "Blessed are all simple emotions, be they dark or bright! It is the lurid intermixture of the two that produces the illuminating blazes of the infernal regions." What Hutton misses is Hawthorne's attempt to re-allegorize that lurid intermixture as "infernal," thus categorizing and controlling this vision of love and horror or at least harnessing it again within the boundaries of an either/or simplicity upon which so much of allegory rests, but his critical move here is decidedly perceptive and strikes at the dark heart of Hawthorne's entangled emotions: "The point and art of this eerie tale lie in the conflict of emotions which Beatrice's true spiritual beauty and malignant physical influences raise in the mind of her lover, filling him with a passion blended equally of love and horror" (Crowley 377). Thus deep within Hawthorne's vision smolders a "weird-like tangle of human elements [exemplifying] his uncanny fashion of awakening the most mutually repellent feelings at the same moment" (Crowley 379).

Of course in nineteenth-century criticism, as I have suggested, man and artist were one and the same; it simply took a weird man, however legitimated and authenticated by his Calvinist genes, to write a weird tale. In Hawthorne we discover, therefore, Henry Fothergill Chorley's "retired and timid man" (Crowley 96), a kind of taciturn mystery and silent soul in which much can be read by the discerning eye. "There was never a man more shrinkingly retiring," declared George William Curtis in the *North American Review* of October 1864: "The truth is, that his own times and their people and their affairs were just as shadowy to him as those of any of his stories" (Crowley 417, 419). Thus, within or beneath his peculiar originality and remote, Puritan gloom, we find a shy, sensitive, brooding, anguished, gracious fellow, a tabula rasa, on which can be written the visions of an era. According to Curtis, Hawthorne knew exactly what he was doing when, in his preface to the 1851 edition of *Twice-Told Tales*, he described himself, "on the internal evidence of his sketches [as one who] came to be regarded as a mild, shy, gentle, melancholic, exceedingly sensitive, and not very forcible man . . . He is by no means certain that some of his subsequent productions have not been influenced and modified by a natural desire to fill up so amiable an outline, and to act in consonance with the character assigned to him" (Crowley 229). The wily Hawthorne's use of double negatives creates a sense of mystery that can only add to his status and presence as an author, particularly in those Romantic times when the doomed solitary sensitive soul incarnated the artist in his full-fledged public role.

Elizabeth Palmer Peabody, in a letter to Horace Mann of March 3, 1838, found Hawthorne cocooned in "a life of extraordinary seclusion" (Bosco/Murphy 20). When he returned to Salem from Bowdoin, Elizabeth Manning Hawthorne, his sister, in a letter to James T. Fields, Hawthorne's publisher, in December, 1870, noted that he "began to withdraw into himself" (Bosco/Murphy 8). Rebecca Harding Davis described him as "Banquo's Ghost" (Bosco/Murphy 106). "There was never a more intense Hathorne than the father of Nathaniel Hawthorne, the silent, somber sailor," explained George Bailey Loring in 1880, as if to find a genetic and historical reason for the author's supposedly intense solitude.

On the other hand, viewing Hawthorne's silence from a more positive perspective, Franklin B. Sanborn in his 1880 essay, "A Conversation about Hawthorne at the Concord School of Philosophy," explained that "You felt, when with him, that you did all the talking and had had a delightful conversation" (Bosco/Murphy 197).

We can watch the gloomier image, the Byronic, troubled, solitary shroud, descend on Hawthorne. In 1853, late in his career, as Ronald A. Bosco and Jillmarie Murphy point out, George William Curtis created as much as he discovered the image of Hawthorne as "an absolute recluse" (Bosco/Murphy 65), a hermit in Salem, a ghost in the Old Manse, "as much a phantom and a fable" (Bosco/Murphy 66) as a living author and as silent as a shadow. In 1864, after Hawthorne's death, Hutton described him "as though he were stricken by some spell which half-paralyzed him from communicating with the life around him . . . His spirit haunted rather than ruled his body; his body hampered his spirit" (Crowley 408). In 1894 Sarah Ann Clarke remembered him appearing "shrouded in a cloak, Byronic and very handsome . . . gloomy, or perhaps only shy" (Bosco/ Murphy xxxvii). Hawthorne became the standardized gloomy romantic icon steeped in what Duyckinck as early as 1841 described as a "sadness deepened into awe and fear" (Crowley 76). His shyness became the shadow of a spell, of a haunted doomed spirit.

Nineteenth-century critics and essayists, in trying to position Hawthorne at the beginning of American letters as well as describe his works, often confused the man and the fiction. They easily moved from one to the other as if personality and fiction must necessarily and seamlessly mirror one another. To a critic of today, these impressionistic ramblings often seem vague and analytically incoherent. Such essayists/critics also relied on rigid polarities to guide them in their speculations. Hawthorne's content was dark and morbid, but his style was elegant and transparent. The morbid vision underscored and did not detract from his embodiment as the solitary, tortured, Romantic genius, a product of New England Puritanism. Some critics attempted to broaden the appeal of his work by pointing out that his particular background was essentially American with its distinct national traits and aspirations. Others tried to make the case that the man himself was not personally melancholy and gloomy, though his work was.

Many essayists and critics saw Hawthorne as having almost single-handedly created or founded a national American literature — prefigured perhaps by Irving, Cooper, and Brockden Brown but risen to genius in his elegantly refined and moral-minded fiction — as well as having been an individual who straddled the shadowed crossroads between the feminine and the masculine, defying the increasingly rigid middle-class gender roles of the nineteenth century, a gentle hermaphrodite of horrors, an ambivalent actor on an elusive stage.

Early in the nineteenth century reviewers and critics were calling for the elevation of a new "American" literature. In November 1828, Sarah Josepha Hale pronounced, among a chorus of others, that "the time has arrived when our American authors should have something besides empty praise from their countrymen . . . [They should not pursue] the vapid and worn-out descriptions of European manners, fashions and vices" (Crowley 42). "Let America first praise mediocrity even," trumpeted Melville in 1850. We should back our artists "against all Europe . . . we must turn bullies, else the day is lost" (Crowley 119, 121). "If we do not assert the claims of our own Literature," bemoaned Charles Wilkins Webber in 1846, "who will do it for us?" He continued: "We do recommend the study of Hawthorne, conscientiously, as the specific remedy for all those congestions of patriotism which relieve themselves in uttering speeches . . . this morbid activity — this vehement and overstraining intellection — concerning which we have spoken so much, as the main and unpleasant characteristic of our age, . . . in him [emerges the] worthy characteristics of a truly National Literature. . . . Hawthorne is national — national in subject, in treatment and in manner" (Idol/Jones 81, 82). Thus Hawthorne's morbidity morphed from his transformation of "vehement and overstraining intellection" into a national phenomenon.

Webber's question about who would "assert the claims" of a distinctly American literature could not go unanswered by the indefatigable Elizabeth Palmer Peabody: "The greatest artist will be the greatest benefactor of our country. Art is the highest interest of our state . . . then, we shall have a country; for then, and not till then, there will be a national character." And her brother-in-law? "He sits at the fountain-head of national character" (Idol/Jones 34, 30). Orestes Augustus Brownson, not a great lover of *The Scarlet Letter*, remarked that he "regard[ed] Mr. Hawthorne as fitted to stand at the head of American Literature" (Idol/Jones 87). Hawthorne's tales "are national in their character" (Idol/Jones 58), declaimed the ever-supportive Longfellow.

The cultural desire and need to create and discover a national American literature, separate from and freed from the cultural dominance of British fiction and poetry, continued to expand and thrive after the Civil War. It was as if the new nation, which had rid itself of British colonial rule, now wanted to override and overcome British cultural influences as well. Claudia Stokes, in her book *Writers in Retrospect: The Rise of American Literary History, 1875–1910*, describes the era as one full of nostalgia and a lust for origins, a time when the writing of popular literary histories became an urgent duty, complete with the fashioning of a canon, the periodization of the literature, and a new attention to literary craft as opposed to mere popularity. The time was ripe to establish a New England tradition once and for all, as Lowell in 1860 had declared that Hawthorne's work was destined to spread out "from a small circle of refined admirers and critics [to] the whole community of readers" (Idol/Jones 251). The industrial era, which was at full throttle with its factories and immigrants, fueled the fears of those who saw themselves — or wanted to see themselves — as preservers of cultural refinement, especially the "Yankees," those Anglo-Saxons from New England who could only locate that refinement in a manufactured past. The Chosen People — or those who identified with them — in their City on a Hill, a sacred space besieged by modernity, craved origins, however morbid and peculiar.

As the nineteenth century congealed into rigid gender roles and performances, and members of the rising middle class slowly costumed and festooned themselves, as well as everything from furniture to architecture, in Victorian decorum, propriety, and often gaudy gables and towers, how could a cultural place or role be found for the elusive Hawthorne? One way was to see in him a strange but fascinating combination of masculine and feminine traits, a kind of androgynous genius that partook of both sexes' generic traits. Waxed Duyckinck in the *Democratic Review* in April 1845: "Imagine a man of a rugged frame of body and a delicate mind . . . fragile and sensitive as a maiden's; the rough hairy rind of the cocoa-nut enclosing its sweet whiteness . . . The perfectness of his style, the completeness of form, the unity of his subject and of all his subjects, are masculine: the light play of fancy, the sentiment, are feminine. There is a deeper vein which no woman could ever reach, an intimacy with the sterner powers of life which we should wish no woman to attain" (Crowley 97). Better the hairy coconut than the unprotected "sweet whiteness" of a woman's fancy! "He is so gentle and mild that you feel as if speaking to a girl," concurred Henry Bright early on in 1852 (Idol/Jones 60). Longfellow would agree: "His genius, too, is characterized by a large proportion of feminine elements, depth and tenderness of feeling, exceeding purity of mind, and a certain airy grace and arch vivacity" (Bosco/Murphy 81). James Russell Lowell in 1848 summarized this combination of masculine and feminine qualities in Hawthorne in verse:

> When nature was shaping him, clay was not granted
> For making so full-sized a man as she wanted,
> So, to fill out her model, a little she spared
> From some finer-grained stuff for a woman prepared,
> And she could not have hit a more excellent plan
> For making him fully and perfect a man.

This dualistic or polarized approach still inhabits and helps shape contemporary criticism, when in fact the various perspectives and often contradictory speculations in his work are more entangled one with another in a kind of dark but dynamic dialectic than assured of their separate existence. At times they suggest possible synthesis and reconciliation, but more often they resist integration and resolution. These identified polarities — light/dark, good/evil, male/female, life/death — interact with one another, but in doing so produce a process of dramatic flux and uncertainty in which each of them breaks down and begins to blur and dissolve. What critics have assumed depends upon how they view the independence of each polarity, whereas in Hawthorne's fiction, he continuously undermines and subverts them, producing a kind of open-ended debate in which all seemingly separate and opposing values are seen as entangled one with the other. The result reveals a dark and often paradoxical, contradictory vision that challenges all certain beliefs, whether in terms of gender and class or moral and spiritual values. His work has often been seen as a threat to conventional and increasingly rigid nineteenth-century morality, as we shall see, his gloomy perspective undermining nineteenth-century American optimism.

The nineteenth century was mesmerized and repelled by gloom in an America that was proclaiming its Manifest Destiny, and so that gloom was always suspicious, vaguely un-American, unsettling. Proclaimed George William Curtis in 1853 in his *Homes of American Authors*, ". . . the imagination of our author treads the almost imperceptible line between the natural and the supernatural . . . But we avoid it. We recoil and hurry away, nor dare to glance over our shoulders lest we should see phantoms" (Bosco/Murphy 74). No "No, in Thunder" — as Melville had described Hawthorne's ultimate view of the world and society around him — for this writer; the headless horseman rides too closely, or as Emerson aphorized: "Hawthorne rides his horse of the night" (Bosco/Murphy 70). For Eugene Benson in 1868, Hawthorne "lures you on and on into the depressing labyrinth of human motives" (Crowley 434). Better to cheer up, and all will be well.

Other critics and acquaintances fought back against the frozen gothic image that seemed to be attached all too easily to Hawthorne. "Hawthorne is not a gloomy writer," insisted Duyckinck in May 1841; "his melancholy is fanciful, capricious" (Crowley 7). Thus was launched the genteel Hawthorne, the kindly homebody, the loving father and husband, the observer of tollgates, drunkards, the Erie Canal, and stagecoach passengers. James T. Fields spun amiable anecdotes about the man in 1871. George Lathrop revealed the everyday and ordinary minutiae of the notebooks. Henry James found him the creator of skillful but artificial and provincial romances.

At Bowdoin College, insisted John S. C. Abbott, one of Hawthorne's classmates, Hawthorne was "universally popular . . . He never seemed melancholy . . . there was nothing in his demeanor to repel the friendly advances of anyone . . . [He was] always meeting one with a pleasant smile, always ready to exchange a few affable words" (Bosco/Murphy 156, 159). "Fantastic romancer as he was," declaimed Henry James in reviewing the

French and Italian Notebooks in 1872, "he here refutes conclusively the common charge that he was either a melancholy or morbid genius." Horatio Bridge, who was also at Bowdoin with Hawthorne, in 1893 also declared that "he was neither morose nor sentimental; and, though taciturn, was invariably cheerful with his chosen friends; and there was much more of fun and frolic in his disposition than his published writings indicate." True, Bridge had written Hawthorne in December 1836 that "the bane of your life has been self-distrust [and] you never look at the bright side with any hope or confidence," but in his *Personal Recollections of Nathaniel Hawthorne*, a compendium of letters, money matters, publication dates, and memories of Bowdoin, in which Bridge presented himself as Hawthorne's principle supporter and cheerleader, he emphasizes Hawthorne's more normal and friend-inspiring traits. At Bowdoin "the customary pastimes included card-playing and wine-drinking, in which he joined his friends through good fellowship; but he rarely exceeded the bounds of moderation . . ."

So what was the standard nineteenth-century assessment of Hawthorne as a man and author? Morbid, maybe, but so were the Puritans. Melancholy, in his works, yes, but not as a man. A genius? Of course! Byronic outcast or at least a tortured ghost condemned to solitude? Yes, but . . . Genteel gentleman who loved kids and cats? Certainly, although . . . We begin to see how the image of Hawthorne over time attracted and supported distinctly polarized views, a perspective his own fiction helped create, as we will discuss below.

We begin to see later in the nineteenth century a very real sense of impenetrable mystery developing at the center of Hawthorne's work that could not be so easily quantified and spelled out. It had always been there, but most early nineteenth-century critics wanted to categorize and codify it as morbid, strange, weird, creepy, and diseased. We see it beginning to emerge in Nathan Hale, Jr.'s review in the *Boston Miscellany* of February 1842: "He contents himself with unveiling the movements of the inner man, and the growth of motive and reflection . . . There is often an air of mystery about the person and actions of his characters . . . he often brings before [his readers] agents whom they almost believe to be shadows from another world" (Crowley 79). Samuel W. S. Dutton in 1847 realized that Hawthorne "sees deeply into the interior of human character. He observes particularly and exactly its outward manifestations . . . and makes his accurate and lively description of the outward but the medium of vision into the inward . . . aware of its dark depths and its universal fountain of corruption" (Crowley 136, 137). In 1852 Edward Percy Whipple described Hawthorne's fictions as exploring "the processes of thought and emotion [along with] the delicate sharpness of insight into the most elusive movements of Consciousness, by which the romance is characterized" (Crowley 267).

The mind and its mysteries came to be seen as the focus of Hawthorne's psychological fiction. "In the region of mystery, the wildernesses and caverns of the mind, [Hawthorne] is at home," wrote Richard Henry Stoddard in 1853, "more at home, it seems to us, than in the upper and outer world" (Crowley 289). This would lead logically to the several interpretations of various events and behaviors with which Hawthorne filled his narratives. "Hawthorne does not clear up his mysteries," asserted Dorville Libby in the *Overland Monthly* of February 1869. "The truly supernatural admits no clearing up. It is the especial privilege of the romancer to make this departure from the strictly probable, and thus avail himself of the charm of mystery" (Crowley 458). This may be one of the reasons that keeps us reading Hawthorne today. The anonymous reviewer in the *North British Review* of September 1868 declares: "His pages are replete with mystery, hintings of an eerie presence, tokens of a power preternatural yet strangely in affinity with human life . . . But this mystery is never revealed; it is a presence without a form, an inarticulate voice, an impalpable agency . . ." (Idol/Jones 451).

By the time of his death in 1864, Hawthorne's fiction and his persona had been thoroughly established. He remained, as anonymous reviewers suggested, "the ghostly genius . . . a psychological dreamer . . . as though he were stricken by a spell" (Idol/Jones 439), sensitive, melancholy, shy, meditative, often ghastly but always ghostly. Such a melancholy genius had, of course, to be "that true child of New England, half shadowed with Puritanism, half kindled with the light and glory of modern thought and feeling," commented yet another anonymous reviewer (Idol/Jones 298). A twilight solitude permeates his work and character, as "The Minister's Black Veil" becomes "a parable of his own life. And this great characteristic of Mr. Hawthorne's imagination which, like aged sight, magnified even while it interposed a separating film between him and the outer world" (Idol/Jones 301). He remained "a Democrat among high-dry Federalists . . . shy as a cuckoo, recluse as a Trappist [monk]" (Idol/Jones 473). As early as 1853 Curtis had declared him "an absolute recluse" (Idol/Jones 65) and created the silent, haunted, gloomy Salemite Hawthorne, an image which has never been totally eradicated.

Writing about *The Scarlet Letter* in 1850, George Bailey Loring suggested that Hawthorne himself might have been personally involved with the impenetrable shroud of mystery that resonates in his fiction: "No author of our own country, and scarcely any author of our times, manages to keep himself clothed in such a cloak of mystery as Nathaniel Hawthorne . . . the strange and shifting picture he gives of the motive heart of man [suggests] an image of himself as a speculative philosopher" (Idol/Jones 133). Perhaps Hawthorne had chosen that "cloak of mystery" as consciously and purposefully as Whitman crafted his image as the swaggering young common man standing in a field and Emily Dickinson her legend as the strange shy poet mysteriously swathed in white.

The gloomy isolated icon that was Hawthorne remained unshaken, a mirror image of his work, as critics and reviewers failed to separate the man from the author. Eugene Benson, writing in December 1868 about both Poe and Hawthorne, saw Hawthorne as one who "brooded over his thoughts; he spent season after season in reverie — reverie which is foreign to our idea of the American man. Out of his loneliness, out of his reveries, out of his dreams, he wove the matchless web [luring] you on and on into the depressing labyrinth of human motives and human character" (Idol/ Jones 468, 467). The anonymous critic in the *Southern Review* of April 1870 described Hawthorne's characters as "essentially phantasmagoria . . . haunted by dreams" (Idol/Jones 475).

Hawthorne as silent icon became a source of much speculation for friends and critics. As his reputation, which they aided and abetted, grew, so did they come to accept as fact the mystery that surrounded him both as a man and as a writer. In their critiques and remembrances, were they consciously and calculatedly trying to create an aura of mystery that the word "genius" inspires? Once the genius label was firmly established early on, did the conjuring up of a sense of mystery necessarily follow? At John S. C. Abbott's 50th Reunion at Bowdoin, he remembered "an indescribable something in the silent presence" of Hawthorne (Bosco/Murphy 157). In 1901 in the *Atlantic Monthly*, Paul Elmore More could identify "the daemonic force of the man himself, the everlasting mystery of genius inhabiting his brain."

Despite the gloom, many nineteenth-century reviewers tried hard to opt for a subtler, softer Hawthorne, someone who would fit the more Victorian mood of sweet melancholy in an ultimately harmonic world. As the writer for the *Southern Review* explained in April 1870, "his sunshine wears often an Indian summer hue to veil its brightness, and sometimes a cloud of morbidness comes over it with an effect unpleasantly chilling; but generally, even his most pensive reveries are pervaded with a sweet serenity" (Idol/Jones 479). Alexander P. Japp, writing in October 1871, made an even stronger case: "He believes in inherited evils [but] also a Divine purpose, which embraces human life . . . Humanity is on the way towards a higher condition . . . But let no man trust in himself in view of the higher ends of life . . . Hawthorne holds by Providence, and not by men . . . Providence needs its human agents" (Idol/Jones 483, 484). Once again when confronting Hawthorne and his work, critics stressed the conflicts, the opposition, the paradoxes, the apparent polarity between gloom and gleam, blackness and brightness.

In 1871 James T. Fields, Hawthorne's publisher, published *Yesterdays with Authors* and in several chapters focused on Hawthorne the man. In his concerted assault on the public image of the gloomy, morbid author, he described him as incredibly handsome, "and although the humorous side of Hawthorne was not easily or often discoverable, yet have I seen him marvelously moved to fun, and no man laughed more heartily in his way over a good story." Fields reports that on August 5, 1851, when he, with Hawthorne, Melville and others, trekked up Monument Mountain in western Massachusetts, armed with food and champagne, "Hawthorne was among the most enterprising of the merry-makers; and being in the dark much of the time, he ventured to call out lustily and pretend that certain destruction was inevitable to all of us."

What we recognize between "the most enterprising of the merry-makers" and the man who pretended "that certain destruction was inevitable to all of us" is once again a description based on a polarized and dualistic perspective. Part of this approach may have been generated by the polarized positions that were already well established in the nineteenth century, the result perhaps of the perilous equilibrium between merriment and gloom, soul and mind, theology and psychology, sentiment and sex. Did Hawthorne, forever entranced and repelled by the solitariness of the individual, caught between these various forces and speculations, recognize, as Edward S. Reed suggests, that "introspection reveals the results of a 'play of forces' and is thus both indispensable and inadequate: indispensable, because the mental forces can nowhere else be observed; inadequate, because it is introspection that makes us wonder what gives rise to the play of forces in the first place"? (85).

Hawthorne recognized the essential aloneness, complicated by the more social aspects and facets of loneliness, that compelled his characters to either seek isolation or reach out for some kind of ever-elusive intimate connection. Was he peculiar? Maybe. Was he a Puritan? You could call him that, but carefully, warily. Was he a Byronic recluse? Hardly. A shrewd Yankee and literary dreamer? Perhaps. Feminine? Masculine? Neither? Both? Yes. Early critics wrestled with such categories, as we are wrestling still. But it is probably that aura of mystery that leads us on, the half-felt desire to move beyond the very polarities that shaped Hawthorne's intellectual and aesthetic makeup. Can we seek new momentary stays against confusion, or must we still grapple with elusive designs, if design governs at all?

The mystery remains intact. The silence of the man is eternal. He seems a handsome presence and an elusive absence, as tantalizing to biographers as perhaps he was to himself, if not downright disturbing. When he confronts the notion of an autonomous self, it becomes a black hole, an absence, a dark unconscious depth that he, as was suggested in the *North British Review* in 1868, makes "sacred by his fear of violation and submission to stronger wills. . . . He seems endowed with a sort of intellectual polarity" (Idol/Jones 464). His penchant for allegory certainly reveals those metaphysical longitudes and latitudes. The key may lie at the crossroads of those polarities, at some slippery center that can never be named nor rigidly located, a kind of entanglement that re-conceives of polarities as both interpenetrating one another and finally indeterminate. Nineteenth-century biographers took it upon themselves to explore these crossroads, that center, and that entangled vision, and it is to them that we must turn to see what they made out of the mysteries surrounding their elusive quarry.

3: Biographical and Critical Veils in the Nineteenth Century

THE NINETEENTH CENTURY declared that Hawthorne was a genius, as if that resolved everything about him and his work, and scattered impressions this way and that about his vision of solitude and isolation, his morbid mind and his solitary ways, his fixation on guilt and sin, sorrow and sympathy, all in an atmosphere of proclaiming the birth of a genuine American literature to counteract the British hold on American culture and fiction. But the man himself managed to evade all would-be critics and scattershot analysts, presenting himself to the world in his prefaces as a pale Romantic fellow, haunted in haunted rooms, and troubled by his fascination with allegory as if it were small recompense for his inability to grapple with the real world that lay around him, opaque, dense, and indecipherable.

Yet another dualism or polarity haunts every Hawthorne biography: how was one to relate the "morbidity" of his vision to the elegant gentility of his style? Was the latter used to disguise the former? Was the vision itself so dark that Hawthorne could only approach it instead of descending into it? How could such a life be lived with this nearly schizophrenic division between the dark romancer who buried himself in solitude in his study and the practical man who worked to obtain political appointments? Biographers would shift back and forth from one to the other, from periods in which the dark romancer took over the center of the tale to the reinstatement of the practical man of letters. Psychological perspectives would deepen both aspects, often in an attempt to see them as flip sides of the same coin. In the more modern era of deconstruction and cultural studies, biographers tended to focus on the enigma of Hawthorne's personality and his life as a male New Englander in the middle of the nineteenth century, freighted with all the racist and sexist myths of the time. This seesawing back and forth marks the general trajectory of Hawthorne biographies.

For example, we can see how the battle between biographies continued over Hawthorne's "essence." In *The Rebellious Puritan: Portrait of Mr. Hawthorne* (1927) Lloyd Morris deepened Hawthorne's Calvinist legacy, for example, by describing *The Scarlet Letter* as not just a historical and Puritan tale but "actually . . . an inexorably realistic study of the world as it is" (230). Hawthorne wrestled with Calvinist conundrums: Can evil contain good? Or as Morris formulates the question: "May not the soul be saved through what appears to be sin; not through repentance, but through consistent adherence to sin? And, conversely, may not consistent devotion to an ideal that appears to be noble bring us, in the end, to evil?" There are no final solutions, but Hawthorne dared "to observe life closely; to project the problems into life and deduce conclusions from what observation revealed; this was all one could do" (143–44).

Hildegarde Hawthorne, Hawthorne's granddaughter, in her genteel, uncritical biography, which was written primarily for younger readers, took up the idea of rebellion but utterly redefined it. In *Romantic Rebel: The Story of Nathaniel Hawthorne* (1932), she simplistically associates rebellion with the act of writing itself and stresses the miracle of Hawthorne's happening to meet Sophia Peabody when he did: "Indeed, there is a sort of miracle in his ever escaping from that haunted chamber, as he himself called it. . . . [He and Sophia] suddenly found themselves within the flaming circle of love" (79, 101). Hildegarde's emphasis on the love story is obviously her attempt to counteract the myth of her morbid grandfather.

The ways Hildegarde and Morris deal with Hawthorne's mother reveals much about their "take" on the writer's life. Hildegarde acknowledges that Elizabeth Hawthorne, after her husband's death, took to her room in the Manning household but remained "friendly . . . lovely . . . fragile in health, but rarely ill [with] a reserved charm that instantly attracted those who did meet her. There was nothing cold or grim in this drawing away from normal human life, she never repelled anyone" (24). Morris paints a different portrait. Madame Hawthorne "passed her days in the darkened solitude of her room . . . a gravely beautiful ghost, whose insubstantial existence, although remote from the routine of domestic life, dominated the household by an unacknowledged tyranny." She kept "a secret rite of perpetual vigil and lamentation . . . In this desolate anti-life her rebellious heart achieved an austere, comfortless peace" (10, 11). Morris seems to be viewing her through the eyes of Hawthorne the romancer, for he, in effect, produces here a thoroughly Hawthornesque character. His Mrs. Hawthorne is the romancer's Mrs. Hawthorne in all her secret, desolate solitude. Hildegarde recognizes the reality but presents a charming, friendly, and lovely woman who repelled no one.

The sense of mystery that has always dogged Hawthorne as a man and writer may be not only the result of the Romantic image of the solitary artist in the mid-nineteenth century but also the result of Hawthorne's own public mystifications of his life and work, through which he participated in the very myth of necessary artistic solitude that haunted his culture and his times. Such a veil is impossible to remove entirely, since both he and his culture wove it together and set it in place, but biographers over the years have tried to peer beneath it or at least describe it in terms of psychological projection, cultural artifact, gender-constructed shield, racist mask, or carapace of self-defense. Each age paints a somewhat different picture of Hawthorne the subject, but the process itself, which is forever ongoing, is always fascinating if never definitive.

Hawthorne's basic biography reveals no extended bouts of madness, no torrid sexual affairs, no wild revels, no misuse of drugs, no fiery feuds, and no great crimes (that we know of, though Herman Melville told Julian Hawthorne that he always suspected that there had been some great dark secret in Hawthorne's life). In fact the outward shape of his life strikes one as staid and almost stolid.

As we have seen, during Hawthorne's lifetime and after his death, the myth of the morbid recluse had taken such firm control of his image that family members and others were eager to sabotage and undermine it. We have seen the twists and turns of early critics and reviewers, attempting to transform such disagreeable morbidity into a version of Puritan and New England history, thus turning Hawthorne into a national, more American writer. His pellucid style overshadowed such dark forebodings every time, its elegance transcending the morbid substance of his fiction, yet how could an author write "The Minister's Black Veil" and "Little Annie's Ramble," the first a dark tale of religious and psychological obsession and a staple of contemporary Hawthorne criticism, the second all but abandoned today because of its sentimentality?

Eleven volumes of Hawthorne's work, from his notebooks to his unfinished romances, were published posthumously between 1864 and 1883, extending his powerful position in American literature. These included Sophia's heavily edited edition of the *American Note-Books* (1868), followed by the *English Note-Books* (1870) and Una's edition of *The French and Italian Note-Books* (1871). *Septimius Felton* appeared in 1872, *The Dolliver Romance* and *Fanshawe and Other Pieces* in 1876, and *Dr. Grimshawe's Secret* in 1883. In 1883 a twelve-volume, complete edition of his works, edited by his son-in-law, George Parsons Lathrop, was published, including Lathrop's own book, *A Study of Hawthorne*, which had been originally published in 1876. Also in 1883 students at Yale could choose to write their junior essays on "Hawthorne's Imagination," the only American to be so honored (Tompkins 29). "In short," as Jane Tompkins has suggested, though Hawthorne's work may not be exactly "the property of a dynastic cultural elite, the friends and associates who outlived Hawthorne kept his fiction up-to-date by writing about it, and then *their* friends took over" (30). Hawthorne's exalted status demanded that family members and others try to present a clearer image of the man to the general public in order to spring him from the gothicized ghetto in which others had imprisoned him.

Julian Hawthorne in his two-volume *Nathaniel Hawthorne and His Wife* — the title of which should make a contemporary soul cringe — published in 1884, determinedly separated the writer from the man and father. While his mother was all of a piece — gentle, optimistic, a kind of

chipper Greek chorus to the great man's work: "The mother sees goodness and divinity shining through everywhere" — the younger Hawthorne
saw his father's attitude as "deductive and moralizing" (324). And Julian
asserted that "it is the biographer's business . . . to confine himself to
putting the reader in possession of this human aspect of his subject, and
to let the rest take care, in great measure, of itself . . . His literary phase
seemed a phase only, and not the largest or most characteristic . . . Any
attempt to make the works throw light upon their author is certain to
miscarry" (244, 243).

When Julian eventually read his father's books, "they struck him as
being but a somewhat imperfect reflection of certain regions of his father's
mind with which he had become otherwise familiar" (245). Determined
to transform his father from solitary soul into genial Victorian patriarch,
Julian assaults the Romantic-Gothic legend that people had built up, "constructing an imaginary Hawthorne from what was assumed to be the
internal evidence of his writings, — a sort of morbid, timid, milk-and-
water Frankenstein, who was drawn on by a grisly fascination to discuss
fearful conceptions, and was in a chronic state of being frightened almost
into hysterics by the chimeras of his own Fancy" (84). His manner had also
been "magnified into a superhuman and monstrous shyness" (84).

"His melancholy," insisted the son, "indeed, belonged rather to his
imagination than to his realities; it was the melancholy of a mind conscious
of power" (126). He goes on to quote his aunt, Elizabeth Palmer Peabody,
with whom he often spoke before writing his book: "[Hawthorne] was not
morbid or gloomy in nature; his peculiar form of shyness was rather the
result of the outward circumstance that he belonged to a family which had
done nothing (as the mother and sisters of a man generally do) to put him
into easy relations with society . . . His reserved manners had come to be
a barrier against intrusion . . . [Sophia] guarded his solitude, perhaps with
a needless extreme of care" (247). Elizabeth, of course, prided herself on
discovering Hawthorne and his work and promoted him and it among the
New England intelligentsia. He may even have been engaged to her at one
time. Sophia also contributed to the portrait of her husband as a congenial
and loving man and father, writing in November 1847 that "Julian idolizes
his father, and will not come to me when he is in the room" (323).

Julian presses his case: "At no time during his residence at Bowdoin
did he have the reputation of being a recluse, or exclusive" (120). He was
not "the victim of an insatiable appetite for gin, brandy and rum" (85).
His presence in conversations suggested a certain aloofness and quality of
observation, but "to be a student of human nature is not the same as to
be a spy upon it" (85). "He had his own views regarding the manner in
which people should be interfered with, even for their own salvation, and
regarding the extent to which such interference was justifiable" (91), a
curious comment, which Julian does not develop, that leaves us wondering

where this sense of interference and "being invaded" (85) comes from. Sophia comes to the rescue, as quoted by Julian: "He has perfect dominion over himself in every respect . . . I never knew such loftiness, so simply borne . . . Happy, happiest is the wife, who can bear such and so sincere testimony to her husband after eight years' intimate union" (373).

Such happiness appears, in Julian's telling of it, to arise from a one-dimensional, child-like, sweet-tempered woman of unshakeable faith and serenity, the perfect counterpart to her husband's "forebodings" (40), a person determined to cling to her vision of Christian goodness. Her beliefs "kept her a child all her life long; [they] drew around her, as it were, an enchanted circle . . . She was disciplined and instructed by pain, as others are by sin and its consequences" (48). Here it is obvious that Julian is drawing the circle, and that as the only boy in a family with two sisters, the same conditions in which his father was raised, he may have felt his own fear of invasion and interference.

Julian certainly took the Victorian gender role of the married woman and mother to heart. In light of this, he attacked the writer Margaret Fuller for her outspoken stand on women's rights. He also accused her of embodying "the *look* of absolute irreligion" (259). According to Julian, Fuller had no womanly charms whatsoever, revealed a strong but coarse nature, was a great humbug living on borrowed qualities and, quoting his father's angry assessment of her after her death (which infuriated Fuller's friends), in surrendering herself to a penniless Italian count gave in to "this rude old potency" of sensual pleasure. No wonder Julian paints Sophia with such broad Christian strokes: she is the Victorian woman on her pedestal, the disciple at the foot of the Great Writer, of whom Hawthorne himself could write, "My wife is, in the strictest sense, my sole companion, and I need no other; there is no vacancy in my mind, any more than in my heart . . . she is always cheerful. Thank God that I suffice for her boundless heart!" (289).

Hawthorne's work, therefore, must have come from some other place, from his observations and assessments of not his particular but the general human condition. In a comment on that condition, he wrote on January 1, 1840, that "nobody would think that the same man could live two such different lives simultaneously. But then the grosser life is a dream, and the spiritual life is a reality" (210). In regard to and support of that spiritual reality, Julian quotes from a letter by William B. Pike to Hawthorne, a man Hawthorne befriended while working at the Boston Custom House: "You probe deeply, — you go down among the moody silences of the heart, and open those depths whence come motives that give complexion to actions, and make in men what are called states of mind; being conditions of mind which cannot be removed either by our own reasoning or by the reasoning of others . . . you show how things take place, and open the silent, unseen, internal elements which first set the machinery in motion . . . You show us that such depths exist" (444, 445, 446). Dualism is enthroned yet again: the outer life, the inner workings, those first bold strokes of psychological romance that reveal the writer's vision but not the man's healthy, family-oriented, optimistic, and loving soul. Adds Hawthorne's sister Elizabeth: "I never heard of any insanity in the family. We are a remarkably 'hard-headed' race, not easily excited, not apt to be carried away by any impulse. The witch's curse is not our only inheritance from our ancestors; we have also an unblemished name, and the best brains in the world" (9).

Julian's second volume begins in England in July 1853, after his father had been recently appointed as the American consul in Liverpool. Here we find more tales of travel and more assessments of Hawthorne's art. On May 15, 1854, Mary Howitt praised Hawthorne's style in a letter to him as pure, transparent, refined, elegant, and exquisite with "all your minute detail, — your working out a character by Pre-Raphaelian touches — your delicate touch upon touch, which produces such a finished whole, — so different from the slap-dash style of writing so common nowadays" (48). He even tries to justify his father's limits of artistic appreciation: "He accepted and respected the Dutch masters because they came into direct rivalry with concrete nature, and he could test the accuracy of their rendering by his own observation . . . A great part of specific art culture consists in learning the limitations of art, and judging, not absolutely, but comparatively . . . [Hawthorne] is continually finding the beauty enhanced by its connection with humanity and antiquity, — a connection, of course, not intrinsic, but created by the observer's imagination" (221).

The dismantling of the myth of Hawthorne's morbidity continued unabated. "He was the *least* morbid of men," insisted Henry Bright, who became one of Hawthorne's best friends in England, "with a singularly sweet temper, and a very far-reaching charity; he was reserved and (in a sense) a *proud* man . . . He was full of a quiet common-sense, which contrasted strangely with the weird nature of his 'genius'" (350). The dualism yet remained as if ingrained in Hawthorne's legacy, the weird genius full of a quiet common sense.

Julian recognized that his father "uniformly chose to anticipate the darker alternative of whatever event was developing" (207), particularly in Rome when his sister Una nearly died of malaria, his mother at the other extreme never giving up the slightest hope. Sophia every once in a while recognized Hawthorne's more shadowy nature. He was always "veiling himself from others, since he veiled himself from himself . . . I never dared to gaze at him, even I, unless his lids were down. It seemed an invasion into a holy place. To the last, he was in a measure to me a divine mystery, for he was so to himself" (352–53). The dark mystery remains intact despite the genial image of father and husband, but in Sophia's own words that mystery remained, of course, divine, emanating from "a holy place" that curiously feared or generated threats of invasion.

Julian's story darkens with Hawthorne's musings on Melville's certainty of annihilation and on the certain doom that came to the life Byron led. He reports on Hawthorne's speculations about the pretext for civil war. If the South remained in the union, would the arrogance of the slaveholders take over? If the union collapsed, the North would be freed from slavery, but would that be the best possible outcome? The war seemed to offer him only "the absence of a distinct, well-defined object to be settled by the fight" (293), and the possible freeing of black slaves only complicated the issues at hand. Upon their return from England to Concord in 1860, Sophia urged Hawthorne to travel more for his health and to stay as long as he must or liked.

Thus in his biography of his father and mother, Julian staunchly separated the loving father from the melancholy writer, confining that melancholy to Hawthorne's imagination, which he saw as distinctly separate from the person. He relied on Elizabeth Palmer Peabody as a witness, and she was also determined to separate the "real" Hawthorne from the public legend of the gloomy recluse. In doing so Julian confined his mother to the role of the Victorian stereotype: the amiable, optimistic, and solidly Christian wife and mother, a wonderfully self-effacing helpmate who stood by her husband and family at all times. Such an image would not be questioned by other biographers in any great depth until late in the twentieth century.

One of the first biographical-critical books on Hawthorne and his work was his son-in-law George Lathrop's above-mentioned *Study,* published in 1876. Lathrop was determined to resurrect a more normal and conventional Hawthorne to diffuse the dark Byronic legend. His critical judgment is certainly unreliable — he says that "*The Scarlet Letter* is perhaps not so excellent as the author's subsequent books . . . there is a harshness in its tone, a want of mitigation . . . *Blithedale* is certainly the most consummate of the four completed romances [with its] appearance of unlabored ease, and a consequent breeziness of effect" (101, 111) — and his book a hodge-podge of letters, opinions, and family legends.

In his rambling overview of the man and his fiction, Lathrop admitted that "his real and inmost character was a mystery even to himself, and this, because he felt so profoundly the impossibility of sounding to the bottom any human heart" (137) — thereby preserving that mystical aura that every writer was assumed to embody — but insisted that the opinion of Hawthorne as an "extremely gloomy" man was dead wrong (131). He recognized the strangeness of Hawthorne's obsessed characters but denied that this was the result of "self-study, — personal traits disguised in fiction; yet this is what has often been affirmed of Hawthorne. We don't think of attributing to Dickens the multiform oddities which he pictures with such power" (132). And Hawthorne? "In truth he was a perfectly healthy person" (132). Though "none can ever be said to know Hawthorne who do not leave large allowances for the unknowable" (138), he was not a fatalist but "an optimist . . . who has a very profound faith in Providence; not in any 'special providence,' but in that operation of divine laws through unexpected agencies and conflicting events, which is very gradually approximating human affairs to a state of truthfulness" (136). The idea of nineteenth-century progress persisted.

Ultimately, then, "the morbid phases which [Hawthorne] studied were entirely outside of himself" (142):

> The psychical conditions described by Hawthorne had only the remotest connection with any mood of his own; they were mainly translations, into the language of genius, of certain impressions and observations drawn from the world around him. After his death, the Note-Books caused a general rustle of surprise, revealing as they did the simple, wholesome nature of this strange imaginer . . . critics have not yet wholly learned how far apart from himself these creations were. (141)

Extracts that Lathrop published from selected Hawthorne letters, much to the distress of Julian Hawthorne and others, were regarded by him "as very important in showing the obverse of that impression of unhealthy solitude which has been so generally received from accounts of Hawthorne hitherto published" (65).

Lathrop concluded that "although his spiritual inspiration scares away a large class of sympathies, and although his strictly New England atmosphere seems to chill and restrain his dramatic fervor . . . I believe there is no fictionist who penetrates so far into individual consciences as Hawthorne, that many persons will be found who derive a profoundly religious aid from his unobtrusive but commanding sympathy . . . he is one of the most powerful because unsuspected revolutionists of the world . . . plac[ing] him on a plane between Shakespeare and Goethe" (151, 152).

Critical attention, however superficial, to Hawthorne and his work began to appear within the same period as the family biographies. In his *A History of American Literature* (1878), Moses Coit Tyler makes passing references to Hawthorne as a successful American writer. Selden L. Whitcomb, in his *Chronological Outline of American Literature* (1894) lists Hawthorne's work year by year like a spreadsheet. "Unnatural as this existence was," writes Brader Matthews in his *Introduction to American Literature* (1896), "Hawthorne kept his health and seldom lost his cheerfulness" (112). The genteel image of Hawthorne had become firmly rooted by the 1890s, as had Matthews's idea that he had mastered the craft of writing better than any other American author who preceded him — with some allowances made for Washington Irving and Poe. Matthews ranked *The Scarlet Letter* second in popularity among American novels to

Uncle Tom's Cabin, insisting that Hawthorne was the "most accomplished writer America has yet produced" (123).

In 1897 Rose Hawthorne Lathrop published *Memories of Hawthorne,* a book that relied on her mother's letters, a kind of response to Julian's manly tome, and like his, overwritten in that lush sentimental Victorian style, reeking of Victorian pieties, in which one hundred words are preferable to ten, akin to Victorian decoration, which leaves no square inch untasselled or unadorned. Sophia is obviously the hero of Rose's book, as Hawthorne was of Julian's. It is as if Rose's own religious convictions also allowed her to view life through rose-colored glasses and contributed to her rhetorically florid Victorian style that transformed Romanticism into a Pre-Raphaelite painting with its jeweled surfaces and incandescent lights.

And what of Rose's father? The campaign to save him from the predominantly public image of the gloomy and reserved recluse continued. He was neither gloomy nor shy but pensive. He loved to read aloud to his family; "every character is unfixed from the page, and stands free in life" (75). He was never ill; "he has no brute force" (136). He was acutely pragmatic when writing letters to friends for jobs and political appointments. Losing his job at the Salem Custom House, he railed against the villainous Charles Upham: "if Mr. U. should give me occasion, — or perhaps if he should not, — I shall do my best to kill and scalp him in the public prints; and I think I shall succeed" (108). He was constantly writing, wrote each morning with a gold pen and led a rigorous existence, determined not to waste any time. He kept his temper, banked the fires of life, managing his "volcanic power" (447). He was temperate, forgiving, and philosophical. "His terrors were those of our own hearts . . . he governed his character by Christian fellowship" (445). In England he presented himself as dignified. Not at all did he seem morbidly shy. In gloomy Liverpool his cheerfulness overruled any traces of morbidity. "His cool command" (214) often took charge of his "half-withdrawn brooding" (361). He was never outwardly perturbed but usually cheerful in a solemn manner. He could see through anyone but with sympathy, not the poison of contempt.

We can detect a young child's adoration of a parent in Rose's description of her father's work as well as her mother's infectious optimism:

> The books my father wrote [in the Berkshires] embrace this joy of untheoried, peaceful, or gloriously perturbed life of sky and land. Theory of plot or principle was as much beneath him as the cobblestones; from self-righteous harangues he turned as one who had heard a divine voice that alone deserved to declare. He taught as Nature does, always leading to thoughts of something higher than the dictum of men, and nobler than their greatest beauty of action. (125)

Back in Concord in 1860 Hawthorne "entered upon a long renuncia-
tion . . . [there were] longer and longer intervals of wordless reserve"
(472) though his sympathy remained intact. The threat and then reality of
the Civil War added to his sudden transformation, for he turned "from
sunshine to dusky cold" (478) and became "an old, old man" (478). He
insisted that after his death all his letters be burned and that no one write
his biography; "he forbade any such matter in connection with himself in
any distance of the future" (477).

As for Rose's final word on her famous father: "He hated failure,
dependence, and disorder, broken rules and weariness of discipline, as he
hated cowardice. I cannot express how brave he seemed to me" (480). In
this he almost sounds like the stereotypical New England Yankee — tough,
mostly silent, stately at times, at times remote and distant, driven by discipline and rigorous habits as rock-solid as his favorite White Mountains,
and always somehow on his guard against unruly pleasures and pastimes.
Writing must have in part secured his release from that "volcanic power"
within. While a Mr. Thompson was painting him as he sat in "a stiff chair,"
he saw himself "a perfect recluse in disposition. So I was under the impression that I was being punished by the invisible powers, which I was conscious of eminently deserving" (372).

The mystery of Hawthorne's true nature and the mysteries that lay at
the center of his psychological romances and tales lingers despite Rose's
rosy ruminations. Almost buried in this long book is a letter written by
George S. Hillard to "My Dear Hawthorne" from Boston on March 28,
1850. Hillard praised *The Scarlet Letter* as "a book full of tragic power, nice
observation, delicate tact, and rare knowledge of the human heart." But
the man continued to baffle him:

> You are, intellectually speaking, quite a puzzle to me. How comes it
> that with so thoroughly healthy an organization as you have, you have
> such a taste for the morbid anatomy of the human heart, and such
> knowledge of it, too? I should fancy from your books that you were
> burdened with secret sorrow; that you had some blue chamber in
> your soul, into which you hardly dared to enter yourself; but when I
> see you, you give me the impression of a man as healthy as Adam was
> in Paradise . . . But . . . let me be thankful for the weird and sad strain
> which breathes from "The Scarlet Letter" . . . . (121–22)

Once again a voice in the nineteenth century wrestles with appearance and
reality, recognizing the morbid as somehow unhealthy but fascinated by it
nonetheless. Is this perhaps the fate that Hawthorne himself experienced,
convinced that he was "punished by invisible powers," the dim secrets in the
"blue chamber" of his soul, and his attraction to twilight tales? For Rose he
remained "this sensitive, warm-hearted, brave, recluse, much-seeing man"
(450), and among such contradictions his biographical incarnation still lies.

Anthony Trollope, in his "The Genius of Nathaniel Hawthorne" of September 1879, wrote perhaps one of the best early summaries of Hawthorne's work, knowing that Hawthorne admired his "beef-and-ale" novels and of Hawthorne's focus on human suffering. Trollope suggested that there was "a certain grandness in nature in being susceptible of such suffering . . . You have been ennobled by that familiarity with sorrow . . . Something of the sublimity of the transcendent, something of the mystery of the unfathomable [suggests] that you too might live to be sublime, and revel in mingled light and mystery" (Idol/Jones 502). Hawthorne never "altogether dispelled . . . some unutterable woe [but] the woe is of course fictitious, and therefore endurable, — and therefore alluring. And woe itself has its charm" (Idol/Jones 501). Trollope recognized that "in no American writer is to be found the same predominance of weird imagination . . . *The Scarlet Letter* is so terrible in its pictures of diseased human nature as to produce most questionable delight" (Idol/Jones 503). Thus does Trollope try to transform "morbidity" into the sublime, one way of combining the shadows with light, while separating the man from the author, and becoming unconsciously part of a network of writers and friends who attempted to refute the image of the shadowy haunted soul of the Old Manse and reveal a more "regular fellow," a family man with a sense of everyday realities and genteel humor.

It may be helpful to consider one final critic-reviewer of Hawthorne's work and background in the nineteenth century, a fellow writer who both wanted to portray himself as a logical successor to Hawthorne and yet wavered in terms of how to deal with him. Henry James' relationship to Hawthorne both suggests a kind of anxiety of influence and a curious blend of praise and criticism of him and his work. To every positive comment, James seems driven to add a negative riposte. In his 1872 review of the selected passages from the *French and Italian Note-books*, he celebrates "our sense of that genius" and then immediately qualifies this statement by asserting that if we were to judge them "with any real critical rigor," we would find them "superficial, uninformed, incurious, inappreciative" (Idol/Jones 355). "These pages offer no adequate explanation of him; [they remain] fitfully diffuse and shallow . . . He walks about bending a puzzled, ineffective gaze at things . . . Never, surely, was a man of literary genius less a man of letters" (Idol/Jones 355, 356). And how would we then define genius? The word had become so associated with Hawthorne by this time, interfused with patriotic needs to proclaim a nationalist triumph over various British writers, that it no longer required any definition or explanation. Does Hawthorne, for James, remain "the last pure American" (Idol/Jones 358), thereby making way for the new "impure" literary realist who covets his status and success?

James joins the genteel allies in proclaiming, "fantastic romancer as he was, he here refutes conclusively the common charge that he was either a melancholy or a morbid genius. He had a native relish for the picturesque greys and browns of life" (Idol/Jones 356). But then, of course, "his taste was not robust," and he displayed "a comfortable want of eagerness in his mind" (Idol/Jones 357). James's position is not quite as radical a flip-flop as Poe's — allegory is all right; allegory proves fatal to a work of art; Hawthorne's work is very original; his work is not original in the slightest — but the same tendency exists.

In 1879 James, in his book on Hawthorne, suggested that the note-books revealed only "an extraordinary blankness — a curious paleness of colour and paucity of detail" (33). They showed only absence, coldness, and vacancy. James used the word "simple" again and again. Hawthorne's life was "as pure, as simple, as unsophisticated, as his work" (144). Bowdoin was a simple place compared to Oxford and Cambridge. Hawthorne's manliness was simple; so was the society he grew up in, as well as the democratic social structure itself, and finally Hawthorne's own modes of contemplation and genius. As a product of provincial New England he might have been shy and reticent, victimized by a pinched moral responsibility, village life, the lack of diversity caused by the lack of immigration, and the "strange, vague, long-dormant heritage of his straight-laced Puritan ancestry" (127). Puritanism, therefore, was but a pigment of Hawthorne's creative fancy, a flavor and aesthetic coloring, not part of a deeper vision. Sin was but an effect, not a state or condition, lending itself to chiaroscuro and local color, not to any kind of penetrating analysis or exploration.

The Scarlet Letter, according to James, while "densely dark [and] the most consistently gloomy of English novels of the first order," lacks real-ity, abuses the fanciful, reduces its characters to types, and remains too ingenious, too fraught with allegorical abstractions for its own good. Spoken like a true literary realist who would praise *The Blithedale Romance* as "the lightest, the brightest, the liveliest . . . of unhumorous fictions" (105); "the effect of [which] is to make one think more agreeably of life" (105); Coverdale "is evidently an excellent fellow" (106). Of course it would follow that in James's opinion *Our Old Home* would display Hawthorne's best writing, the most charm, and that *The Marble Faun* (known to James as a resident of England by its British title, *Transformation*) would appear to be "less simple and complete" (131), a popular success that pushed unreality too far and left its faulty narration fatally vague" (131, 134).

For James, surely the more cultured, more cultivated, more cosmo-politan American, the Civil War marked the end of a less critical era and brought forth a world far more complicated and complex than the simple, provincial Hawthorne could ever fathom. He praised "Roger Malvin's Burial," "Rappaccini's Daughter," and "Young Goodman Brown" as Hawthorne's masterpieces, although he also suggested that they really had nothing to do with Hawthorne's state of mind and were essentially "little tales of New England history" (45).

William Dean Howells, the reigning novelist of manners after the war, in 1880 chided James for just such issues. For him James too often describes the people of Salem and Concord before the war as provincial. Howells goes on to draw a clear distinction between the romance and the novel, which we will explore in the final chapter, and chides James for confusing apples with oranges: "No one better than Mr. James knows the radical difference between a romance and a novel, but he speaks now of Hawthorne's novels, and now of his romances." He explains that James's "defect, or his error, appears oftenest in his discussion of the notebooks."

Howells praises James for his critical take on *Our Old Home* and himself would "place *The Blithedale Romance* before *The House of Seven Gables* [*sic*]" — the literary realist and novelist of manners cannot resist sticking to his creed — but also agrees with James's assessment of Hawthorne's character as "innocent, affectionate . . . extremely domestic [with] an unperplexed intellect." James's book remains "skillful and manly . . . a miracle of tact and of self respect," another one of those impressionistic Victorian phrases that drove the New Critics to try and create a literary criticism that was more scientific and analytical.

By 1896 in his essay on Hawthorne, written for the *Library of the World's Best Literature Ancient and Modern*, vol. XII, James had changed his tune a bit. He not only recognizes "that feeling for the latent romance of New England" but credits Hawthorne with having looked for it "in the secret play of the Puritan faith," thus focusing on "a life of the spirit more complex than anything that met the mere eye of sense. It was a question of looking behind and beneath for the suggestive idea, the artistic motive," a process similar to James's own. He admits that "*The Scarlet Letter* lives, in spite of too many cold *concetti* — Hawthorne's general danger," and concedes that it is "the closest approach we are likely to have to the great work of fiction, so often called for, that is to do us nationally most honor and most good," but he holds his highest artistic praise for *The House of the Seven Gables* and *The Blithedale Romance* because they push "more closely [to] the surface of American life" and come "a trifle nearer to being . . . novel[s] of manners" with their "certain value as a picture of manners."

James castigates the author's fancy in *The Marble Faun* "for freakish correspondences," adores Hawthorne's "exquisite women such as Hilda and Priscilla" (!), and comments on Hawthorne's ultimate aloofness — "He is outside of everything, and an alien everywhere. He is an esthetic solitary" — all of which contemporary critical perspectives would have trouble with, except for the solitariness, which seems to be one of the touchstones of the modern era of Hawthorne criticism. He may be right in his assessment that Hawthorne went out of his way not to plunge into the depths of human tragedy — "he preferred to remain . . . on the surface" — but he acknowledges the "faculty that gave him much more a terrible sense of human abysses than a desire rashly to sound them and rise to the surface with his report," something he seemed reluctant to do in 1879. Yet James ends his essay by stating that "the subtleties [Hawthorne] spun are mere silken threads for stringing polished beads. His collection of moral mysteries is the cabinet of a dilettante." What James offers with the right hand, he withdraws with the left.

James's last assessment of Hawthorne's work appeared in a letter he wrote to celebrate the commemoration of Hawthorne's centennial in 1904, and his appraisal and respect for Hawthorne's work had deepened further. He praises Hawthorne for describing "the romantic side . . . of man's relation to his environment," though Salem remains "sunny and shady . . . the blissfully homogeneous community of the forties and fifties." He allows that Hawthorne did manage to see "the quaintness or the weirdness, the interest *behind* the interest . . . as something deeply within us, not as something infinitely disconnected from us, [saw] the real as distinguished from the artificial romantic note." *The House of the Seven Gables*, for instance, now "takes up the parti-coloured angular, audible, traceable Real, the New England earnest, aspiring, reforming Real." Thus it and Hawthorne's other works become literary classics "by the manner in which later developments have worked in respect to them . . . in spite of themselves." Of course, James being James, classics become such in comparison to contemporary works in his time, in which journalism had routed fiction in "these days of huge and easy and immediate success." Hawthorne has survived, he has passed the tests of time, and once this has occurred, "[he had] become one [who] may be left to the light and the ages." Do we detect a touch of envy, a smidgen of jealousy? Perhaps, but at the very least and at the last James had given Hawthorne his due by declaring him a classic writer, albeit "blindly, brought about, for the author on whom the crown alights, by the generations, the multitudes worshipping other gods, that have followed him" (web).

Moncure D. Conway met Hawthorne twice, in July 1860 at a dinner of the Literary Club in Boston and again in either 1862 or 1863 at the home of James T. Fields, Hawthorne's publisher. His first wife was a cousin of Sophia's, and he was shocked by the change in Hawthorne from "his great athletic frame . . . softened by its repose" in 1860 to a man "who appeared vague and lost amid the whirl of events, about which he was inclined to be silent" (204) in 1863. In his *Life of Nathaniel Hawthorne* (1890) we have the first attempt at a critical biography, a delightful patchwork of mini-essays, chatty glimpses, asides, and episodic tangents, many of which came from Elizabeth Palmer Peabody, who was still alive at the time, and the writings of Thomas Wentworth Higginson, a famous cultural critic of his day who wrote for *The Atlantic Monthly*, and W. W. Story, the sculptor whom Hawthorne had met in Italy. The genteel portrait reigns.

According to Conway, Hawthorne's morbid streak was derived from his pedigree, his ancestors "the Nero and Caligula of Salem" (171); from his mother's "morbid anxieties" (17), from his solitary years as a boy in Maine, and from his "hermit years" in Salem (29). Hawthorne himself was doomed to an essential shyness, but there was nothing morbid or gloomy about him, Conway went on to insist, thus contradicting his earlier position. He wore his shyness as a shell and displayed "a certain morbid susceptibility to the influence of persons" (58), being shy as well of other literary men, but "what a ruddy heart was masquerading in that somber Salem raiment" (100). In Conway's time "ruddy" meant healthy and robust. Emerson, Conway suggested, "feared everything morbid, everything superstitious" (99–100), and, not having gotten deeply enough into Hawthorne's fiction, overlooked that ruddy heart. Ultimately "ever in reserve, [Hawthorne] was an uneventful person" (117).

For Conway, Hawthorne's life appeared as a religious journey, perhaps due to his own experience as a Southerner having seen the light in regard to abolition; he described the Italian notebooks as "a religious autobiography" (181). We can perhaps detect in this the 1890s fascination with the aesthetics and art of Catholicism, an attraction to the Celtic revival that was occurring at the time. Hawthorne's fascination with Catholic Italy, its rites, such as the confessional, and its images, such as the Virgin Mary, as well as its art, which the iconoclastic Puritans had not only frowned upon but destroyed during the Reformation, fascinates Conway as well: "Hawthorne's new spiritual vision now recognizes evergreen growths where his religious training taught him to see only crumbling idolatry" (170). As a result, "a transformation in Hawthorne preceded the transformation of his Marble Faun. He had not the least interest in pope, priest, or pious ceremonies, but the religion pictured in galleries and monuments entered the sacred retreat where eloquent preachers had, for a generation, knocked in vain" (173). The sheer historical presence of Rome all but overwhelmed him, Conway maintains.

Once Hawthorne's alleged religious nature was reawakened, he was overpowered, Conway insists, by paintings, sculptures, churches, temples, and shrines that threatened his proto-Calvinist perspective, which viewed art, if it were at all necessary, as moral parable. It had to be functional in terms of a moral message. The mark of Cain that shadowed *The Scarlet Letter* and the curse that haunted *The House of the Seven Gables* became in the notebooks an acknowledgment of the Virgin Mary's powers: "Puritanism had eliminated the Madonna, but for Hawthorne, and other hearts that flowered above that thorny stem, Jesus has absorbed the Madonna and revealed her gentle features . . . It was in Florence that Hawthorne first began to observe carefully pictures of the Virgin" (184).

Conway's religious sensibility and perspective makes for a nice narrative trajectory, but we appear to be getting more of Conway's cryptic conversion than Hawthorne's.

Conway discusses the necessity of impersonal laws that work themselves out in *The Scarlet Letter*. He admires Clifford's recovery in *The House of the Seven Gables* but sees Judge Pyncheon as just the ordinary cardboard stage villain. He mentions the possible connections between Zenobia in *The Blithedale Romance* and Margaret Fuller but not surprisingly focuses most on *The Marble Faun*: "It is in [this romance] that his inner history is told, — and therein all the evolutionary years of New England, whereof he was the characteristic flower. Having come so far the book reaches far: it has had the phenomenal success of becoming at once the tourist's guide and the scholar's interpreter" (162). Conway is correct about Hawthorne's last romance's becoming a guidebook for tours of Italy, but Hawthorne's "inner history," if this final book reveals any of it, remains as muddled, contradictory, and fragmented as the narrative itself.

For Conway *The Marble Faun* should not have been called a romance; it "is rather a realistic drama" (165), and as such, "Hawthorne has projected, as it were, [on Hilda's virginal essence] his own soul . . . The pilgrimage of New England from deified despotism to the maternal deity, in all but sex . . . was on the same spiritual path that led Rome to build the Madonna's shrine" (169). Conway's insistence on religious revelation in its more aesthetic forms, however, reveals more about American culture in the 1890s than it does about Hawthorne's own mysterious quest.

Conway attacks Hawthorne for his views on slavery, an issue that had riled the abolitionists of Concord in Hawthorne's own day. His support for and loyalty to Franklin Pierce, for instance, Emerson saw as the most grievous fault in American literary history up to that time. Conway, who says he was "a Virginian who had known the loneliness of social exile on account of my anti-slavery views" (205), was shocked "to think that such a man should speak — with a sincerity that itself seems deplorable — of the anti-slavery movement as 'the mistiness of a philanthropic theory;' still more that his hero's [Pierce's] share in the proslavery robbery of Mexico — euphemistically called 'war' — should be extolled without any intimation of the indignation felt by every other northern thinker in America" (146). Such views on slavery have been thoroughly examined, explored, and often condemned in much of the criticism of the 1980s and beyond.

Conway did allow for Hawthorne's pragmatic streak in dealing with politics, despite the fact that he was no politician, but he was appalled by his wishy-washy stance on slavery, his political quietism, which he recognized in a letter from Hawthorne to Elizabeth Palmer Peabody: "The good of others, like our own happiness, is not to be attained by direct effort, but incidentally. All history and observation confirm this . . . God's ways are in nothing more mysterious than in his matter of trying to do good" (156). Subscribing to such a stance leads only to political paralysis, the kind that infuriated Conway and others in Hawthorne.

George E. Woodberry in his *Nathaniel Hawthorne* (1902) in Houghton Mifflin's American Men of Letters series, depicts the practical, poor, grateful Hawthorne who gladly accepted the Boston Custom House job in order "to have a material task to do, something with the stubbornness of fact in its resistance, a practical duty such as belongs in the ordinary lives of men . . . He felt the need of a fuller, earthly, practical life, a real life, as he would have called it by contrast with the impalpable things of his genius [if only] as 'a means'" (91, 98). Woodberry's biography bolsters this pragmatic outlook throughout, grounding his subject in the daily and necessary tasks of life and supporting a family.

Woodberry confronts Hawthorne's aloofness as a product of his mind — "there was this temperament of the solitary brooder upon life" — but explains how "this absorption in the moral sphere was due to his being a child of New England." Such an upbringing in that region led to "an intense self-consciousness of life in the soul . . . he thought about nothing else" (155), but he experienced a "pendulum of temperament . . . a certain lethargy of life," a certain "dullness" and torpidity "with as little indebtedness to personal experience as ever an artist had" (159, 153). Hawthorne had "no inward life of his own that sought expression. He was not even introspective. He was primarily a moralist, an observer of life, which he saw as a thing of the outside, and he was keen in observation, cool, interested. If there was a mystery in his tales, it was in the object, not in the author's breast . . . he describes the thing he sees . . . Hawthorne left himself out of his work, so far as a man can . . . He had the indolence of the meditative habit" (150, 152). Yes, he was temperamentally an aloof and dreamy soul, but that was only part of his gentle, spare, frugal, practical, decorous, calm, and quiet demeanor and essence that Woodbury takes careful pains to present and authenticate.

The separation between man and artist, between what T. S. Eliot referred to as the man who suffers and the artist who creates, led Woodberry into a critical assessment of Hawthorne's art that seems surprisingly modern and prophetic, particularly in a biography that traces Hawthorne's life in such a matter-of-fact and deliberate manner. He dealt with the "morbid solitude" issue by concentrating on the craftsman of the artist, the cool observer, who, however shy, could never have been so morbid and solitary as many of his critics had suggested. In a sense Woodberry anticipates the New Criticism, which generally separated the work from the life of the author and focused on the inner workings of the text, often at the expense of its context. Thus he discusses Sir Walter Scott's pictorial and theatrical influences on Hawthorne's methods and approaches in terms of set speeches, vivid tableaux of characters, and elaborately set scenes within which different forces of history confront one another (the

Calvinists versus the merrymakers in "The Maypole of Merrymount," for instance). Hawthorne's sketches become illustrations of provincial, rustic New England village life, "transcripts of life" (128), conjuring up "the power of peace in quiet places . . . a faithful reproduction of the common-place . . . a past that was countrified and old-fashioned" (130, 133), akin to Thoreau's vision of the woods and Wordsworth's solitary musings in natural settings. Stories like "The Gentle Boy" and "The Gray Champion" become historical fables that recognize the pieties of the times.

For Woodberry, something in Hawthorne's work always remained "countrified in the mode of handling, something archaic and stiff in the literary mould, something awkward, cramped, and bare in the way his art works in its main motions" (156), and thus solitude and isolation, rather than personal paralysis, became "a fixed idea in his imagination, an integral part of life as it was viewed by him" (149). The key here is, of course, the word "integral" to convey a larger, more personable portrait of this practical man.

Woodberry is again prophetically modern when it comes to his explanations of Hawthorne's use of allegory, his concentration upon particular objects and images as symbolic icons to build his fictions upon, and his appreciation of *The Scarlet Letter*'s relentless examination of the human soul, "the record of a prison-cell, unvisited by any ray of light . . . [in which the prisoners] are seen. But they do not see" (202). Still a creature of nineteenth-century ideas of Christian faith and progress, Woodberry declares that "in the highest sense, it is a false book. It is a chapter in the literature of moral despair" (203) because it has no redemption, no real atonement, and no Christ in it. On the whole sin continues to breed sin, there can be no forgiveness, and the complexities of the human condition outrun the moral scheme, a realization that has haunted most Hawthorne critics ever since.

Woodberry's understanding of Hawthorne's use of allegory raises the kinds of critical questions that are still being raised today. Hawthorne's allegorical method, he suggests, "is not employed with any exclusiveness, but takes its place with other resources of his art" (140), at times more prominent than in others but not the essence of Hawthorne's literary arsenal: "It is said that he had, artistically, the allegorizing temperament, and he in fact did use all those forms of imagery — the fable, allegory, parable — which belong to this mode of presentation, but in his more effective work the allegory is more subtly embodied — it exists in suggestion, and its appeal is as much emotional as didactic" (143–44).

For Woodberry, the object or image that Hawthorne seized upon or that seemed to possess him — the scarlet letter, the black veil, the marble faun, the poisoned plant — inhabits the center of his fiction. "It becomes more than pure symbol," Woodberry explains, "and sometimes it is almost vitalized into a life of its own. This power of such an object to become the medium of thought and emotion as well as to convey merely allegorical meaning he gradually discovered" (144). Woodberry deepens this line of analysis: "He has fully seized the power of the physical object, plainly sensible to all as matter of fact, to serve as the medium for moral suggestion often difficult to put into words . . . like fears in an anxious mind" (136, 139).

The image persists in Hawthorne's imagination, becomes its own obsession, possesses the writer's mind and had to be exorcized in fiction "like a text which gathers atmosphere and discloses significance under the special treatment of a preacher" (143). Woodberry's choice of tales to examine — "The Artist of the Beautiful," "The Minister's Black Veil," "Young Goodman Brown," "Rappaccini's Daughter," and "Roger Malvin's Burial" — are among the very tales that fascinate most contemporary critics. Hawthorne's "literary habit was to let the story tell itself from within according to its impulses" with no predetermined shape or idea in the way that "a pure allegorist would've done . . . This may account for the indefiniteness and mystery of effect often felt . . ." (148). It's as if Woodberry subscribes to the concept of anti-allegorical allegories that many present-day critics have found in the structure of Hawthorne's work.

Woodberry's assessment of the other three romances still rings true today. *The House of the Seven Gables* displays "a glamour of reality" but also a "lax unity" in its succession of stories and pictures painted with a Dutch faithfulness (218). *The Blithedale Romance* he dismisses outright as inferior but praises its "external realism" (232). *The Marble Faun's* weak plot and structure as well as its ethical meanings are as vague as those in *Gables*. The book, "though it is all surface . . . solves nothing and ends in futility" (271, 277), despite Hawthorne's attempts to work out a moral design. Finally, for Woodberry, the many art treasures that are described and meticulously explored in the romance disrupt its already muddled moral theme.

Others wrestled with the Hawthorne icon: Katherine Lee Bates, an editor of a Hawthorne edition, in 1902, Richard Burton in his "Class Book" of 1904, Barrett Wendell in *The Mystery of Education, and Other Academic Performances* (1909), and Theodore Stanton in *A Manual of American Literature* (also 1909), who summarized the conventional wisdom when he declared that Hawthorne was "the greatest genius among American writers of romance, by many held to be the supreme literary artist of America" (155). Stanton's book was published in Leipzig, and it seems likely that it was a reader for German students of English, thus presenting a representation of American literature to foreigners. Most would also agree with both Burton and Stanton, who viewed Hawthorne as a product of his specific geographical region, an active and outgoing young man who was nevertheless strange, and a writer who, as Stanton maintained, "constantly describes the unseen in terms of the seen, the spiritual world by means of the every-day material world" (161). For them "he was in his work the New England conscience made flesh; surely an important role and mission" (Burton 115).

He compared *The Scarlet Letter* to Euripides and Goethe's *Faust* with its mystery of sin, adding that its very publication "distinguishes the year in American letters as Tennyson's 'In Memoriam' and Wordsworth's 'Prelude' do in English poetry" (158). Stanton, however, in his cultural era of social realism and the novel of manners, pronounces *The Blithedale Romance* "the most perfect of Hawthorne's works" since it "may be said to approach more closely to real life than any other of the greater works" (163, 164). For him Hawthorne is the "interpreter of spiritual mysteries" (165).

Perhaps one of the last early twentieth-century biographers to maintain and transmit the genteel portrait of Hawthorne as a pragmatic, relatively good-natured man — and genius — was Frank Preston Stearns in *The Life and Genius of Nathaniel Hawthorne* (1906). Stearns had met the Hawthorne family in the spring of 1862, delighted in their "purity and refinement" (405) but was then shocked when he once again came into contact with Hawthorne in November 1863, finding him now "tremulous" and "betray[ing] the weakness of his nerves" (408). Even then, however, "his features were not only classic but grandly classic; and his eyes large, dark, luminous, unfathomable — looking into them was like looking into a deep well." Stearns recalls the morning of May 20, 1864, "when Julian Hawthorne appeared at my room in the Massachusetts dormitory [at Harvard] and said, like a man gasping for breath, 'My father is dead, and I want you to come with me'" (418).

Stearns thinks of Emerson as day and Hawthorne as night, and quotes "Miss Rebecca Manning, Hawthorne's own cousin, still living at the age of eighty and an admirable old lady [who] distinctly confirms my statement, that 'wherever Hawthorne went he carried twilight with him'" (438). He takes issue with Julian's attack on Margaret Fuller and attempts to locate Hawthorne in a broader spectrum of other writers and art in general, with references to Carlyle and Dickens, Italian art, Leonardo da Vinci, Beethoven, Richard III, William Cullen Bryant, and Longfellow.

Stearns, with his own cosmopolitan interest in art, also produces a short biography of Hawthorne's life. He also believed that Hawthorne as a writer ranked with Fielding, Pope, Scott, Wordsworth, Shelley, and Emerson among others, but that writers such as Homer, Aeschylus, Sophocles, Cervantes, Descartes, Voltaire, Swedenborg, Chaucer, Shakespeare, and Milton, among others, outranked him. Ultimately "Hawthorne was simply impenetrable . . . but his sympathies were as profound as the human soul itself" (166).

Stearns insists on Hawthorne's purity of mind as if he could in no way be besmirched or corrupted by the world at large. He remained a "pure-minded, closely observing man," neither an optimist nor a pessimist but decidedly pursuing "a middle course." His bashfulness arose from the kind of fits "that sometimes overtake supersensitive natures," and "he was emphatically an idealist, as every truly great artist must be," who believed utterly in the "essence of Transcendentalism[:] the assertion of the indestructibility of spirit, that mind is more real than matter, and the unseen than the seen." In this Hawthorne embodied for Stearns the most positive aspects of nineteenth-century American optimism and progress, revealed no ultimate skepticism about such matters, and produced a style known for its "exquisite refinement and feminine grace": "It is a pleasure to read him, simply for his form of expression, and apart from the meaning which he conveys in his sentences." As for tales like "Young Goodman Brown," "it would have been better perhaps if [it] had been used to light a fire at the Old Manse . . . The plot is cynical, and largely enigmatical [and] the effect is decidedly unpleasant." "'Rappaccini's Daughter,'" Stearns says, "might serve as a protest against bringing up children in an exceptional and abnormal manner"! (183).

Stearns saw Hawthorne's politics as preserving the status quo. He wrote that "in order to practice his art, he must devote himself to it, wholly and completely [and] separate himself from all existing conditions, as Beethoven did" (147). Such a stance toward politics had much in common with Stearns's own. A community like Brook Farm would "destroy the sanctity of family life; and it would also include a tendency to the deterioration of manliness" (149). One must face the evils of the world and build both character and virtue, according to Stearns, for "the true object of life is not happiness, but development . . . if we pursue happiness directly, we soon become pleasure-seekers, and, like Faust, join company with Mephistopheles" (151). Were true Victorian pieties ever more baldly expressed? Stearns meticulously discusses the various presidential elections between 1840 and 1852 and examines Hawthorne's role in all of them, as well as his apt descriptions in his journals of men like Jonathan Cilley and Franklin Pierce and his dismissal from the Salem Custom House. He also decides that Hawthorne's idealism remains undaunted.

Stearns sees Hawthorne's art, on the other hand, as dealing with sin in its many guises. Concealment and its consequences darken *The Scarlet Letter*, which is totally fictional as opposed to historical, since "what is called history is fiction after all [and] nothing that Hawthorne published himself is to be considered of historical or biographical value" (221). Women's purity would always triumph over men's laws. *The House of the Seven Gables,* with its ingenious plot, exposed layers of social hypocrisy, and *The Blithedale Romance,* so much freer from Dutch realism than the former, explored "the sin of moral affectation" (368); however, the final catastrophe and the plot itself are mismatched and unbalanced. *The Marble Faun* dealt with original sin on a grand scale, steeped in Hawthorne's Italian notebooks, which are as rich and full-bodied as Byron's, Shelley's,

Ruskin's, and the two Brownings'. The fortunate fall into sin, however, left poor Hilda traumatized like Hamlet: "what Hilda ought to have done was, to leave Rome at once, and forever," unable to resolve her dilemma over Miriam, whose persecutor "was evidently a husband who had been forced upon her by her parents . . . Yet Hawthorne repeatedly intimates that there was something more in this. Let us not think of it" (374).

Stearns was determined, therefore, to present Hawthorne as an idealist at all times, progressive, genteel, and more domestic than demonic in his interests. He went out of his way to deny that Hawthorne was ever skeptical or dour, linking him to writers and artists in particular and to the artist's lack of interest in political and social issues in general. Hawthorne was, thus, dedicated to his art and, as a result, an upholder of the status quo in all things. As for his dark tales and the persistent melancholy, uncertainty, and self-doubt that erupt within them: "Let us not think of it."

Stearns concluded that "Hawthorne had died in his sleep as quietly and peacefully as he had lived. There is the same mystery in his death that there was in his life," but "the deeper a man's sense of the awe and mystery which underlies Nature, the less he feels inclined to expose it to the public gaze." Hawthorne was never a skeptic, according to him, for "in regard to the great omnipresent fact of spirituality he has no doubt." Stearns goes on to quote A. E. Schenbach, whom he calls "one of the most recent German writers on universal literature," who praised Hawthorne's writings and the psychological exploration of his characters. Hawthorne becomes for Stearns "essentially a domestic writer, — a poetizer of the hearthstone" (431). There the nineteenth century takes leave of him once and for all. In the years that would follow, Paul Elmore More, an influential cultural and literary critic in the early years of the twentieth century, would emphasize that "the penalty of solitude laid upon the human soul" would override such genteel visions and lead to the darker depths of Hawthorne that linger still (590).

Yet Carl Van Doren in his entry on Hawthorne in *The American Novel* of 1921 works hard to try to reconcile both points of view. He mentions Hawthorne's "seclusion" in the Maine woods and his mother's living "in a rigid seclusion, which naturally influenced the entire family, confirming in her son an original tendency" and suggests that in *The Scarlet Letter* he "seems sterner than the elder Puritans, for he admits into his narrative no hope of providential intervention." He mentions "those profound studies of conscience, 'Young Goodman Brown,' 'Rappacccini's Daughter,' 'The Christmas Banquet,' and 'Roger Malvin's Burial' . . . side by side with . . . [the] smiling and elusive exercises of Hawthorne's fancy, 'The Celestial Railroad' and 'Feathertop.'" He briefly describes Hawthorne's reliance on tableaux to tell his tales in his austerely economic manner but wonders about the scarlet letter itself, as it "assume[s] an entity of its own — tending inevitably on such occasions to be a mere frozen fancy," the allegorical perspective sustained by "his felicitous conception of Pearl" (112).

Literary realism seems to be the touchstone for Van Doren: the pictures in *The House of the Seven Gables* render it memorable, and *The Blithedale Romance* survives because of its "touching charm that springs from the very tenuousness of its substance." His decline more or less coincides with New England's, a theme that will be elaborated by other critics in the early part of the twentieth century. Sin becomes "a violation less of some supernatural law than of the natural integrity of the soul . . . where human instincts are continually at war with human laws," but Hawthorne finally produced "an art finely rounded, a rich, graceful style, a spirit sweet and wholesome . . . by lifting [the Pilgrims's stony province] into enduring loveliness." At the last, says Van Doren, "Always Hawthorne stands with society and sunshine against pride and gloom" (113). He may stand with them, but he certainly writes, in his more complex tales, of unending and relentless pride and gloom, as the New Critics were about to discover and explore.

As we have seen, early biographers mixed life and art at will, slipping from biographical tales into critical assessments of Hawthorne's works. Each infiltrated the other with impressionistic ease suited to fit a particular perspective on Hawthorne's life. It was such imprecise impressionism and biographical "slipperiness" that the New Critics, beginning in the 1920s and 1930s, would oppose vociferously, as we shall see in chapter 5, treating literature more scientifically and psychologically, relying both on T. S. Eliot's idea of literary criticism as a careful and precise analysis of texts and Freud's ideas of the individual self as a battleground of libidinous desires, social repressions, and the ever-present confrontation between sex and death. Twentieth-century biographers wrote in such a critical atmosphere, focusing on these psychological depths as precisely as possible, attempting at all costs to avoid the impressionistic approaches of their predecessors. Yet the battle between the "Dark" Hawthorne and the "Normal" Hawthorne would continue unabated.

4: Biographical Visions of the Twentieth Century

A T THE TURN OF THE TWENTIETH CENTURY, psychology as the new science, based almost solely on Freud's descriptions of the Oedipal complex, social repression, and the unending battle between *eros* (love/sex) and *thanatos* (death), permeated the popular American consciousness so that "repression" became the buzzword of the 1920s. The impressionistic, genteel biographies and critiques of Hawthorne by his heirs, Julian (1884) and Rose (1897), and by such writers as Moncure D. Conway (1890), George E. Woodberry (1902), Frank Preston Stearns (1906), and Carl Van Doren (1921), gave way to the more deeply psychological portraits of a solitary and tormented Hawthorne as conjured up by Paul Elmore More in "The Solitude of Nathaniel Hawthorne" in the *Atlantic Monthly* of November 1901, and especially Newton Arvin's Hawthorne in 1929. This view of Hawthorne is still with us in the later critical biographies by Frederick Crews (1966), Gloria C. Erlich (1984), and Edward Haviland Miller (1991), culminating in T. Walter Herbert's presentation of the Hawthornes' middle-class marriage as a psychological battle of wills (1993).

Despite the several attempts to humanize Hawthorne and present him as both a genteel and pragmatic soul, the vision of solitude and strangeness did not so easily disappear. It lay at the heart of the notion of the solitary artist, the New England proto-Puritan with his basic Yankee reticence and diffidence. Even though More did "not wonder that his family, in their printed memoirs, should have endeavored in every way to set forth the social and sunny side of his character and should have published the Note-Books with the avowed purpose of dispelling the often expressed opinion that Mr. Hawthorne was gloomy and morbid . . . The predominant trait of Hawthorne's work [remains] the penalty of solitude laid upon the human soul . . . and by right found its deepest expression in the New England heart." The Hawthorne image, however questioned and interrogated, remained intact, underscored yet again by his regional background.

Slowly but inevitably as the world changed, as writers such as Darwin, Marx, Freud, and Nietzsche began to dismantle old half-truths and Romantic conventions, Hawthorne's portrait changed with it. Evolution, class warfare, the tragic combat between ego and id (more of a "duel-ism" than a dualism in Freud's vision), the will to power, and the division of labor amid the horrors of burgeoning industrialism began to undercut the notions of the autonomous individual with an autonomous soul, linked to some overarching trajectory of human perfection and historical progress. The German "Higher Criticism" of the Bible in terms of historical analysis as opposed to prophetic truths — reason replacing revelation — assaulted absolutism in any form and in every direction, as psychology by the end of the nineteenth century continued to undermine the theological beliefs of the past. A new sense of social realism appeared in the novels of Henry James, William Dean Howells, Mark Twain, Stephen Crane, Kate Chopin, and Harold Frederic, undermining the Romantic faith on all levels. This emphasis on realism focused more on the social aspects of loneliness in such novels than on the more existential recognition of aloneness, which lay at the center of much Romantic fiction and poetry.

More thought he recognized a Hawthorne who "was singularly lacking in the political sense, and could look with indifference on the slave question," a Hawthorne whose "novels are full of brooding over the past . . . Hawthorne saw only the infinite isolation of the errant soul." For these reasons he praised the obsessive and intense symbolism of "The Minister's Black Veil," the isolation and disconnection among the four major characters in *The Scarlet Letter*, the working out of the evil curse in *The House of the Seven Gables,* and the lengthy exploration of Miriam's suffering in *The Marble Faun.* Here the modern Hawthorne of the twentieth century was fully embodied. We don't weep over Hawthorne's characters but see in them that solitary despair "that must seem to us now as old and as deep as life itself."

Newton Arvin in 1929 conjured up at that time the apotheosis of this "queer changeling" (9), the Romantic loner, and the strange man with his "passion for isolation" (105), which proved to be "incurable" (168). While Arvin indicts Hawthorne as a writer, he sees him as a forerunner to the modern alienation that had come into its own in poems like T. S. Eliot's "The Waste Land" and would perhaps reach its fullest fictional incarnation in William Faulkner's novels *The Sound and the Fury, Light in August,* and *Absalom, Absalom!* "Dispersion, not convergence, has been the American process," explains Arvin. The explorer, the colonist, the Mormon: they were "united after all in their common distrust of centrality, their noble or their ignoble lawlessness, their domination by spiritual pride" (203). Thus Hawthorne's "very estrangement from his fellows was but emblematic of their own estrangement from one another or their collective estrangement from the main body of human experience" (204). His own family's traditions produced a realm "in which seclusion . . . was the very principle of household ritual" (31). Hawthorne was no longer unhealthily morbid but a prophet of modern times immersed in "the essential tragedy of pride" (286).

Psychological explanations and visions had smoldered and surfaced in the nineteenth century, often inchoate in Hawthorne's case or described imagistically by him as the dark dank cavern of the human heart wherein lurked all kinds of monsters and motives that were better left untouched and unexplored. He knew they were there in the unconscious minds of his obsessed male characters in pursuit of their female victims — Rappaccini's Beatrice, Ethan Brand's Esther, Goodman Brown's Faith, Aylmer's Georgiana, Hester, Zenobia, and Miriam. For Arvin, Hawthorne had no more Puritan blood in him than Emerson. His main vision involved "the ubiquity of secret guilt, the fatal connection between isolation and evil, the flagrancy of spiritual pride . . . not of any Calvinist theology, but of his own somber consciousness of separation from the ways of his fellow men . . . All that isolates, damns; all that associates, saves" (134, 59). He had experienced such a saving association in the form of love with Sophia Peabody, but his "dusky fatalism" (65) drove him to write the stories he felt compelled to write.

Once again Arvin picks up on the divided Hawthorne, the one who remained loyal to ambitious politicians such as Pierce and Cilley and to his college friend, Horatio Bridge, in his various incarnations, "drawn strongly, by every impulse of his under-nourished imagination, to the brisk and noisy facts of the coarser world, [the world that] was warm, gross, sweaty, muscular, unilluminated, crass" (72). For that reason Hawthorne appreciated the sweat and toil of his work in the custom houses, the heft of salt and coal, and for that reason he went to Brook Farm, armed by the idealistic notion that manual labor and writing could only support and assist one another. Arvin quotes George Ripley, the founder of Brook Farm, who described the vision that appealed to Hawthorne: "We are striving to establish a mode of life which shall combine the enchantments of poetry with the facts of daily experience" (98).

"As a writer of fiction," however, Arvin declared that "Hawthorne is plainly not of the first order" (207–8). His *Twice-Told Tales* are not great literature "because of the factitious fatalism that pervades them" (67). He lacks Fielding's, Balzac's, and Tolstoy's knowledge of the full-bodied human condition. Hawthorne appreciated Trollope's solid and substantial work, but his own, a psychological projection of estrangement and distance, failed the "test of observable reality" (208). Here again we come upon the conventions of social realism, still thriving in its reaction to the Romanticism that existed before the Civil War. While Hawthorne is excellent at creating atmosphere and aura, the action of his fictions "is halting, torpid, and badly emphasized" (212). He is good with pictures but not with drama: "We miss the easy gestures, the impulsive motions of real life" (214). We get more masque, pageant, and procession than we do the heart's blood of fiction. His characters exude their own isolation and distance from one another; they are "the prey of forces against which it is useless for them to struggle" (218). Everything becomes Chillingworth's dark necessity, the product of an allegorizing mind, the stuff wherein allegory itself strangles real imagination; "we miss . . . the touch of illusive personality" (221).

Arvin's is a strange but mesmerizing performance, allegorizing Hawthorne the man as the solitary soul who foreshadows the modern age and accusing him of using too much allegory in his own work, which stifles the dimensions and intimations of symbols and suggestions. Hawthorne "simplifies the drama of human struggle at the expense of dramatic truth, and is essentially false to the facts of personality" (221), but that personality is precisely what Arvin celebrates for its experience of estrangement and difference. Hawthorne embodies "the spiritual isolation in which Americans on many levels have preferred to live rather than lend themselves to a general and articulated purpose" (204). How can his "allegorized" Hawthorne not write allegories?

Hawthorne's tragic awareness was, therefore, preferable to the transcendentalist faith in the autonomous self, a false faith partly initiated by Emerson. It was very difficult, to say the least, to appreciate anything transcendental after the First World War and, eventually, the Great Depression of the 1930s. It was precisely the transcendental belief in individual expansiveness and intellectual pride that led to the creation of an Ethan Brand, according to Arvin, who is consumed finally by the very fires he cultivates and commands. While Hawthorne may have had "something very like a fear of fixity, an undefined dread of the static" (150), he still constructed that fixity in his work, and for Arvin, who became fixated on this "queer changeling," he embodied the fixed fatalism and psychological tremors of the modern era.

Vernon Louis Parrington, in his two-volume *Main Currents in American Thought: An Interpretation of American Literature from the Beginnings to 1920* (1927), and Fred Lewis Pattee, in *The First Century of American Literature: 1770–1870* (1935), deepened the Arvin-More image of solitariness but more or less dismissed Hawthorne. Pattee referred to him as a strange "suicide-haunted man" (544). His isolation was the result of his "self-imposed solitary confinement between the age of twenty-one and thirty-three, confinement almost dungeon-like in its solitude" (540). *The Scarlet Letter* appears artificial and unnatural, Pearl is unreal, and the final scaffold scene is ludicrous (547). Pattee preferred *The Blithedale Romance*, the book that had seemed to critically flourish during the time of literary realism and novels of manners in the 1880s and into the twentieth century.

Parrington railed against New England's "absolutist theology" and praised the "liberal political philosophy [of] English Independency" (iv). Progressive and democratic, he lambasted "the Puritan conception of human nature as vicious [and focused on] the conception of human nature as potentially excellent and capable of indefinite development" (v), the progressive and Romantic idea that he celebrated in direct opposition to the Puritan vision. Not for him the "*saeculum theologicum*" of seventeenth-century America but the "*saeculum politicum*" of the eighteenth century.

By the time Parrington wrote his second volume, *The Romantic Revolution in America: 1800–1860*, which led eventually to *The Beginnings of Critical Realism in America: 1860–1920*, he saw Hawthorne as a skeptic, "detached, rationalistic, unhopeful, skeptical about Utopias . . . but curious concerning evil . . . like Jonathan Edwards in probing the psychology of sin" (xxi). Parrington considers him in part 4 of the volume, "Other Aspects of the New England Mind," where his neighbors include Longfellow in the subsection, "The Reign of the Genteel," and Oliver Wendell Holmes and James Russell Lowell as representatives of the Boston Brahmin tradition in "The Authentic Brahmin." Parrington admits that he is not greatly concerned with aesthetic values or judgments and delights in the overthrow of the older colonial America, which "had been static, rationalistic, inclined to pessimism, fearful of innovation, tenacious of the customary" (iv). The more liberating ideas of democracy had been hindered by the Civil War, and Parrington wanted to place those ideas on a firmer footing.

From Parrington's perspective, therefore, Hawthorne emerges as a kind of throwback, a skeptic who can only slow down the inevitable democratic process and progress that are slowly working themselves out: "He was the romancer of a dead but unforgotten past," and thus he remained cut off from the thriving national scene, remaining "to the last isolated, a frequenter of the twilight." His was "the romance of ethics — the distortions of the soul under the tyranny of a diseased imagination" (444). While the country surged and seethed with the political and economic repercussions of the slavery question, Hawthorne remained introspective, an aloof brooder: "He was the extreme and finest expression of the refined alienation from reality that in the end palsied the creative mind of New England" (450). Time had passed that creative mind, and thus Hawthorne himself, by. The region was played out on all levels, and Hawthorne's solitude could thrive only in his own morbid fantasies and remote imaginings.

Van Wyck Brooks in 1940 added to the dismissive picture that Pattee and Parrington painted but with a more positive spin. In *The Flowering of New England, 1815–1865* he created a Hawthorne who embodies the decay of his native Salem, "a ghost himself . . . dark and picturesque, tall and rather imposing [but] something vaguely foreign" (214–15). Brooks buries Hawthorne in his own gothic images, interweaving Hawthorne's words with his own, stranding him in the Castle Dismal as if spellbound, trapped in a life as "deep as a nightscene by Albert Ryder" (216). He reads Hawthorne's life through Hawthorne's own dark imaginings, confusing the man with his own fictional devices and techniques, framing him in art-ful paintings like Ryder's.

Brooks also displays a fondness for colorful lists in his often vague and impressionistic style, filled with references to painters. In fact the style often suggests Washington Irving's fascination with abundance and lar-gesse, sunlit and luxuriant, the kind that can conjure up a Hawthorne only as its dark opposite, a creature of the shadows, reflected in the chiaroscuro that Hawthorne often employed in his fiction: "Old houses and antiquated customs charmed his imagination, but he dwelt on the poisonous influ-ences that gathered about them"; "He scarcely thought of the world as real, either to be seen or touched or lived in, or, for the rest, altered and improved. It was a film on the breast of Maya, the goddess of illusion" (231, 282).

Brooks does recognize Hawthorne's "sensible double-ganger" (224) as the practical man of business but underscores that old dualistic dilemma: "Which was the true Hawthorne, which the phantom"? (225). Lest there be any doubt, the phantom wins hands down, the culmination of More's 1901 portrait, anchored to a politically reactionary perspective that mar-ginalizes him in an America addicted, at lease publically, to the vision of prosperity and hope. From that position he could only look out upon the world with a sidelong glance, by a certain indirection, [which] was second nature with him, and this was the mood his romances conveyed . . . It was this that gave him his effect of magic and made these beautiful books, with their antique diction, something other than novels can be" (387). The "phantom" wrote the fiction, therefore, from his marginalized position, while the practical man navigated the murky waters of political appoint-ments and favors, a fragile balancing act that Brooks never really explicates or probes.

In 1948, Malcolm Cowley's essay, "Hawthorne in Solitude," contin-ued the tale of the dark angel from New England. Returned to his native Salem after Bowdoin in 1825, he pictured himself, according to Cowley, "as a man completely alone. He began to be obsessed by the notion of solitude . . . as a ghostly punishment to which he was self-condemned" (4–5). He was again a man divided; "one was the storyteller and the other his audience . . . Divided between his two impulses, toward secrecy and toward complete self-revelation, he achieved a sort of compromise: he revealed himself, but usually under a veil of allegory and symbol . . . He was one of the loneliest authors who ever wrote, even in a country of lost souls . . . his four novels are full of anguished confessions" (8).

Cowley firmly grasps and embroiders the myth of Hawthorne the Byronic rebel, the man whose life reveals doubleness throughout: "proud and humble, cold and sensuous, sluggish and active, conservative and radical, realistic and romantic . . . a recluse who became involved in party politics and a visionary with a touch of cynicism" (12). That curse of polarities, however, "foreshadowed the ideals that later American writers would try to realize and fixed the patterns that many of them would instinctively follow" (17). His formal and decorous style nevertheless incarnated strange and Romantic tales and effects, as inner dreams and outer actualities clashed and confronted one another. One often undermined the other, but in the spirit of the New Criticism, Cowley praised Hawthorne's modern techniques, "stories built around a single effect and having the unity of a lyric poem . . . He was the first American writer to develop this architectural conception of the novel . . . consist[ing] of *interactions* among a few characters . . . and the result is that each book becomes a system of relationships, a field of force as clearly defined and symmetrical as a magnetic field" (25). That system and field, as we shall see in the next chapter, reveal the persistent recognition of that textual unity that New Critics exploited and admired.

The symmetry of Hawthorne's architecture speaks directly to the New Critics, who analyzed texts for their elaborate tapestry of irony, paradox, and ambiguity, all beautifully balanced into a final unified "system." Ambiguity implied that perilous equilibrium, rarely with any loose ends, that emerged from carefully constructed symbols, relationships, and fields of force, and the psychological depths of such fiction assured Hawthorne's survival, in Cowley's view: "It is only the surface that is censored in Hawthorne and it is chiefly the surface that has aged; his underlying problems are as real today as when he first presented them" (26). Hawthorne's solitude produced not social realism but a psychological vision, the projection of that reclusive solitude that he was never able to shake. Like the mother skunk in Robert Lowell's "Skunk Hour," it "would not scare."

In "The Hawthornes in Paradise" (1958) Cowley fleshed out his version of Hawthorne by documenting his courtship and happy marriage with Sophia Peabody. The wary recluse had been rescued by love, despite the machinations of Sophia's sister Elizabeth and his being "secretly involved with a Salem Heiress" (32). Cowley then identifies the heiress as Mary Crowninshield Silsbee, who fabricated a tale of how badly Louis Sullivan had mistreated her, so incensing Hawthorne that he challenged him to a duel. Sullivan wrote and told Hawthorne the truth — no such treachery ever took place — but Hawthorne himself, according to his son Julian's biography, which kept Silsbee's identity a secret, "was uniformly quoted by his friends as the trustworthy model of all that becomes a man in matters of honorable and manly behavior" (173). Hawthorne's college friend, Jonathan Cilley, who had also been challenged to a duel, accepted it after his doubts were assuaged by Hawthorne's example and was killed. Julian suggests that Hawthorne may have felt responsible or at least guilty for his friend's death. In any case Hawthorne and Sophia become the new Adam and Eve in the Old Manse, underwritten by "the sense of almost delirious gratitude that both of them felt for having been rescued from death-in-life" (40). *The Scarlet Letter*, Cowley decided in the same year, "recaptured, for [Hawthorne's] New England, the essence of Greek Tragedy" (55). "As a Racinian drama of dark necessity" (51), it arose from Hawthorne's true, suggestively demonic depths.

Looking ahead for the moment, it is interesting that both Lionel Trilling's "Our Hawthorne" (1964) and Alfred Kazin's "Hawthorne: The Artist of New England" (1966) compared Hawthorne with Kafka, although Trilling described Hawthorne negatively within the comparison, and Kazin viewed Hawthorne more positively. They both, while praising some of Hawthorne's accomplishments as a writer, marginalized his work and found it out of step with the modern world. Trilling praised Kafka's "great tyrant dream" (457) but found that the actualities of the world cramped and constricted Hawthorne's vision, that "he always consented to the power of his imagination being controlled by the power of the world . . . the modern consciousness requires that an artist have an imagination which is more intransigent than this" (454). Kazin, on the other hand, while viewing Hawthorne as too much the product of an old-fashioned New England consciousness — "Twentieth-century American writers do not generally feel much relation to Hawthorne . . . for the New England character is a fixed quantity in everybody's mind . . . [an] anachronism" (458) — favorably compares him to Kafka as another writer "able to capture in fiction the reality of a moral tradition that has just lived itself out as religion but has not yet dissolved into mere culture." Both, however, set Hawthorne's influence and work aside, Trilling because "he is, in Nietzsche's phrase, one of the spirits of yesterday — and the day after tomorrow" (458) and Kazin because the New England mind has more or less played itself out: "This is why there are so many theological and psychoanalytical interpretations of Hawthorne; they fill the vacuum created by our modern uncertainty about the use and relevance of Hawthorne's art."

Trilling also dealt with Henry James's interpretation of Hawthorne and his work, finding it limited by James's inability to believe in the true darkness of Hawthorne's vision and relegating Hawthorne's Calvinist-influenced gloom to an aesthetic as opposed to a genuine personal vision. For Trilling the dark Hawthorne is the truly modern Hawthorne, especially because of the role of ambiguity in his work, which led to multiple interpretations and always more analysis.

Even suggesting that it was within the advent of the New Criticism that "the Hawthorne of our day came into being" (435), Trilling lambasts Parrington for representing "Hawthorne as being virtually an enemy of the common people because of the delicacy of his art" (437) but also worries that the explosion of criticism all around us may have interfered with our own personal relationship to Hawthorne, a worry he finds also expressed by T. S. Eliot.

Trilling describes acutely and accurately the twentieth-century shift in Hawthorne criticism from impressionistic charms to psychological and quasi-religious tensions, but then explains that because of "the intractable weight and actuality of the world" (449), Hawthorne's imagination, never "boldly autonomous," fails to grip us and finally lets us down: "Over Hawthorne's imagination, the literal actuality of the world always maintains its dominion" (451). His is a lost world, an old-fashioned world, and as Kazin concludes, "he stimulated new thinking among psychologists and theologians, because he had become a problem safely established in the past" (451). Both he and Trilling agreed that "our Hawthorne" is finally too self-circumscribed and provincially handicapped to account for much in the modern age.

The wheel of biographical fate turned when both Randall Stewart and Robert Cantwell in separate biographies published in 1948 conjured up a more practical and down-to-earth Hawthorne, as did Mark Van Doren in 1949 and both Arlin Turner and James Mellow in 1980, but the doomed, damaged Hawthorne, whose work suffered as a result of the doom and damage and was marginalized by some of his critics, did not fade away. By the 1940s the impressionistic, genteel Hawthorne was all but dead, shredded by the astute and scientifically constructed New Criticism with its keen eye for ambiguity and paradox, leading to some already presumed unity. The dark solitary soul had risen from the depths of popular psychology and Freudian fiat, as allegorical sign and symbolic icon incarnated the unconscious, the id, the murky cesspool of compulsions and instincts bubbling up from a more naturalistic view of humanity. The pendulum would swing again, as it always does, as the dark Hawthorne, soon to become the darling of the New Critics in the 1950s and 1960s, barely withstood the assault of the more balanced biographies by Stewart, Cantwell, Mark Van Doren, Turner, Mellow, and Moore.

Armed with the knowledge and experience he gained from the editing of some of Hawthorne's notebooks, Randall Stewart's *Nathaniel Hawthorne: A Biography* was immediately acclaimed when it appeared. Here was a more normal Hawthorne, a more pragmatic fellow, a more conventional, "anti-Arvin" creature, sprung from the dark chrysalis of the solitary, angst-driven hermit, who somehow drifted through the world amid his own dreamscape and occasionally touched down on our common earth to land a few political appointments, father three children, and mingle with his fellow men and women. Stewart's factual style leaves his Hawthorne as the antithesis of Arvin's view of him, a tepid but shrewd individual who employed social and political strategies, was involved in the selling of his books, and managed to save $30,000.00 from his consulship in Liverpool.

Lest we miss Stewart's well-honed point of view, he made it perfectly clear: Hawthorne "had enjoyed a healthy participation in the social and intellectual life of the college community [at Bowdoin] . . . One looks in vain for evidence of social isolation in the Berkshires . . . he was scarcely the lonely hermit of romantic legend who was rescued from solitude by the good offices of the Peabodys" (25, 107, 51). To secure a political appointment, he knew how to wield "a subtile [sic] boldness, with a veil of modesty over it" (139). His "solitary years" from 1825 to 1837, as described by Stewart, were actually extremely productive and busy: "Doubtless they were solitary to an unusual degree, but not in the sense of a hermit's deliberate withdrawal from the world" (27). "One needs to be reminded, for the sake of a true perspective, that Hawthorne was a writer by profession, not a receptionist, and that he liked the people he liked" (222). His jobs, his travels and his visits to friends undermined that old charge about the morbidity of the man: "A morbid solitariness is hardly compatible with such mobility" (40). He was always in control, never completely derailed or overcome by the artist in him; hence his style often appeared to be objective and cool, rarely fevered or flagrant. According to Stewart, the scenes in the notebooks where Hawthorne describes his reading of *The Scarlet Letter* having given Sophia a headache, and the earlier deathwatch at his mother's bedside "are the only recorded instances of uncontrolled emotion" (95). He was engaged with the pressing issues of the day such as abolitionism and slavery, however obliquely and remotely, and was determined to see both sides of every issue, the kiss of death in a situation of impending war. Harriet Beecher Stowe considered him a traitor to the abolitionists' cause, as did many of his transcendental neighbors, albeit not in such strident terms.

For all of his balancing the Hawthorne persona with his facts and figures, however, Stewart concludes with a kind of timid summary of Hawthorne's themes and vision. Hawthorne's Puritanism predates the neo-orthodoxy of the Cold War era, that darker, more troubling view of the paradoxes and contradictions contained within the Christian faith. He opposed the liberal reforms and public optimism of his day. He saw evil as real, intertwined as it was with his notions of fate and providence. Skeptical of all faiths, he believed only that any regeneration of the spirit must come from within, not from any human policy or program. Operating between "a cold aloofness and a warm sympathy" (251) — balance is all! — he savaged instances of pride in his work, "the root evil, for pride is voluntary separation" (250), for masters, armed with their private obsessions and upheld by their excessive pride, could cast spells on slaves to do their bidding. A human equilibrium in all things underscored Hawthorne the man, much as it underwrote the New Critical faith in the unity of the text. Stewart's Hawthorne, for a time, was the man of the hour.

Robert Cantwell's *Nathaniel Hawthorne: The American Years* (1948) bristles with lusts, landscapes, political chicanery, family relationships and alliances, fortunes made and lost, networks of cousins and aunts and in-laws and ancestors, Salem's China trade, the history of the Hawthornes' house, colorful characters and skyrocketing careers. The sheer "busy-ness" of this richly detailed book creates a vigorous, politically savvy, and actively alert Hawthorne who worked carefully to maneuver his way through the various relationships he cultivated. There are hints of the dualistic Hawthorne — these probably will never die, however much they are more a product of language and logic than of the man himself — in Cantwell's judgment of the author's portraits and photographs. In portraits he "looked startled, shy, beardless. And gentle . . . he seemed a poet." In photographs "he looked mean . . . he seemed a square-jawed son and grandson of sea captains and privateers" (288). Rita K. Gollin's *Portraits of Nathaniel Hawthorne: An Iconography* (1983) is the perfect place for the reader of images of Hawthorne over the years to start and see, among other things, if Cantwell's case, however naïve, holds up.

Cantwell devotes considerable space to events that happened to Hawthorne's close friends, however peripheral to Hawthorne's work, such as Horatio Bridge's loss of his fortune and his house, invested totally as he was in building a dam across the Kennebec River in Maine; Jonathan Cilley's duel as the result of Congressional politics; and the Joseph White murder trial, which involved people whom Hawthorne knew. During the brouhaha over the trial Hawthorne left Salem as if to distance himself from the public furor.

One of the best examples of Cantwell's method is his exploration of the origins of the tale, "Ethan Brand," which Hawthorne describes in his notebooks in 1838 on his trip to North Adams, where he encountered various characters at local taverns, saw lime kilns burning throughout the night, and an old Dutchman who traveled about with his flimsy diorama. Cantwell investigates with a relentless ferocity, detail by detail, concluding finally that "Ethan Brand" "was not fiction at all. It was a literal description of a place, with imaginative meanings and interpretations cementing the blocks of reality together" (285). This strikes me as too harsh in its appraisal, since Brand himself transcends the details and circumstances of the tale, both of which often reflect his own brooding and self-destructive manner.

Most biographers love to nail a tale or poem to a specific event or encounter, but Cantwell does it so thoroughly and exhaustively that for him "Ethan Brand" is "not a convincing story . . . the story is static" (285). He reveals how much of reality Hawthorne incorporated into it and then concludes that that reality weighed down his imagination, as if the real folk, transported into Brand's suicidal final night on earth, could only posture, "somewhat uncomfortably at being brought on the stage . . ." The story, says Cantwell, "is a kind of Berkshire landscape, mountain scenery, clouds and thunderstorms, brightness and gloom intermingled, faithfully reproducing the mood of his notebooks" (285–86). We will see the same problem in *The Marble Faun* and somewhat in *The Blithedale Romance*, where actual events threaten to disrupt Hawthorne's story and render it sluggish and fragmented.

Cantwell's only lapse, and it looms large enough to raise questions about his biography, is his sensationalistic idea that Hawthorne may have been an undercover agent for the treasury or state department, that his trips may have been consciously planned to undertake some secret investigation of the explosion of the public powder magazine in Pittsfield or the smuggling of arms across the border from Canada. The missing pages from the 1838 notebooks, which seemed to be torn out, made Cantwell suspicious. He wondered, "Did he have a conscious purpose on this journey?" (276). Fire destroyed the records of the Boston Custom House in 1894, so we can never know exactly what Hawthorne was up to: "He was probably a government agent . . . When he left Salem . . . he entered the customs service, and from that time on was usually in the employ of the government in some investigating capacity . . ." (149). In fact, when it came to their engagement, "the secretiveness of Hawthorne and Sophia was an accomplishment that would have done credit to a pair of secret agents" (262). Hawthorne led

> an active and vigorous life of considerable excitement and some hazard. He was an active politician in the Democratic party, a circumstance which has made me [Cantwell], in view of its treatment of him, and insofar as [he has] any political opinions on the issues of the time, a Federalist. He was a skillful journalist. The depth and nature of his political work is mysterious. That is the true mystery of his life. He was forever visiting scenes where explosions had occurred or where violence of some sort was threatened or where smugglers were active. Loneliness and seclusion were his portion certainly, but they had less to do with his writing and with his view of the world than with his duties in the customs service. (ix)

Such unprovable speculations may generate more of the same, but one longs for Stewart's down-to-earth biography in these matters, since Cantwell's assumptions seem as over-the-top as those that produce the dark, morbidly shy, hermit-haunted Hawthorne.

Cantwell castigates the myth of the solitary years: "The legend was unusual on the face of it. Moreover, it left unexplained a great deal more than it explained. Yet it persisted as the basic story of the greatest American novelist" (66). Here Cantwell agrees with Stewart and finally decides that the image Hawthorne created of himself in his prefaces is just that: a public veil. The real Hawthorne "was as hard as nails" (386).

In his essay, "Hawthorne and Delia Bacon," which Cantwell includes at the beginning of his biography, he makes it very clear the kind of people that Hawthorne had to deal with as consul in Liverpool, from vagabonds and alcoholic priests to imposters and mistreated sailors, as well as lunatics, wastrels, and other miscreants, including Delia Bacon and her idea that Shakespeare's plays may have actually contained the secrets of a philosophical society that she alone attempted to decode. Cantwell concludes his biography with the triumphant publication of *The Scarlet Letter.*

The very next year, 1949, Mark Van Doren, Carl's son, produced his biography of Hawthorne and joined the chorus of those intent on portraying a balanced, reasonable man, who nonetheless remains virtually impenetrable, and who barely managed to straddle the gap between the world and his imagination. He remains "a mild, shy, gentle, melancholic, exceedingly sensitive, and not very forcible man" (3) who dug deep into that imagination in his romances only once, in *The Scarlet Letter,* and avoided those depths thereafter. Van Doren's Hawthorne "was so alone, so aloof, because he found so few around him whose seriousness equaled his . . . If one were serious, one never forgot the eternal importance of every soul, and never doubted that the consequences of deeds, even of impulses, last forever" (162). As a skilled negotiator, "he was not a man of doctrine. He was a story-teller" and "unimpeachably loyal to his friends" (203, 98).

Van Doren from his New Critical perspective discusses the tales that New Critics wrestled with, darker ones than the nineteenth century usually celebrated. In "Young Goodman Brown," "the hum of supernatural energy is authentic from beginning to end" (79); the withered bow at the end of "Roger Malvin's Burial" embodies as much symbolic power as do Faith's pink ribbons; the night scene of Ethan Brand's suicide is superb. Only in regard to "The Minister's Black Veil" does Van Doren waver, discovering "a certain irresolution in the moral . . . The veil 'obscurely typifies' some mystery . . . Obscurely, yes. But even the mystery is obscure" (87).

Only in *The Scarlet Letter* does Van Doren see Hawthorne achieving "a perfect balance": "Hawthorne has at last found individuals who can hold all of his thought" (163, 148). Sin and secrecy rule over and undermine all, since they lie at the heart of Hawthorne's vision. Hester, an erotic suffering goddess, transfixed her creator: "Hawthorne went to the center of woman's secret, her sexual power, and stayed there" (155), and none of the evil in the romance can "be relinquished" (161). After that fictional triumph, *The House of the Seven Gables* remains almost purely pictorial, the weak wispy characters in *The Blithedale Romance* are undermined by the material from Hawthorne's notebooks and are viewed by an unreliable and unscrupulous narrator, Coverdale, who "is an ass" (226), and the many morals in *The Marble Faun* clog the tale itself, in which the facts of Rome also bury the vague interpretations of myth.

Stewart and Cantwell would probably agree with Van Doren's idea that Hawthorne distrusted and feared both himself and the dark depths of his imagination — "its very depth made him distrust it, and its terrors were distinctly not to his liking" (42) — that he clung to the ordinary daylit world as a way of trying to avoid it, and that "he never fell out of love with the 'real world' of 'broad and simple daylight' which half the time he treated as the foe of his fancy, the enemy of his art" (63). Even "his descriptions of himself . . . are tentative; they give the impression that he is trying to make up his own mind concerning the sort of soul he carries" (54). He remains a mystery to himself, walking "through the world like one both in it and not in it" (54).

Everything originated with Hawthorne's experience of solitude, says Van Doren: "It terrified Hawthorne . . . not [as] an idea [but as] a fact with which he lived . . . He knew it was more powerful than he; it was the dark angel whom no Puritan had conquered either; it was the vacuum of ennui and despair which no religion ever filled — indeed, to recognize it was what religions were for" (126). Cantwell added that Hawthorne had not yet "recognized that his intellectual homelessness was a distinction and an asset . . . that his very aloneness made him not a survivor from an older order but a hesitant spokesman for the new" (288). Existential dread, however circumscribed in these biographies, haunts them in full.

For me, Arlin Turner's *Nathaniel Hawthorne: A Biography*, overshadowed by James R. Mellow's *Nathaniel Hawthorne in His Times*, published in the same year, 1980, reads like a sober and solemn accumulation of facts. Turner chose to create a compulsively detailed biography that remains timid when it comes to criticism and interpretation. Like many incidents and descriptions in Hawthorne's notebooks, Turner sees his task as "to perceive and record, not to proclaim — though possibly to suggest — sympathy, pity, or condemnation" (93). He recognizes in his preface that "the inclination toward solitude . . . has not been easy to reconcile with his activities in the world about him" (v) but chooses "to place Hawthorne's works . . . in the context of his life in such terms as he might have used himself, and leaving readers . . . to supply their own interpretations and applications [since] there are likely to be as many interpretations as there are spectators" (vi, vii). Turner's knowledge of such things as salaries, publication dates, the numbers of books actually sold, the Mary Silsbee affair, the spoils system of the day, Hawthorne's relations with John O'Sullivan, and Cilley's duel is prodigious.

For Turner, Hawthorne's years of solitude turn out to be a self-chosen literary apprenticeship, exaggerated by him in terms of his isolation later on so that he could be rescued even more completely by Sophia's love. His own description of these dismal years constitutes "a portrait, not a photographic reproduction . . . [but a] metaphoric reading in a symbolic portrait" (90). He comes across as Duyckinck's "fine ghost in a case of iron" (213), his silences as astonishingly "*sociable*" (214) according to Melville, and, quoting Hawthorne himself, burdened with an English reserve, "shy of actual contact with human beings, afflicted with a peculiar distaste for whatever was ugly, and, furthermore, accustomed to that habit of observation from an insulated stand-point which is said (but, I hope, erroneously) to have the tendency of putting ice into the blood" (291).

Turner describes Hawthorne's basic vision in rather simplistic and thematic terms, but they serve as a touchstone to his work. He accepted human nature "as man's fate to survive," was convinced that "every heart contains inner secrets that can be revealed to no other," knew that one must "face inevitably such consequences of guilt, whether assumed or concealed [since] every choice, every action, brings inescapable consequences" (308), saw "man as imperfect with propensities for evil, and the victim of forces beyond his control" (307), and generally recognized that each of us is bound by some form of psychological determinism, the artist especially having to "find his reward within himself" (327). Turner recognizes development in Hawthorne's art — "since about 1830, he had consciously adjusted the romance of adventure and the romance of effect, dominant at the time, to serve his own purpose of psychological delineation" (232) — but sees his primal vision as having remained intact and undaunted.

James Mellow, on the other hand, planned a series of biographies that would place Hawthorne, Margaret Fuller, Thoreau, and Emerson in their historical and cultural contexts, but he only managed to write the one about Hawthorne. Still he was determined to record — and for the most part succeeds in recording — various encounters and events as if "held in continuous solution, never allowed to crystallize out into falsifying summary assessments," eager to display "versions of the truth, private records, personal fragments — bits of wreckage borne on the surface of the broad, indifferent stream of time" (7). In doing so he hoped to conjure up "a kind of Proustian awareness of the power of objects to preserve some fleeting human reference out of the flux of history" (482). He attempted to both pursue and deconstruct the polarities that have hounded Hawthorne from the beginning — imagination/reality, gothic/genteel — flip sides of the same coin, and in locating Hawthorne in his cultural and historical milieu tried to re-create "two such different lives simultaneously" (208), as if Hawthorne were wandering through a corridor of expanding and darkening mirrors, entranced by such uncertain mysteries of his times as mesmerism and intrigued by a vision of the primal human condition, that between master and slave.

In such a manner Hawthorne's various guises seem to perform within and against a fluid and very populated background; he is a creature both of conscious strategies and of a proto-Puritan temperament, a dreamer and a pragmatic political appointee: each incarnation is dependent upon the situation of the moment. His own view of himself readily encompassed the seeming abyss between his external and internal lives, but such a view may have been part of the social and psychological environment of the time, a product of an emerging middle class's image of itself, more psychological than theological and polarized by a society moving in too many directions at once.

Mellow opens his biography with Hawthorne's calling on the Peabody family in November 1837, thus initiating "the classic elements of a romance: the chance meeting, the instant recognition — love at first sight" (7). From then on both Mellow and Hawthorne take delight in various characters and personalities, life and career, contretemps and connections: "In his youth, Hawthorne displayed none of the irascible temperament of the genius and little of that pose of the artist-as-romantic hero. He remained remarkably level-headed about his profession" (36) and does so throughout the biography. The doubleness, of course, persists, with Hawthorne's feet on the ground and head full of dark dreams, however bothered and disturbed by his own psychological dilemmas. "An aura of unresolved paternity seems to cling to Hawthorne's heroes" (14); "the theme of dark nuptials . . . occurs with such persistence in Hawthorne's early stories that it also suggests a more deep-seated psychological prohibition against marriage and happiness" (69). Mellow also subscribes to Emerson's idea that each man becomes his own private theater, thus attempting to play out Hawthorne's various performances, at the same time recognizing the critical revolution that by 1980 had restored Emerson from being the Lucifer of Concord to our greatest philosopher-poet.

We already are aware that Elizabeth Palmer Peabody loved "Sunday at Home," "Sights from a Steeple," and "Little Annie's Ramble," but Mellow clearly joins the modernists in his appreciation of those dark tales that Hawthorne left out of the first edition of *Twice-Told Tales* in 1837: "My Kinsman, Major Molineux," "Young Goodman Brown," "The Wives of the Dead," and "Roger Malvin's Burial." In all he discerns "a recurring theme of the end of innocence . . . with the skill of a surgeon probing diseased flesh" (63, 58). "Ethan Brand" is much too mechanical and moralistic but reveals Hawthorne's concerns with "the cruel intellect with an infernal laugh" (45). The man himself remains a puzzle, but Hawthorne operated well and fruitfully in his era. He really may have felt responsible or at least guilty for Cilley's death. The tale of Martha Hunt's suicide by drowning in Concord, the description of which Hawthorne relied upon to depict Zenobia's suicide in *The Blithedale Romance*, first appeared in Julian's biography, faithfully culled from his father's notebooks. Was there ever an engagement or the possibility of one between Hawthorne and Elizabeth Peabody? Was his final assessment of Melville as neither a believer nor an unbeliever really more about his own skeptical view of the cosmos? Could he have been a repressed homosexual involved in "helenized friendships" that were as fraught with sexual possibility, or so we think today, as were "Boston marriages" between women?

Even Cantwell had earlier mentioned Hawthorne's beauty and raised the question of homosexual intimations. Although adult men sharing beds was not an uncommon occurrence in the nineteenth century, had his Uncle Robert molested or made improper advances to him when they slept together for several years? Was Melville right when he suggested to Julian that Hawthorne harbored some ultimate secret? Was Hawthorne right to view the Civil War not as some moral crusade but as revealing the incompatibility of the North and South in some permanent state of union?

For Mellow *The Scarlet Letter* "enabled [Hawthorne] to maintain contradictory views in precarious balance" (305), balance being both a New Critical article of faith and the thrust of Mellow's book. *The House of the Seven Gables* may have been his better book; it certainly was a bigger success immediately. As for *The Blithedale Romance*, it is "an autopsy report on the rationalized morals" (394) of Hawthorne's characters and replays the obsessive dualism of Dimmesdale and Chillingworth in the figures of Coverdale and Hollingsworth — Hawthorne and Melville? As for *The Marble Faun,* Mellow's critical approach remains intact as he concentrates on the dualistic separation of plot and scenery, although the novel appears "like a sculptured frieze-in-the-round. It moves by way of brief and brisk episodes in a circle" (523).

Offering one more incarnation of Hawthorne as a social and historical personage, Margaret Moore in *The Salem World of Nathaniel Hawthorne* (1998) declares gleefully that "in the tangled web of Salem genealogies, anything is possible" (212) and then goes on to prove it. Here is a volume filled with historical lore, teeming with characters and odd circumstances, an entire region and era conjured up: murder trials, the religious battles between fading Calvinists and the more optimistic, upstart Unitarians; schools, politics, and a plethora of friends from Caleb Foote to the insane poet Jones Very, whom Emerson and Thoreau celebrated as an outstanding transcendentalist. We learn that African Americans in Salem lived in a segregated space called "The Huts" and that Charles Wentworth Upham went to Harvard with Emerson and, before launching his campaign to evict Hawthorne from the Salem Custom House, had extended Very's incarceration at the McLean Asylum in Charlestown. It was John Endicott who named the Indian port, "Nahum-Keike" or "Naumkeag," Salem, and the war of 1812 that permanently damaged the town's trade, which could account for 225 ships before the war and only 57 afterwards. Moore describes Hawthorne's fascination with the "fireside traditions" of legends and tales, conveyed by aged aunts and grandmothers and undermines the myth of his mother's seclusion, promoted by the Peabodys so that they could come to his rescue. And I love her quote from Father Taylor, a local minister, who described the Transcendentalism of his day "like a gull — long wings, lean body, poor feathers, and miserable meat" (115).

Hawthorne emerges in Moore's book in his pragmatic, realistic guise, filled with the inherent pride and reserve of old New England families. She portrays him as having enjoyed a happy childhood and paints a very different picture from Erlich's, Miller's, and Herbert's biographies. Yet the man remains mysterious: "If we change our minds, we can find enough substance to prove the opposite . . . His conclusions were tentative. That is the reason he spoke more in the subjunctive mood rather than in the indicative" (253, 256). Moore quotes Sophia's suggestion of 1863, "He is very all sided and can look serenely on opposing forces and do justice to each" (184). He was after all a Salem boy, a Massachusetts lad, a New England character, and perhaps the frigidity of New England winters and the stultifying humidity of New England summers, as Henry Adams suggested, may have helped generate that ineradicable duality in the man that even he himself had recognized.

Psychological analysis was not new to Hawthorne criticism. It had eroded the more theological arguments and approaches over the years while religion had receded from the conventional vocabulary of the culture, a battle between emerging psychology and traditional theology fought in the nineteenth century and continued somewhat in New Critical analyses, but Frederick Crews's *The Sins of the Fathers: Hawthorne's Psychological Themes* (1966) revolutionized its importance. Hawthorne was at once "a self-divided, self-tormented man" (7), and the New Critical fascination, as well as Crews's, with Eden and the fall (fortunate or otherwise), neo-Christian paradigms, religious symbolism and the like trembled at the onslaught of his Freudian fulminations. What Hawthorne really did was "to make psychological metaphors out of history and ancestry, God and Satan" (263). Real, dangerous knowledge lay beneath such traditional trappings and veils.

In 1680 Nicholas Manning, the first Manning to arrive in the New World and a direct ancestor of Hawthorne's mother's family, committed incest with his sisters, Antriss and Margaret. He fled into the wilderness, but the sisters were tried and forced to wear the word "INCEST" on their caps. Philip Young in *Hawthorne's Secret: An Un-Told Tale* (1984) makes much of this sordid history, as if discovering the ultimate clue to the origins of *The Scarlet Letter*. For him Hawthorne's ancestry was all about "incestry" (167). On March 29, 1681, the sisters, Antriss and the seven-months-pregnant Margaret, were "sentenced to be imprisoned a night, whipped. Or pay 5 pounds, and to stand or sit, during the services of the next lecture day, on a high stool, in the middle alley of Salem meetinghouse, having a paper on their heads with their crime written in capital letters" (115). The pattern may have continued, Young suggests, with Hawthorne's incestuous feelings for his sister Elizabeth, the "Dark Lady of Salem" (103), who, according to him, hated Sophia, loved "Alice Doane's Appeal," and was not repelled by tales of Byron's incestuous lusts. In

"Appeal," "My Kinsman, Major Molineux," and "Roger Malvin's Burial," "three fathers have been supplanted . . . and two daughters freed for brothers. Altered but audible are the vibrations of an ancient triangle" (74). However audible to Young, these vibrations remain highly speculative and virtually unprovable.

In *Salem is My Dwelling Place: A Life of Nathaniel Hawthorne* (1991), Edward Haviland Miller elaborates upon Hawthorne's Oedipal uncertainties and anxieties, laced with rage, grief, and fantasies of incest, and is eager to prove that the Freudian family romance is more Hawthorne's dwelling place than his native Salem. Here is the tale of the completely dysfunctional family, the abandoned child, the cold mother, the absent father. Miller quotes Hawthorne's abandoned manuscript on Dr. Grimshawe, in which the narrator wonders, "Each son murders his father at a certain age; or does each father try to accomplish the impossibility of murdering his successor?" (488). Thus Hawthorne and many of his characters, to quote the same narrator again, "do not take root anywhere" (398), and his fictions become a series of veils that, according to Miller, "for the most part successfully concealed the sexualized environment, the almost prurient interest in sadism, voyeurism, incest, and male terror of sexuality and marriage" (116). Hawthorne understands the master-slave dynamics of sexuality, recognizes "his intuitive awareness of his own lusts and the compelling attractiveness of incestuous and deviant sexual desires" (101), and celebrates his role as a spiritualized Paul Pry, the role he sees himself playing as he gazes down upon the town of Salem from the heights of a church steeple in "Sights from a Steeple" (1831), since as a spectator, "it was one way of keeping hell-fired emotions under seeming control" (33). When Owen Warland in "The Artist of the Beautiful" finally succeeds in creating his mechanical butterfly, Miller suggests that it "may represent the soul, immortality, death, or the winged phallus or indeed all of these" (253). Then again, maybe it's just a mechanical butterfly.

Miller rightly assesses much of the criticism of Hawthorne's fiction, finding that "interpretation is limited to the head-heart conflict, which in its either/or orientation washes out Hawthorne's complexity with a neat but unsatisfactory formula; or to the historical-social significance, when clearly Hawthorne is more than a historical or social commentator; or to the treatment of evil or original sin, when skepticism and agnosticism characterize his perspective . . . Some critics seek to resolve his inconclusive conclusions, when his obvious intention is to posit several possibilities, sometimes even contradictory" (108–9). These contradictory and entangled possibilities lie at the center of Hawthorne's art.

Miller's idea that "all slavery is reciprocal" (245) in terms of psychological dynamics coincides with the Freudian perspective, but he oversimplifies the parts of Hawthorne's biography that seem to fit all too easily into such psychological categories. Hawthorne's art, like every artist's, can be described as "veiled autobiography" (298), but the veils are what make this art possible, created in terms of gothic conventions, proto-Calvinist musings, allegorical obsessions (of both Hawthorne and his characters), and symbolic encounters. One veil leads only to another, and though the winged phallus may be one object used to shred them, they still reveal yet another veil.

For Miller the people in Hawthorne's life also wore veils that he must strip away. Elizabeth Palmer Peabody, for instance, "lived more or less securely inside the shelter provided by fantasies of innate goodness which reduced human complexities to a comforting symmetry" (144). Melville's "extraordinary idolatry had a sexual resonance" (359). Hawthorne's children turn out to be unsocialized because they were kept apart from others. Julian's morbidity (412), Una's emotional and physical instability, and Rose's marriage to an alcoholic all proved that Sophia, armed with her "iron-butterfly" optimism and faith, devoted to her "humorless, duty-driven regimen" (410), lost control of "three unruly, essentially troubled children . . . she never realized how she had hurt her children by denying them peer relationships and the socialization schools provide" (523). Hawthorne, as a creature of his time, agreed with such a division of labor, as sexist as it appears to us today.

In his art, according to Miller, Hawthorne found no repose or resolution but created psychological pictures (106), dreamscapes "in constant flux" (108), and a sense of mystery that remained the ultimate veil that he used so as not to look too deeply into his own dark depths, clinging to his "elegantly conservative, fastidiously correct prose style . . . that beautiful placid façade, underneath which gyrated the shadowy phantoms" (49, 92). *The Scarlet Letter* becomes "a veiled resume of his life" (296) with its relentless sense of guilt, isolation, sin, and separation and the dynamics of masochism and sadism that are played out between Dimmesdale and Chillingworth. In *The House of the Seven Gables* a gleeful Hawthorne grotesquely dances around the corpse of the dead judge. *The Blithedale Romance* reveals only "disintegration and futility. Everything is fluid, and values are in doubt" (369). Everything is reduced to the dramatic encounters of theater "in a carefully structured series of confrontations" . . . (369). Nobody changes at Blithedale, [and] because Hawthorne did not resolve mysteries and ambiguities, there will never be a consensus in the critical interpretation of the romance" (268).

Miller quotes Emerson's reference to *The Marble Faun* as "mush" (447), as the novel "moves in interlocking circles — setting, history, myths, and religions merging and separating the endless repetition of human acts and fantasies . . . in the manic-depressive rhythms of people adrift . . . the romance at times seems overcontrolled, as though he was straining for resolutions of personal conflicts which art cannot provide"

(459). The romance does, however, anticipate "symbolism and the twentieth-century allusive fiction of art, history, religion, and psyche" (449), and as such "the wastelands of Hawthorne and Eliot are the same" (452). Perhaps, but Eliot's "The Waste Land" (1922) is all of a piece, while Hawthorne's romance remains scattered and fragmented.

Lest we think that the reign of the psychological in understanding Hawthorne's biography and art was coming to an end, T. Walter Herbert's *Dearest Beloved: The Hawthornes and the Making of the Middle-Class Family* (1993) purports yet again to strip away the civilized masks that repress the individual, claiming to reveal "a world of sexual politics" (9) in which Sophia and Nathaniel fought to the death. For Herbert, Crews confined such horrors to the literature, Turner and Mellow only perpetuated the myth of their placid family life, and Erlich and Miller had only begun to plumb the depths and damage of wounded psyches and sexual tensions. Herbert's is a world of Nietzschean proportions within which "the emerging middle-class obsession with maintaining self-control in the face of sexual desire" (142) reveals only the tip of the iceberg.

Beneath Sophia's insistent faith and optimistic prattle, claims Herbert, lies a vital self-assertion, forced to authenticate herself in the Cult of Domesticity by submitting to her husband's will. Such submission contributes to the middle-class myth of the self-made man but comes with a heavy psychological price, producing a kind of "moral tyranny" (105) that masks "her equally repressed impulse to take charge of him" (133). The domestic ideal places women and children in a subordinate position from which they can devote themselves to the man-in-the-making, but once he achieves the status of the self-made man, "the ideal loses its imperative agency and its power to hold conflicts in abeyance" (209–10). Of course the whole concept of self-making remains problematic, since no one is ever certain when the process ends, if it ever does. And if it doesn't, the constancy of struggle simply continues unabated.

Hawthorne, abandoned and alone, was according to Herbert "dominated by an inward unburied father, who disabled him from participating in the 'world of men'" (258), and the struggle to create his own manliness in terms of work and life fostered a grief that festered into rage and finally flowered into guilt, all of which "are held at bay through a vehemently asserted innocence" (260). That "lost purity of boys" (260) finds itself projected onto women as domestic angels who will contribute to the male's carapace of innocence, while he projects his own anti-patriarchal rage and guilt upon the rebellious women in his romances: "Innocent boyishness was the keystone of a defensive psychic structure that shielded him from an evil he projected into . . . tyrants (like Chillingworth, Jaffrey Pyncheon, and Westervelt)" (264). Did these flawed father figures represent his own self-loathing? Was the angel/whore dichotomy merely a projection of his own innocent boy/dirty-old-man self? Did

Hawthorne cultivate his aloofness to repudiate surrogate fathers at the same time he longed for them? Was it finally not enough for Sophia to be seen or to see herself as "the repository of his self-in-the-making" (230)? Herbert would answer all these questions in the affirmative, though they do raise psychological possibilities that cannot be so easily defined and circumscribed.

Sophia accordingly had sublimated her very real physical pain into a kind of spiritual triumph, convincing herself that evil could only be non-being (53). She worked hard to keep all of her children entirely dependent on her, thus barely concealing a "repressed motherly and matrimonial fury" (175). Herbert goes on to suggest that female sexuality became a fatal flaw in Hawthorne's work, though Sophia in her role as the dutiful Victorian middle-class domestic angel may have feared poverty more than sexuality and cultivated, along with the Peabody family, intellect and virtue as a way to compensate for the lack of wealth (54).

For Herbert, Una, as a victim of the middle-class marriage, learned to quash her own desires and cultivate the proper role of self-effacement for women in the Victorian era, which led to unsustainable contradictions in her personality and eventually to a mental breakdown. Is it any wonder that the Hawthorne children, according to Herbert, turned out to be "a saint, a criminal and a madwoman" (xvi)? Hawthorne could appreciate the sensuality, animality, and androgyny he saw in the marble faun, but in Margaret Fuller he felt such a presence was disgusting and threatening. Herbert suggests he was always "overwhelmed by psychic torment and confusion" (247) and could have had homosexual longings and experienced the fear of homosexual rape by his Uncle Robert. Is that why Coverdale fled from the masculine, authoritative, and handsome Hollingsworth? Is that why Dimmesdale didn't flee Chillingworth? When giving birth Rose went mad and had to be treated for insanity as Una had to be treated by shock therapy to restore her fragile mental balance. According to Herbert this is the upshot of Hawthorne's experience of life and fiction, a grim account based on his psychological speculations.

Brenda Wineapple's *Hawthorne: A Life* (2003) opens with Julian Hawthorne in the dock for his crimes. He was charged with and served time in prison for the "misuse of the United States Postal Service, a catchall complaint designed to nail the defendants, whose real offense, according to Judge Mayer, wasn't selling shares in a worthless silver and iron mine so much as the exploitation of their recognizable names" (5). Wineapple's book is at once lyrical and sure-footed, written with a poet's eye and with a novelist's sense of drama and suspense. She carefully explores Hawthorne as an enigma and keeps that enigma intact, not reducing it to some psychological grid, combat amid class warfare, or a class-bound product of a repressive culture, though all of these perspectives are woven into her biography. She manages to hold Hawthorne's contradictions in a dynamic equilibrium, neither fused nor transcended, not as a problem to be solved but as the crossroads of the human condition, "'the Actual and the Imaginary' — implicitly warring factions of experience coaxed into a 'neutral territory' by an author sensitive both to inner vision and to outer exigencies" (63). Everything can be taken in at least two ways, the multiplicity and complexities of experience as well as the limitations of language, making substantive what may only remain shadows. Wineapple captures the dynamic entanglements of the man without reducing him to an example of a particular theory or argument.

What Wineapple calls Hawthorne's "great subject" (125) becomes the terrible conflict between the past and the present. Each is entangled with the other, "interminably, relentlessly interlinked" (124) with no relief in sight, forever a "dark and deep, an imagined place" in which one could get lost. Perhaps his sense of homelessness and gnawing self-doubt contributed to that conflict, resulting in his awareness of the teeming absence at the heart of things. He seeks presence but has experienced only absence: "He wraps anonymity about him like a dark cloak. Itself a kind of monastic identity that protects him from — terrifying to consider — nothing at all" (86). He is an ultimately existential soul. He was, therefore, always a fatalist, "apprehensive of action — associated with aggression — skeptical of result" (332): "To give himself was to lose himself, and he couldn't afford to lose what he wasn't sure he had in the first place" (247). The man is the mystery, and "the past intrudes in present life every day, at every juncture, demanding something: the impossible settling of old accounts by means as reprehensible as the initial crime" (305).

Events and people transcend single interpretations for Wineapple. As for Hawthorne and Melville, their friendship has been "probed, sexualized and moralized, Hawthorne cast as a repressed and withholding father-figure, ungenerous to a fault, and Melville, needy son, rebuffed by the elder writer. Whenever Melville effused, Hawthorne shrank, or so it seems" (227). There is no doubt that he viewed blacks, Jews, and Italians as inferior to Anglo-Saxons, the racist paradigm of his age. Wineapple writes in a chapter called "Chiefly about War Matters," the title of Hawthorne's infamous article in the *Atlantic Monthly* in 1863, that he could "lampoon the slave-holding South and the censorious North," counseling inaction and viewing abolition as yet "another instance of noxious pride" (351, 332). We can abhor such an attitude, but they were also a part of himself and his age.

As a writer Hawthorne became the chronicler of "an imagination of unbelief and dislocation [filled with] melancholia and stark existential dreads" (364). Writing ushered him into a heart of darkness and shame, "an isolation no one could fathom or relieve" (365). "Hawthorne's best stories penetrate the secret horrors of ordinary life, those interstices in the general routine where suddenly something or someone shifts out of place, changing everything" (87). "The allure of his best prose derives from the tension between regulation and psychological — even ontological — pandemonium" (228). His fiction chronicles and creates such horrors, focused as it is upon "alienation, duplicity, and the sense of living double, not being what one seems or what others take one to be" (231). Sexual confusions smolder: "Chillingworth, no less than Hester, is Dimmesdale's lover and Hawthorne's double" (213). Hawthorne plays his own Westervelt in creating the convoluted plots within plots in *The Blithedale Romance*, with Coverdale as "an antebellum Prufrock" (250). The only lesson of Rome in *The Marble Faun* seems to be that all the defenses against ruin "are doomed to failure" (321); all finally seems "a heap of broken rubbish . . . shored against one another — plotline and characters and rumination and guidebook" (328). The rotting corpse of the old city spells "the death of romance" (321).

At the center of Hawthorne's art, for Wineapple, lies his ability to "transform[ ] a troubled consciousness into concrete emblems difficult to interpret, the case of the minister's black veil being the most obvious" (94–95). His style moves from phrase to phrase, building "a complex of meaning that at worst seems halting, artificial, and prim" (65) but at best as "phrases and clauses well-calibrated and modulated into sentences . . . [that accrue] a meaning far beyond the literal" (76).

In a recent article, "Nathaniel Hawthorne, Writer; or, The Fleeing of the Biographied," Wineapple, borrowing Emily Dickinson's line, "Biography first convinces us of the fleeing of the Biographied" (197), insists that no matter what perspective the biographer takes on her subject, that subject always remains one step ahead of her. For instance, she explains that "the years of Hawthorne's so-called seclusion (bachelorhood sans Sophia) have become a presumptive psychological conjecture based on the absence, rather than the presence, of evidence" (186). Some critics "accuse Hawthorne of what he didn't do and call it 'cultural work'" (189). Wineapple finally concludes that "such contradictions need not be separated into two different Hawthornes: the isolato, in one instance, and the public man — writer or politician, or both — in another." Hawthorne can be both "sociable and recluse" (197), but the biographied will always finally elude his biographer.

It is appropriate perhaps to end this overview of biographies of Hawthorne with the mention of yet another veil and of meanings far beyond the literal. From the genteel Victorian father to the solitary tortured soul, from the pragmatic man of business who seized a good political opportunity when he saw it to a creature besieged by feminist furies, and from the tormented psyche with all of its repressed, suppressed, and expressed desires and demands to the stolid example of his class and gender, we have passed from veil to veil like one of Hawthorne's characters trying to peel them away one by one, coming to realize that each veil contains some truth, some revealed facet of his personality. The prominence of certain veils comes and goes as the critical terrain shifts and shivers, but the work remains.

5: Entangled Polarities: The New Criticism

DIFFERENT ERAS OF LITERARY CRITICISM and biography always overlap and interact with one another, complicit in each other's confrontational positions or interpretations, but we can still detect important shifts in emphasis and method as we move forward chronologically from the nineteenth century into the twentieth century, with its focus on texts as aesthetic objects to be "de-coded" and meticulously analyzed in the New Criticism and its interest in psychological patterns and paradigms, the ambiguities implicit in Hawthorne's style, the mythic overtones and resonance of many of his plots, and the religious underpinnings of much of his vision. Until the turn of the twentieth century criticism tended to be impressionistic, spasmodic, and scattered. Critics interwove a writer's life with his or her art as if one easily explained and reflected the other and pursued various tangents, depending whatever seemed to arise as long as the general narrative followed the overall trajectory of the writer's life. From a contemporary perspective, such criticism looks blurred and diffuse, meandering and aimless as it veers from the life to the art in no rigorous or carefully constructed manner. Much of it is maddening for one trying to track down a critic's position or stance. Much of it proclaims the critic's point of view and ideological stance in no uncertain terms, doggedly and repetitiously, yet wading through Hawthorne criticism and biography in the last half of the nineteenth and early decades of the twentieth century is by and large a thankless task, searching for nuggets of insight and perspective that are often difficult to locate.

Much of that early criticism clung to a dualistic or polarized view of Hawthorne's work, revealing those oppositions, paradoxes, and contradictions that still haunt our own critical perspective. The rambling celebration of his decorous, elegant, and Augustan style clashed with the sense of the dubious content of his tales and romances, which often struck earlier readers as morbid, gratuitously dark, and downright weird. He was certainly a genius, they declared much too often, but were uncertain as to where and how that genius actually functioned. Was he just a regional writer, or was he a national one? Desperate at the time to find and praise anything national, readers and critics worked hard to build a national perspective into his fiction. Did he write allegories, or was he up to something else entirely? Was the Calvinist darkness in his fiction there merely for aesthetic reasons, or was he an unregenerate believer in some form of Calvinist dogma? He said he wrote romances, but how, exactly, were they different from novels?

Hawthorne's very approach to writing fiction generates and sustains such a dualistic perspective as described above, as we can see in the critical appraisals by such writers as D. H. Lawrence and Newton Arvin in the early twentieth century. Our sense of logic also relies on either/or, neither/nor, or both/and situations in order to construct a thesis or set up an argument. In Hawthorne's case a dynamic and consistently unresolved dialectic, a negative dialectic or entanglement if you will, saturates his vision and the resulting criticism of it. Jacques Derrida, among others, made us more aware of how these dualisms create hierarchies and priorities, so that male was more valued than female, good more than evil, etc. Romantics, on the other hand, suggested that each could not exist without the other, that each defines and complements the other in some ultimate harmonious synthesis. Daylight needs night in order to define itself and vice versa, thus forming a kind of electrical circuit where both positive and negative poles must exist to complete the whole. Hawthorne, however, creates polarities that spawn other polarities, leading to an ultimate uncertainty about all absolute beliefs and perspectives, about the meaning of meaning itself and how we and his characters create it.

Hawthorne created these endless polarities in his fiction, defining romance as that shadowy territory somewhere between the actual and the imaginary. He was fascinated, therefore, by mirrors, reflections, and the haunted mind that was drawn to them. For him, romance exposes and exploits this dualism, seeing the world in terms, however, not of synthesis but of entanglement, estrangement, and disconnection. In a sense this reflects Keats's notion of negative capability, "when a man is capable of being in uncertainties, mysteries, doubts, without an irritable reaching after fact and reason," but mystery for Hawthorne was murky, troubling, often frightening and never far from the everyday surfaces of life.

In his fiction Hawthorne often relied on an allegorical scaffolding to provide a precarious structural balance, a kind of perilous equilibrium that usually, once established by him or one of his characters, begins to disintegrate and dissolve almost immediately. Various interpretations collide and confront one another in an ongoing combat among contradictory visions and values. Dream and reality fight it out, each attempting to overwhelm the other. Thus Hawthorne's self-described "neutral territory," the phrase he used in "The Custom-House" to depict the twilight realm where romance takes place, reveals its artifice, the contrivance of a kind of artificial space that establishes distance from both dream and reality, from the actual and imaginary. Here he could choreograph his differing ideas, show how consciousness and the world were never fully integrated, and create those specters of guilt, doubt, uncertainty, and fear that erupted from the dark, cavernous human heart. He would go no further than to suggest the darkness of that heart: "It is dangerous to look too minutely at such phenomena. It is apt to create a substance, where at first there was a mere shadow" (*CE* XVI, 462). He would hint at unconscious depths, but he would not plumb them. Crime lurked there, the "sin" of consciousness itself that recognized its own isolation in and from the world as well as from others. Momentary stays against confusion, the dualistic/dialectical categories of his fiction and his characters, emerged and then crumbled as the process of romance continued forward, raising questions, sowing doubts, resolving nothing but producing the ongoing process itself.

Hawthorne's dualisms and polarities reveal what I have chosen to call entanglement, borrowing a term from quantum theory. Entanglement suggests that at the heart of things, in the subatomic realm, lies a perpetual flux, a kind of chaos that registers as particle and wave, as word and sentence, as sign and symbol only when we name it, measure it, and perceive it as such. We give form to that realm when we create particular categories, as if the conscious mind must name and number the traces and tracks of what we see emerging from the unconscious, as invisible and inaccessible as the quantum realm itself. In the quantum realm nothing seems independent or particular. Everything is entangled with everything else in a kind of fluid fog or miasma, a murky swarm where all remains indefinite until our consciousness registers and records it.

For example when an electron is expelled from an atom, we see only the trail that it leaves and the mark that it makes on a photographic plate. How we set up the experiment will determine whether we see the electron as a wave or as a particle. It is both, but neither can be seen simultaneously. It is like that image in which one can see either a vase or two heads facing one another. We can register only one at a time, when the actual image contains both at the same time. Thus entanglement speaks directly to what the interior of the quantum realm, and by analogy the unconscious, invisible and inaccessible, might actually be like, a murky foam or flux from which we determine what can be seen in our world by the way we measure the electron's trajectory and signature. This also suggests how we register unconscious thoughts or feelings by naming them and by doing so restricting them to the name that we create for them. We, therefore, disentangle what appears to be completely entangled within its unseen and unseeable domain.

As Louise Gilder describes it, "in entanglement, the quantum state the particles find themselves in is *indefinite* — neither here nor there, neither this nor that, neither yea or nay — but if one is measured and found to be 'yea,' the other is 'nay'" (66). Heisenberg adds to the assault on classical physics and our three-dimensional world: "What the word *wave* or *particle* means, one no longer knows . . . Classical words like *wave* and *particle* are all we have. The paradox is central" (100). Measurement itself disturbs the flux and renders the results as particles or waves, depending upon what measuring device is being used at the time, similar to Hawthorne's idea that once you use a word to name something, it hardens and falsifies what otherwise should remain shadowy and fluid. As he wrote Sophia in 1840, "Words come like an earthly wall betwixt us. Then our minds are compelled to stand apart, and make signals of our meaning" (*CE* XV, 440). Words "are at once our medium of expression, and the impediments to full communication" (*CE* XIV, 606).

Hawthorne recognized the dark entanglement of all things, especially in his time when psychology and theology were in a fight to the death, their assumptions and interpretations undercutting one another, creating a "lurid intermixture" that suggests a threatening vision (for Hawthorne and his culture) of ultimate uncertainty, invisibility, and inviolability. For Hawthorne, confined to his world's view of such things as gender and race, as well as perplexed by the very existence of the soul, which New England had been celebrating for centuries, could it be that the soul was merely mind, that the forces of mesmerism were really what existed and that the soul was just a name that was created to "measure" and "describe" their yet undiagnosed powers? Could all be a kind of self-projection and solipsistic hope? Such uncertainty could only appear dark and mysterious, frightening and isolating. The separation of things might only be an illusion, and words could never hope to capture the "lurid intermixture" of his world.

As we have seen, the dualistic perspective — either/or, neither/nor, both/and — has been deeply rooted in Hawthorne criticism from the very beginning. Polarities seem built into the very fabric of such criticism, a trend that would continue well into the twentieth century and beyond, no matter the focus of the analysis from formal structure and style to such wider social and cultural issues such as gender, race, sexuality, and class. Randall Fuller, for example, in his 2007 book, *Emerson's Ghosts: Literature, Politics, and the Making of Americanists,* locates yet another incarnation of these polarities in Van Wyck Brooks's *America's Coming of Age* (1915): the battle between high-brow and low-brow literature. Fuller also believes "that American culture was divided between 'vaporous idealism' and the self-interested business class" (81). We find such dualistic visions again and again in Henry Nash Smith's *Virgin Land* (1950), R. W. B. Lewis's *The American Adam* (1955), and particularly in Richard Chase's *The American Novel and Its Tradition* (1957), which we will discuss in some detail below, in their broad attempts to locate the pulse of American culture somewhere between technology and nature, innocence and experience, the romance and the novel.

D. H. Lawrence in *Studies in Classic American Literature* (1923) relied upon these persistent dualisms and polarities in terms of his psychological description of the human mind in general but the American mind in particular. For him, "man is made up of a dual consciousness . . . We are divided against ourselves" (91, 112). This results in "a basic hostility in all of us — the physical and the mental, the blood and the spirit. The mind is 'ashamed' of the blood. And the blood is destroyed by the mind" (92). His is the essentially tragic Freudian vision of eternal warfare between the relentless and unending combat between *eros* and *thanatos*. Such a perilous equilibrium always threatens to break down, as super-ego, ego, and id wrestle for supremacy.

In Lawrence's view, Hawthorne knew of this perpetual warfare but the "sugary, blue-eyed little darling of a Hawthorne" (8) managed to hide it all too well: "[The reader in this case] must look through the surface of American art, and see the inner diabolism of the symbolic meaning. Otherwise it is all mere childishness" (89). For Lawrence, Hester's blood seduces the more contemplative and spiritual Dimmesdale, and Dimmesdale is so overwhelmed by that blood knowledge that his self-flagellation as punishment for his "sin" is really nothing more than a form of masturbation that re-enacts his sexual experience without any outside help or support. Freudian sexuality overthrows Calvinist conscience, particularly as this perspective gets developed by the New Critics. It was not the sex that destroyed Hester and the minister but their belief that what they were doing was wrong "that constituted the chief harm of the act. Man invents sin, in order to enjoy the feeling of being naughty" (108). The belief that one cannot or should not do wrong is, for Lawrence, wrong in and of itself. The body will have its way no matter what; the rest is mere subterfuge and disguise. Freud had it right: Pearl represents the demonic, willful, and spontaneous child of an American sexual union, whereas Chillingworth represents a throwback to European manners, "the old male authority" (105).

For Lawrence, to know things mentally is to kill things physically. Hester knows and embodies this and therefore corrupts Dimmesdale's spirit: "The blood *hates* being KNOWN . . . Blood-consciousness overwhelms, obliterates, and annuls mind-consciousness" (91). This is Hawthorne's vision, dressed up in his quiet elegant prose. If man cannot in some way control woman, Lawrence suggests, all is lost. She becomes demonic and boundless and sends "out waves of silent destruction of the faltering spirit in men" (99). Such a vampiric battle of wills lurks at the center of Hawthorne's vision, which is why he is both attracted to and repelled by women. Lawrence suggests that Hawthorne attempts to plumb the depths of that yearning that man, trapped in his own rigid beliefs and mental conceptions, both desires and fears: dual consciousness again, "of which the two halves are most of the time in opposition to one another

— and will be so as long as time lasts" (112). Blood must triumph against the rigid, all-consuming spirit of American belief, however relentless the contest. This vision, of course, underlies modernism in its belief in the basic brutality and animality of man, particularly relevant after the First World War.

F. O. Matthiessen in *American Renaissance: Art and Expression in the Age of Emerson and Whitman* (1941) continued this dualistic outlook along with his New Critical approach but expanded it to include a broader, more cultural perspective. For Randall Fuller, writing in 2007, Matthiessen's view corresponds with Murray Krieger's: "The self-reflexive nature of the aesthetic provides a 'subversive antidote to the political abuse of discursive power'" (84). For Matthiessen, Hawthorne's haunted mind undermines the Genteel Tradition of America literature, however conservative Hawthorne's politics and public values were. His fiction shadows American democracy and culture in their ongoing progress toward a more egalitarian age, a necessary brake to such a trajectory, but his politics is cousin to V. S. Naipaul's notion of hating the oppressors and fearing the oppressed. The result leads to political paralysis, as Hawthorne acknowledged the wrongs of slavery but also feared the violence implicit in the abolitionists' stand against it.

For Matthiessen, "Hawthorne could conceive of evil in the world, but not an evil world" (334); thus his politics should be rejected. In Matthiessen's view, Hawthorne's basic isolation and loneliness marked a condition that he, Matthiessen as a literary scholar, outwardly rejected, hoping to inject the scholar's point of view into a more progressive version of political action, particularly on the eve of the Second World War and its crusade against fascism. Hawthorne wrote about the reality of suffering, the tragic disequilibrium between reason and passion, thought and emotion (345), but 1941 was not the time to celebrate that vision as a way of dealing with the world.

Matthiessen saw Hawthorne much in the way that Henry James did, as a New England provincial trapped in his own self-consciousness and the desiccated traditions of witchcraft and Calvinist darkness. Without much of a literary tradition to support him, although "he saw the empirical truth behind the Calvinist symbols" (199), Hawthorne took his first literary cues from Sir Walter Scott in the way of dividing his characters up into various groups and classes, creating spotlit scenes and exalted speeches that highlighted their points of view (203). His general sense of evil "came to him directly from theological tradition" (355), but his reliance on allegorical constructions provided a "picturesque arrangement but not composition" (301).

While Matthiessen trumpeted Whitman's vision of the heroic man, of "Man in the Open Air," he nevertheless focused on "man's inexorable will to power" (656), a will that had been very much on display in the 1930s and that was far more tragic than optimistic. A sense of the burden of the past much like Hawthorne's seemed to weigh Matthiessen's volume down despite his progressive political views. It seems as if, once he employed the New Critical tools of close reading, with a sharp, ever-vigilant eye on the lookout for paradox, contradiction, and ambiguity, his progressive view lost its cutting edge.

Matthiessen was determined to commemorate "our first great age" (xv) of literary masterpieces between 1850 and 1855, especially Melville's *Moby-Dick* and Whitman's "Song of Myself," which for him represented genuinely new and American voices in their assertion of self, in order to showcase the possibilities of American democracy and strengthen the myth of the common man. He was also determined to analyze literature as literature from several historical and cultural perspectives as a way of reacting against much of the impressionistic, biographical criticism that had preceded him. He was searching for the voice of the age, relying on Emerson's theory of expression, which viewed poets and novelists as seers and prophets. He was out to undermine and replace the sentimental and diffuse views of Van Wyck Brooks in *America's Coming of Age* (1915) and *The Flowering of New England* (1936), as well as Lewis Mumford's *The Golden Day* (1926), with a deeper understanding of Hawthorne's work, for "when dealing with Hawthorne, [they have] deprived one of our few tragic writers of his chief significance" (xvii). For Matthiessen both Coleridge's organic idea of art and T. S. Eliot's concept of the artist as craftsman provided the foundation for his critical claims. Today his book seems elementary in its criticism, diffuse and digressive in its presentation with its references to Joyce, Kafka, Mann, Chekhov, Yeats, and Dreiser, and filled with "old-fashioned" summaries of various books, but for years it reigned as the bible of American Studies.

Matthiessen's shift from the dualistic vision as a description of the human condition to a literary technique linked to allegory trumped his politics. In his discussion of *The Scarlet Letter*, he focuses on Hawthorne's "devices of multiple choice," going on to say that "He does not literally accept his own allegory, and yet he finds it symbolically valid because of its psychological exactitude" (277). Today we may look upon Hawthorne's multiple choices as an extension of that allegorical structure in an either/ or, neither/nor manner, considering that Hawthorne's various interpretations and suggestions are not so much a matter of choice as they are inherent in his characters and situations. For instance when Young Goodman Brown on his way into the forest comes upon a "second traveller," that second man is described as "apparently in the same rank of life as Goodman Brown, and bearing a considerable resemblance to him, though perhaps more in expression than features." Does he resemble him or not? Hawthorne continues: "The only thing about him, that could be fixed upon as remarkable, was his staff, which bore the likeness of a great black snake, so curiously wrought, that it might almost be seen to twist and wriggle itself, like a living serpent. This, of course, must have been an ocular deception, assisted by the uncertain light" (*CE* X, 76). Is it a deception or not? Hawthorne leaves both possibilities intact, a dualistic choice that Matthiessen saw as a primary example of his literary technique. For him Melville created in his white whale a symbol that is more fluid and dynamic than the static image of the pink ribbons in "Young Goodman Brown," for example, but Matthiessen's notion of multiple choice, which for him embodied "a sense of the intricacy of any situation for a perceptive being" (276), carried critical clout throughout the New Critical era and beyond.

Even though he did not describe it as such, Matthiessen's account of Hawthorne's device of multiple choice became one way of characterizing the form of romance. Yvors Winters's *In Defense of Reason* (1987) would strengthen this idea and tie it directly to Hawthorne's romance as what he called "the formula for alternative possibilities" (170), still insisting on the basic either/or perspective that viewed interpretations as binary alternatives as opposed to more multiple possibilities. Dualisms did help define Hawthorne's own analysis of his fiction — actuality and imagination, dream and reality, etc. — and they did emerge from his fondness for allegory, however deconstructed and scrutinized, but in the era of the Cold War and the neo-orthodox notions of a humanity flawed by original sin, they took on a more permanent form. In fact the American Studies program founded at Yale in 1952, based on Harvard's American Civilization program (which was the first of its kind and had been founded by Perry Miller and Matthiessen in the 1930s), was originally "designed as a positive and affirmative method of meeting the threat of Communism" (Fuller 112). The Cold War with its demonic dualisms, the Legions of American Light versus the Forces of Atheistic Darkness, revived the interest in Hawthorne, and his restoration as a major writer emerged in such "allegorical" times, just as critics became more intrigued by and drawn to his awareness of Luciferian conditions in the human heart.

The New Critics championed their sense of ambiguity and paradox, which successful literary texts managed to balance and uphold within an ultimate unity of form and content. Such New Critics such as I. A. Richards, Robert Penn Warren, Austin Warren, and Cleanth Brooks regarded texts as unified objects, which they would then meticulously analyze, almost as if they were scientifically examining a particular object, to reveal how all the ambiguities produced a unified whole. "Ambiguity" became the favorite word of such critics, and each author's works that they chose to analyze appeared to balance such ambiguities perfectly.

In 1970 John Caldwell Stubbs, for example, championed this point of view in *The Pursuit of Form: A Study of Hawthorne and the Romance,* and in his discussion of ironies and contradictions — the crux of the New Critical fascination with such things, particularly as represented in lyric poetry — praised the ambiguity of vision as embodied in the unity of the text. Hawthorne did not write allegory, because nothing in his work was fixed or static: "Distance provided him with the freedom to conduct a dialectical investigation of the conflict . . . a complex questioning process" (43). The artifice of romance specifically called attention to itself with its stories within stories, visible narrators, and various speculations about specific events, so that Hawthorne could "gain an artistic distance from human experience" (5) and probe the larger pattern within it. Hawthorne's ambiguity was not boundless, "for his complexity has its defining boundaries" (81), suggests Stubbs. Hawthorne also "calls attention to his own presence as the mind in the act of weighing and evaluating the action of the work" (78). This was the New Critical goal: ironies may multiply and flourish, but the best texts always managed to encapsulate them in some final harmonious vision, however tragic.

In 1952, Richard Harter Fogle argued decisively in *Hawthorne's Fiction: The Light and the Dark* for Hawthorne's "clarity of technique and ambiguity of meaning" (32), for the often perfect "fusion of surface simplicity and underlying complexity" (33). Roy R. Male's *Hawthorne's Tragic Vision* (1957), Harry Levin's *The Power of Blackness: Hawthorne Poe Melville* (1960), and Hyatt H. Waggoner's *Hawthorne: A Critical Study* (1953) and *The Presence of Hawthorne* (1979) would follow in Fogle's critical footsteps and deepen his critical vision. Fogle explained that Hawthorne "is more Manichean than most theologies would approve" (220), an idea I explored and nurtured in *In Hawthorne's Shadow* in 1985 in terms of such a perspective's influence upon later and more contemporary writers such as Harold Fredric, Faulkner, Joyce Carol Oates, Joan Didion, John Gardner, John Cheever, Norman Mailer, John Updike and others. For Fogle, clearly definable theses and antitheses existed in Hawthorne's fictional world: "His only reconciliation is acceptance of life's differences and contradictions" (220). Order vanishes when Hawthorne's mind begins to probe it: "The dark is better material than the light. All action is imperfection, and all plots are about something that has gone wrong, set over against a norm of rightness by which we judge them. Hawthorne's darkness has the structural and dramatic value of contrast" (221).

For Fogle light represents the clarity of Hawthorne's designs, embodied in his lucid language and classic balance. Matthiessen's diagnosis of Hawthorne's device of multiple choice and Winters's formula of alternative possibilities are not so much techniques as "a pervasive quality of mind" (11). Thus Hawthorne's structural clarity encompasses the ambiguous interminglings of good and evil, dream and reality, as well as "human uncertainty, flexibility of relationship, and ambiguity of emphasis" (54).

100 ♦ Entangled Polarities: The New Criticism

The conceptual framework manages to unify and balance all contradictions and polarities. His characters are allegorical and do suggest certain types and ideas, "but they become complex human beings" (81) as the tales and romances unfold. "The framework of Hawthorne's fiction," contends Fogle, "is customarily a doctrine, a belief, or a moral proposition which he proceeds to test by using his imagination" (80).

At times, says Fogle, too many possibilities can undermine the text, as in "Rappaccini's Daughter." Hawthorne's "skeptical indecision" (182) in the voice of a Miles Coverdale in *The Blithedale Romance* can distort the narrative flow of a decent yarn, and the "knotted entanglement" (211) of ideas and speculations in *The Marble Faun* can undermine the inflexible and allegorical values of a character such as Hilda. By and large the definite design of composition neatly balances the ambiguities in the text itself: contrast, action, character, and structure intimately reflect one another, and if contradictions remain unresolved, and if there can be no forgiveness and no ultimate solutions in the human world, the tragic vision remains intact, the framework as carefully constructed as the scaffold in Puritan Boston. Light and dark balance one another in their Manichean universe, and thus, contends Fogle, "Hawthorne, while refusing to provide a natural or human solution, balances his tragic earth with a clear vision of heaven" (234).

Roy R. Male conceived of Hawthorne's unresolved polarities as a kind of struggle between the head, represented by masculine speculation (he chooses the monetary terms, "speculation" and "investment," to contrast gender roles in Hawthorne's fiction) that champions experimentation, taking chances, and "penetrating into space, sparked by Promethean fire," and the heart, represented by feminine investment that exists to conserve traditions and the family (8). The vision remained a tragic one, since neither of these allegorical positions could be reconciled with the other. In their search for a home, many of Hawthorne's characters attempt "to combine the masculine protestant vision of America with the feminine catholic communion of Europe" (45). For Male "without the humane clothing of a sympathetic imagination, penetrative insight is like rigorous Freudian literary criticism; it plumbs the surface" (166).

Male moves from the tongue of flame as witnessed in *The Scarlet Letter* — the light of intuitive vision and the riddle of moral growth through entanglements of guilt — to evolution and regeneration in *The House of the Seven Gables*, pausing to note what he calls the "abortive catastrophe" (155) of *The Blithedale Romance* with its failure to achieve any redemption through tragedy, "a kind of Walden in reverse" (144), before promoting the possible transfiguration of various characters in *The Marble Faun*, despite its incoherent structure. Hawthorne's tortuous paths of possible redemption fulfill the proto-Calvinist vision of the New Critics, focused as they were on sin and guilt, and do so in the traditional fashion of ultimate dualisms: head vs. heart, male vs. female. Polarities proliferate and remain intact.

Harry Levin acknowledges in his book, *The Power of Blackness,* the darkness in the visions of Hawthorne, Poe, and Melville. Writing in 1958, he does concede that as for slavery, "this was blackness with a vengeance" (34), but in the New Critical manner he explores blackness more in terms of theology, psychology, and myth, concentrating on Manichean dualism, the Jungian union of archetypal opposites, primal darkness, and biblical imagery. He decides that Hawthorne must be "a Calvinist in psychology, if not in theology" (55), that he practices "the cult of antithesis" (37) — "Hawthorne's affirmations are double negatives, the author's repudiation of his characters' denials" (58) — and suggests that in the tales, for instance, "once the hypothesis has worked itself out, its interpretation is hedged with uncertainties" (47). The form of the romance, "the traditional medium of American fiction" (18), supplies the symbolic structure of American writing with the blackness that lies at the center of the American nightmare complete with journeys, quests, dreams, and voyages of discovery, even though, Levin admits, "blackness is merely one side — the less popular side — of a famous polarity. The union of opposites, after all, is the very basis of the American outlook" (xi). That union underscores the New Critics' quest for unity in all the texts that they explored.

Levin summarizes his analysis of Hawthorne succinctly:

> In his vignettes of the American scene, in his appraisals of historic tradition, in his anxiety over the self-isolated individual, and in his curiosity to read the cosmic scheme of things, Hawthorne is truly the founding patriarch of our fiction, and sits upon its grandfather's chair with an air of authority. His position is so strategically taken, between the ethical and the esthetic spheres, that he retains his residence in both. As a moralist, he propounds an austere message; as an artist, he gracefully illustrates it. (68)

One cannot help but notice, however accurate or inaccurate Levin's estimation of Hawthorne's role in American fiction, that his references to "historic tradition," "founding patriarch," and "air of authority" shape a distinctively cultural path that American professors, male, of course, have followed as successors to the Puritan divines who preceded them: from Jonathan Edwards to Emerson to Perry Miller to Matthiessen to Levin (In fact Levin was one of Matthiessen's first students and suggested "American Renaissance" as the title of his masterwork). "Man's habit of telling stories as a means of summarizing his activities and crystallizing his attitudes" (ix) also shores up his position in the historical and traditional family tree of male ministers and critics. Not for nothing does Levin invoke the image of Hawthorne sitting on the "grandfather's chair with an air of authority." Whiteness plays an even greater role in that long descent, within which blackness must be ultimately absorbed and diffused; "the cult of antithesis" becomes the primary focus of American Studies programs, which both accommodated and resisted the often shrill nationalism of the Cold War.

Hyatt H. Waggoner in *Hawthorne: A Critical Study* (1953) epitomizes the best and the culmination of the New Criticism in his well-developed idea that the device of ambiguity lies not only at the core of Hawthorne's art but also inheres in myth and symbols as well. He elaborated upon and explored, for example, the complex vision of the Fortunate Fall in *The Marble Faun*, not that Hawthorne believed it in terms of some dogmatic doctrine but that he recognized that there could be no moral growth and no truly human comprehension of humanity in general without the acknowledgment of sin and suffering. In any case in *The Marble Faun* Hawthorne and his character Hilda, to whom Male attributes "icy rigidity" and "repulsive" purity (172, 173), reject Kenyon's argument precisely because it is a line of reasoning . . . it becomes a frozen creed that is at best a paradox, at worst a mockery of true morality . . . moral truth must be apprehended as a narrative, a parable, an allegory — not as a line of reasoning" (176). Narrative as parable with its religious and moral overtones speaks directly to the concerns of the New Critics.

Although he doesn't mention it by name, Waggoner has clearly responded to the patterns of myth and literature in Northrop Frye's *The Anatomy of Criticism* (1957), the bible of its day that dazzled students with its wheels and patterns, its progressive stages of epic, tragedy, comedy, and irony but that virtually made no aesthetic judgments, brimming with mythical archetypes and founded on an analysis of the neo-orthodox Protestant vision of human limitations and derelict gods, forever tragic, complex and convoluted. Waggoner also acknowledges his debt to Fogle's work and writes in such a clear, thoughtful, and jargon-free manner that one can observe how completely assimilated and understood the New Critical vision and techniques had become. Hawthorne's seriousness is foregrounded and accepted without question: "He could be described as a Christian humanist . . . the most important shaping force behind Hawthorne's art is the special character of his religious belief [which] was existentially oriented, not institutional or traditional" (264). From Henry James's description of Puritanism as a mere pigment in Hawthorne's palette, we have arrived, with Waggoner, at a full-blown, religiously existential belief system. The literal, the symbolic, and the mythic all participate in Hawthorne's practice, which falls somewhere between "traditional Christian allegory on the one hand and . . . modern symbolism on the other." For Waggoner this "seems hardly open to question" (261). Hawthorne's best art, Waggoner believes, emerges from the dream Hawthorne expresses in "The Haunted Mind."

Waggoner's is one of the best descriptions of Hawthorne's style on record:

> It is the style of a man whose insights are too qualified to be succinctly summarized . . . the antithesis of Emerson's staccato sententious style, his pulpit exhortation. (173, 172)

> His style . . . was a little old-fashioned even when he wrote it. It is slow-moving, with its pace slowed down still further by his very heavy punctuation. It is rhetorical . . . It circles around its subject, enveloping it in balanced clauses and phrases that make qualification after qualification . . . It is marked by a strong preference for the abstract or generalized word over the concrete or specific one . . . It is a formal, public, "literary" style of a man of letters, quite different from the private, undressed, colloquial, imagistic style modern writing has taught us to prefer. (255–56)

Such a style suggests Robert Frost's description of a poem as a momentary stay against confusion amid a Heraclitian flux of character and consequence. It reflects thinking in terms of images and episodes, working out various interpretations as the text proceeds. It makes great use of New England history, discovering and exploring meaning as it continues, while feeding deeply on primal religious myths, Christian sin, atonement, and the psychology of guilt: "All the best of Hawthorne's tales exist in the area bounded by allegory and history, archetype and myth" (125). As in *The Scarlet Letter*, Hawthorne occupies that neutral territory between various polarities: Hawthorne's "relations between nature and man, fact and value, and the physical and the spiritual are neither those of identity nor those of total disparity" (151).

Waggoner concluded that Hawthorne and Poe created a new kind of romantic American fiction in opposition to the English realist tradition that featured such writers as Defoe, Fielding, Austen, Scott, and Dickens. Hawthorne worked with epic and myth, the same kind of romantic vision that fascinated James, Conrad, Kafka, and Faulkner. In every case the truth of the human heart would usually transcend the social realism of such English fiction: "The most striking way in which Hawthorne's work is seminal for modern fiction is the mythopoetic aspect of both his theory and his practice" (251).

In *The Presence of Hawthorne* (1979) Waggoner collected eight of his essays from 1962 to 1979, looking back upon the New Critical neo-orthodoxy of the 1950s and finding Hawthorne's tragic affirmation and his fixation on images and their implications basically humanistic and perceptive. He recognizes "the bulk and general excellence of the great outburst of Hawthorne criticism of the 1950s — since ours is an age that has found irony, ambiguity, and paradox to be central not only in literature but in life" (13). Hawthorne remains relevant because the evil buried in the human heart will always remain relevant: "Hawthorne has never been wholly out of favor since the publication of *The Scarlet Letter*, but in the half century following his death he seemed much more old-fashioned than he does now," most likely because of his "antirealist fictional practice . . . in a period of literary realism" (38, 39). Waggoner asserts plainly: "The farther the New Criticism recedes into the past, the better it looks to me . . . Never forgotten, Hawthorne has never needed to be rediscovered" (124, 143).

In 1974 Waggoner edited and published Hawthorne's *Lost Notebook*, including 329 separate entries from May 28, 1835, to June 29, 1841. He noticed, for instance, that Sophia had scratched out the world "squalid" from one of Hawthorne's original lines, which read: "In this dismal and squalid chamber fame was won." If there were no ultimate revelations about the significance of his twelve solitary years between 1825 and 1837, there was enough evidence to counter the view of Hawthorne as a recluse, even though, as Waggoner put it, there was "more than a touch of the 'morbid' in a good deal of what he wrote" (105). He did suffer from "unusually strong guilt-feelings" (105), possibly linked to mastur-bation. We should not forget the extremely negative descriptions of and reactions to the practice of masturbation, particularly for males, in the nineteenth century, sapping not only one's strength but also disconnect-ing one from social intercourse, as evil in its own way as the anti-social aspects of incest, hence the reference to the "squalid" chamber. Waggoner, however, took issue with Frederick Crews's "absurdly reduc-tive reading" in *The Sins of the Fathers* (1966): "Reductive psychologizing about works of art not only diminishes the art but fails to explain what it professes to explain" (108–9). Waggoner did discover that Hawthorne often noticed young women's legs, his comment on which led to what he found to be an amusing newspaper headline that came out at the time of the publication of the notebook: "Hawthorne a Girl-Watcher, Professor Says" (110).

Sharon Cameron in *The Corporeal Self: Allegories of the Body in Melville and Hawthorne* (1981) deepened the dualistic perspective as both vision and technique by linking the idea of allegory in general and in Hawthorne and Melville in particular to the mutilation of the body, in which a part, say, the heart, represents the whole: "The self is distilled to a representative bodily organ" (2). Allegory, thus, reduces the complexities of identity and the self to a single trait or sign, "the reduction of a thing to a representative emblem" (82), which essentially disfigures and mutilates the actual living body. She describes identity itself as a form of allegory, and goes on to contemplate what she calls the various bodies mutilated by this procedure in both Hawthorne's and Melville's works. She makes her position very clear when she explains that to allegorize is "to dichotimize" (102), an act that by its very nature falsifies the more complex experiences in life and literature. Dualism itself becomes an allegorized category as it externalizes internal divisions, confusions, and fissures of and in the self, replicating itself again and again in such polarities as inside/outside, soul/body, body/bodies, and body/world. One thinks of the minister's black veil and of the various rigid categories that Hawthorne's male characters cling to no matter what may happen to them: "Hawthorne both allegorizes his subjects and is simultaneously critical of characters who attempt allegorizations" (86). Thus the self for Cameron is reduced to a specific allegorical meaning in much of Hawthorne's fiction, a process she sees occurring both in Hawthorne's male characters and often in Hawthorne himself.

I would agree with most of Cameron's argument, in which dualism becomes a strategy, a technique, and a structure, though her emphasis on mutilated bodies as an analogy to allegorical meaning seems to confuse the issue. Still, I agree with her analysis of the interrelationship among various opposites and polarities, which she views as contingent upon one another and her decision that nothing can be allegorically "pure": "If allegory is clear, history is incomprehensible" (153). The problem with Hawthorne's characters that reflect Hawthorne's own dilemma is that by using allegory or envisioning the world around them and the other people in it in allegorical terms, they wish to make things conform to an external meaning or significance and to remain that way when "meanings in the temporal world are ambiguous and multiple" (152), as Hawthorne himself recognized.

The New Criticism always made use of Freudian insight — Freud is a kind of New Critic when he describes the psychic levels and layers of a self that longs for some unified vision of itself but can never succeed because of the ongoing warfare between the various layers — whether dressed up in mythic garb or theological robes, but the primary focus remained that of an allegorical religious vision. Frederick Crews, in his highly influential *The Sins of the Fathers: Hawthorne's Psychological Themes* (1966), however, brought such themes out into the open and tied them directly to Hawthorne's fiction and biography. Suddenly it seemed as if the New Critical approach, involving the analysis of patterns of images and symbols, was revealed as a mere mask, which disguised Hawthorne's keynote condition as one of "ambivalence," his status, as Crews points out, that of "a self-divided, self-tormented man" (7). Crews also exposes Sophia's use of euphemisms in editing Hawthorne's notebooks to replace what she considered to be his more psychological and scatological phrases, scratching out "animal desires" and writing "temperament" and substituting "fancy" for "itch."

Oedipal struggles between fathers and sons appeared everywhere in Hawthorne's fiction, according to Crews, aggravated by the fact that he had lost his father at age four; psychological necessities undermined all conscious moral choices; history and ancestry, Satan and God became

"psychological metaphors" (263). Characters, willingly or not, gave vent
to their unconscious and, therefore, virtually pre-determined compulsions
and urges, however obsessive, incestuous, and murderous: "The emotional
sense emanating from a deed like Aylmer's is one of satanic triumph, of
momentary victory over inhibition. The truth is out at last, and it is murderous" (265). In Hawthorne theology and morality conspired to weave
black veils beneath which seethed all kinds of unmentionable forces. One
thinks again of Dimmesdale's self-flagellation: he must punish sexual
desire, but the punishment takes the form of sexual gratification. No wonder Hawthorne's characters are doomed, repetitiously re-enacting their
psychological and often allegorically constructed roles as the desiring
young man, the bad and authoritative father, and the sexually intriguing
— or alternatively, the genteelly idealized — woman.

As Pierre Walker explains, "In *The Sins of the Fathers*, Crews provides
blatantly Freudian interpretations of all of Hawthorne's romances and
best-known tales. When we re-read this book from our perspective [over]
forty years later, we may be tempted to find almost laughable the inevitable
turn in Crews's interpretation of each tale and romance to Freud's Oedipus
complex . . . [it] quickly becomes predictable" (web). Consider, for
instance, Crews's description of Hawthorne's style in contrast to Waggoner's
cited earlier in this chapter:

> Hawthorne's balance between confession and evasion is reflected in
> his style, whose distance and abstraction are often confused with
> Augustan serenity. The meditative poise, the polite irony, the antith-
> eses, the formal diction, and the continual appeal to sentiments that
> are generally shared, all serve to neutralize the dangerous knowledge
> that lies at the bottom of his plots. For Hawthorne regards language
> as a fearful thing. (12)

While both Waggoner and Crews mention the balance and the often
abstract nature of Hawthorne's style, Waggoner emphasizes its rhetorical
qualities, such as the use of clauses and phrases, its calculatedly slow pace,
and its self-consciously literary qualities. Crews, on the other hand,
describes that balance in a more negative, almost dismissive manner as a
kind of "cop-out" between confession and evasion. He also mentions that
Hawthorne's "distance and abstraction" are often mistaken for what other
critics have celebrated as his "Augustan serenity" in Hawthorne's attempt
to "neutralize . . . dangerous knowledge." For Waggoner Hawthorne's
style reveals "a man whose insights are too qualified to be succinctly summarized," not that of an author trying to hide "dangerous" secrets that
Crews too easily reduced to Freudian categories. Finally Crews mentions
Hawthorne's sense of language "as a fearful thing," while Waggoner views
it as a formal and public literary style consciously chosen by Hawthorne as
a man of letters.

So much for Hawthorne's self-declared "neutral territory," now become a smoldering abyss of primal urges and primitive yearnings. No wonder Hawthorne refused to dive any deeper than his descriptions of the human heart as a dark cavern, littered with corpses: in the pit he may have come across too many loathsome things to write about. Better to hint at a further darkness than to descend into it. Better to bind such horrors in allegorical and/or symbolic structures and artful dodging while recognizing, as Crews does, "a sense that nothing in human behavior is as free or fortuitous as it appears" (17).

Crews points out that Freud himself suggested that "No one who, like me, conjures up the most evil of those half-tamed demons that inhabit the human breast, and seeks to wrestle with them, can expect to come through the struggle unscathed" (271). No wonder the master-slave dynamic from Crews's perspective appealed to Hawthorne and appeared so often among his characters; each reflected the other, locked in a fierce battle that could only end in death. Incest and other sexual fantasies prowled within Hawthorne's tormented psyche, resulting in fiction of "a highly energized struggle between inadmissible fantasies and the punishment and denial of those fantasies" (267). Such analysis becomes in Crews's criticism a closed circuit wherein the hero "*becomes an image of what he loathes*" (249). How could one deny such a perfectly circular argument? And how perfectly it reflected the New Critics' compulsion to find unity in all texts.

In 1980 Crews finally, however, parted ways with his Freudian view of Hawthorne, which he decided was too pat, too circular, and too self-absorbed. Admitting that Hawthorne's fiction contained "some paradigm-independent traits" (275), he thought it best to transcend Freudian logic and consider more religious and social contexts for Hawthorne's work. From his later perspective he saw Freud as "yet another instance of allegorical criticism" (281) and recoiled from its simplicities. Hawthorne and Freud were "two of a kind — introspective and prying Romantics who distrusted appearances, brooded over the poisonous effects of long-held secrets, and harbored a tragic sense" (277), yet it was the business of literary critics to pay more attention to the "surface features, including the extraordinary self-control with which [Hawthorne] simultaneously manipulated literary conventions and ironically distanced himself from them" (281).

Yet despite Crews's change of heart, he had opened a Pandora's box of psychological forces that critics could not ignore. In 1970 the French critic, Jean Normand, in *Nathaniel Hawthorne: An Approach to an Analysis of Artistic Creation*, set out to describe and explore Hawthorne's creative process in terms of various spells, exorcisms, and haunted minds, but he sought refuge all too simplistically in Freudian analysis, emphasizing Hawthorne's hungering for the return of the maternal woman and the absent father. Such patterns are softened somewhat by Normand's evocative and sinuous prose style that emphasizes mystery, obsession, and the web of the creative process. "All art," he observed, "proceeds from the dialectic of the divided self . . . a mind whose activity relies upon perpetual antagonisms" (222, 241), but according to Normand, Hawthorne saw himself as a haunted Oberon, a vagabond storyteller, an enchanting nomad and caster of spells, a kind of wizard who constantly lurked within the outward appearance of the dedicated civil servant: "Hawthorne is always two . . . his own labyrinth of contradictions" (19). He remained "the eternally youthful elf, ironic and ardent, tender and cruel" (84), for his soul remained profoundly dualistic.

Hawthorne, according to Normand, delights "in mystifying us, assumes poses, feigns inscrutability and lack of ambition, obscures his own traces by burning manuscripts, letters, documents" (xxvii). He advances and retreats, creating in his fiction and biography a strategy that generates "a multiple and protean reality absolute only in its ambiguity" (114). Dualities shape his entire vision, accompanied by images of the labyrinth, the isolated soul, and the solitary quest: "There was always a static (moral) element and a dynamic (psychological and esthetic) element, each counterbalancing the other" (142). Ambiguity and allegory always signal divisions and polarities. Hawthorne's use of chiaroscuro suggested modern cinematic techniques: "in order to 'see,' Hawthorne needed darkness. He could not grasp objects effectively except through veils, through the mystery with which he surrounded them in advance and which alone spurred him on to examine them from every aspect and in depth. Hawthorne used shadows in order to make light spring forth, confused the trails in order to find himself again, and created closed spheres in order to penetrate them" (149).

In Normand's view such themes and techniques emerge most successfully in *The Scarlet Letter* and "Ethan Brand." His labyrinthine sentences anticipated Faulkner's, and haunted by dualisms in all things, he could only write about the isolated guilty soul, the solitary individual burdened by such a bifurcated vision. Dualisms can stand alone or interpenetrate one another, such as Freud's assessment of *eros* and *thanatos*, but they can never be resolved or overcome: "Hawthorne, like all poets, was a martyr to his own contradictions" (63).

Normand's elaborate and labyrinthine speculations overcome his rigid Freudian framework and create a multi-layered vision of Hawthorne's frame of mind when writing fiction, but their roots remain firmly in Freudian soil. In the battle between psychology and theology, however modernized and updated in the New Critics' version of Hawthorne's fiction, psychology had won. Compulsion conquered consequence, bound by rigidly dualistic contradictions. Once viewed as a cultural, religious, and historical phenomenon, polarities now seemed to be rooted in the human psyche, unshakeable, irrefutable, and immutable. Everything was perpetually at war with itself, lodged in the unconscious mind, a point of view that in its own way became as orthodox and rigid as the New Critics' love of mythic patterns and religious allegory, disconnected as they often appeared to be from historical and cultural phenomena.

In *Family Themes and Hawthorne's Fiction: The Tenacious Web* (1984), Gloria C. Erlich acknowledges the "psychic antitheses" (136) exposed and exploited by Crews and relates them directly to Hawthorne's biography. Hawthorne, according to Erlich, internalized the mercantile values of his mother's family, the Mannings, and realized that life for him would always be a continuous struggle between bookkeeper and poet. To be manly was to be like Uncle Robert Manning, an ambitious and successful merchant; to be an indolent writer was to be "unmanly." Hence the antitheses between Clifford and Judge Pyncheon in *The House of the Seven Gables* and Owen Warland and Peter Hovenden in "The Artist of the Beautiful." Vacillation, ambivalence, and dependence fostered such fictional struggles even as Hawthorne's quest for an actual father figure always collided with his resistance to father figures, as if the absence of his own father was the only intimidating presence of a father he could know. Erlich disagrees with James Mellow's claim that Uncle Robert homosexually assaulted Hawthorne, having both slept in the same bed for years, but she still views Robert as a potent force in shaping Hawthorne's internally divided sense of self.

Thus psychological criticism, especially in its Freudian guise, gained the upper hand in relation to if not entirely supplanting the New Critics' love of image patterns and mythic archetypes. From being relegated to the sidelines in the 1920s and 1930s by the likes of Brooks and Parrington, Hawthorne as a major writer had come into his own in the 1940s and 1950s, aided by the New Criticism and the Cold War culture, both fascinated by a rigidly dualistic vision of the world, whether ironized or politicized. As already mentioned, Crews finally turned against his stark Freudian interpretation and began to reconsider the "surface features" of Hawthorne's texts, in particular how he manipulated literary conventions at the same time he distanced himself from them. This debate had been going on since Hawthorne's own lifetime in terms of whether he wrote romances, as he insisted, or novels and whether there were major differences between the two. This particular dualistic perspective persists to this day.

Formal Warfare: The Romance vs. the Novel

The debate about the romance as a genre opposed to the novel has long raged in American letters. In 1851 Evert A. Duyckinck described Hawthorne's establishing the separation between the novel and the romance, the latter leaving him "the privilege [to set] up his claim to a certain degree of license in the treatment of characters and incidents . . . in the direction of the spiritualities of the piece, in favor of a [semi-allegorical] process . . . an apology, in fact, for the preference of character to action, and of character for that which is allied to the darker elements of life — the dread blossoming of evil in the soul, and its fearful retributions" (Crowley 192). While Henry James in 1879 criticized Hawthorne's provincialism and his interest in New England history as a romance in its own right, he had acknowledged, however grudgingly, that Hawthorne also explored a much deeper psychological as well as moral realm, thus suggesting that his romances were far more concerned with mysteries and other subtleties than history. In remarking on Hawthorne's aloofness — "He is outside of everything, and an alien everywhere" — in 1896 he withdrew his earlier comments on Hawthorne's psychological depths while suggesting that his investigations of human consciousness "gave him much more a terrible sense of human abysses than a desire rashly to sound them and rise to the surface with his report. . . . He lingered, to weave his web, in the thin exterior air" (1896). As usual in his relation to Hawthorne, James equivocates and often contradicts himself.

Instead of defining the romance as a genre, James, in his 1904 letter celebrating the hundredth anniversary of Hawthorne's birth, wrote that we use the term in order to "comfortably escape the challenge to define [it] precisely because *The Scarlet Letter* and *The House of the Seven Gables* have made that possible to us under cover of mere triumphant reference to them." He still linked the "romantic spirit" in Hawthorne not to any particular literary strategy but to Hawthorne's years spent in Salem. Hawthorne could cast a spell in his fiction, but it was more a quality of tone than of vision. Romance, whatever it was, remained unfocused in James's early critical view, more atmosphere than actual outlook.

When William Dean Howells reviewed James's 1879 study *Hawthorne* in 1880, he made it very clear that he was troubled by James's confusion of the romance with the novel:

> No one better than Mr. James knows the *radical difference* between a romance and a novel, but he speaks now of Hawthorne's novels, and now of his romances, throughout, as if the terms were convertible; whereas *the romance and the novel are as distinct as the poem and the novel.* Mr. James [takes exception] to the people in *The Scarlet Letter*, because they are rather types than persons, rather conditions of the mind than characters; as if it were not almost precisely the business of the romance to deal with types and mental conditions. Hawthorne's fictions [are] *always and essentially, in conception and performance, romances, and not novels* . . . (emphasis added)

Lionel Trilling in 1954 reintroduced the idea that the American romance was indeed a particular American genre that was different from the social realism of English novels. In *The Liberal Imagination* (1957), Trilling linked the romance form to the idea of American exceptionalism. This, of course, played very well in terms of burgeoning American Studies programs and the Cold War division of the world between godless Communism and god-fearing liberal democracies. For Trilling the English novel of manners dealt more specifically with "the world of ordinary practicality," shaped by "money as a social element," creating a world of status and snobbery, of social classes that embodied "a culture's hum and buzz of implication" (202, 203, 201). Such novels avoided more romantic territory, such as Cervantes's world of inner reality, "the wildly conceiving, the madly fantasying mind of the Don" (203). As Trilling puts it, "The reality we admire tells us that the observation of manners is trivial and even malicious" (210).

Richard Chase further developed Trilling's idea in *The American Novel and Its Tradition* (1957) and attempted to describe the American romance as its own specific genre. Though he admitted that it was often difficult to define exactly what the American romance accomplished, he suggested that it was freer than the English novel of manners, more abstract, that it dealt with moral issues that often bordered on allegory, tended toward melodrama and the idyll, and displayed "a tendency to plunge into the underside of consciousness," a kind of poetry of disorder with the power "to express dark and complex truths unavailable to realism" (viii, ix, xi). Relying on Lawrence's dualistic vision of "the Manichaean quality of New England Puritanism" (11) and tracing the romance to writers such as Sir Walter Scott, James Fenimore Cooper, and William Gilmore Simms, Chase decided that "for the first time the psychological possibilities of romance were realized" in Hawthorne's fiction (18). Thus "consciousness itself becomes a participant in the drama" of *The Scarlet Letter* (69). In the final analysis, as Chase makes clear in his introduction, "the fact is that the word 'romance' begins to take on its inevitable meaning, for the historically minded American reader, in the writing of Hawthorne . . . namely, the penchant for the marvelous, the sensational, the legendary, and in general the heightened effect" (20–21).

Chase dislikes the pictorial and static quality of Hawthorne's fiction, linking it to allegory, and finds "no coherent politics" (74) in his work at all. For Chase, the characters more or less remain types, from the eternal woman to the cold, intellectually willful man and, as most New Critics did, he preferred Melville's white whale as an expansive, dynamic, organic, and more poetic symbol than Hawthorne's more dramatically static emblems such as black veils and Roman ruins. Of *The Blithedale Romance* Chase bemoans the fact that Hawthorne was unable to write a novel "without imparting to it a preponderance of romance" (83), but that, of course, was Hawthorne's intent: to write a romance not a novel based on his experience at Brook Farm. His aloofness underscored his inability to bring characters to life. For Chase, realism is fundamental for the novel, and when romance arises in it, it is only to modify that realism. Hawthorne thus fails as a novelist, for he lacks the "solid moral inclusiveness and massive equability . . . the great practical sanity [and] a normative view of life" (viii, 2) that can be found in the best English novels. Hawthorne even lacks any unifying cultural myth but possesses "only a clear perception of historical facts . . . no theory or consistent view of history is presented" (76).

Richard Brodhead began his discussion of the romance in terms of the time-honored dualistic tradition but then moved on to a wider and more expansive analysis of it. In *Hawthorne, Melville, and the Novel* (1976), he concentrates on the gap between subject and object, between consciousness and physical objects, and on Hawthorne's often precarious shifting from one to the other, from Hawthorne's meticulously realistic descriptions that reflect the style of Dutch paintings in *The House of the Seven Gables*, for instance, to the more romantic elements of the Pyncheon family curse: "The gap between his 'fancy-sketch' [Hawthorne's often dismissive reference to his own romantic vision] and his lifelike tints . . . corresponds to the tension in all his work between a fiction that creates the imagined world of romance and a fiction that creates a semblance of reality" (113).

Hawthorne and Melville, says Brodhead, were both committed to telling stories from different perspectives, never settling for one particular mode or method. No one style spoke to them directly. Instead they easily interrupted the traditional linear narrative with legends, stories, symbolic asides, and sudden epiphanies. In Hawthorne "what we see . . . is a mind playing across objects, allowing them to enkindle reflections and projecting onto them its own thoughts and feelings" (16). For Brodhead it is this playing that fuels the narrative with different voices and speculations. In *The Scarlet Letter*, for instance, he explores "a haunted interconnectedness" between images, objects, events, and consequences: "The scarlet letter itself becomes, in effect, a character, insisting upon itself" (56) as people gaze at it from different perspectives and positions. The multiple points of view, he insists, are not random but precisely articulated. In terms of the letter on Dimmesdale's chest, for instance, we are offered four possibilities: it is the product of "self-inflicted penitential torture"; it is magically produced by "Chillingworth's potent necromancy"; it is "the work of remorse"; or it is not there at all, Dimmesdale's "confession" being more of a parable than the "revelation of personal guilt . . ." (67, 68).

For Brodhead, then, Hawthorne recognizes and manipulates this gap in his fiction, at times creating romantic tales told by characters within the romance — such as Holgrave's tale of Alice Pyncheon, Zenobia's of the silvery veil, Coverdale's of Fauntleroy, and Hawthorne's own dark design as he stops the action of his romance to dance around Judge Pyncheon's corpse — at others arranging tableaux, emphasizing contrasts and oppositions in a proto-allegorical manner, and peopling his fictions with wizards, mesmerists, mediums, and witches. Both Hawthorne and Melville finally "resist acceptance of any code of final belief, religious, cosmological ethical, or aesthetic" (200). They move between possible cosmic designs to laws inherent in the purely physical world, creating fictions that occupy the gap between. The opposition "between a transcendent and an experiential vision [is] placed in dramatic conflict . . . Romance is the fictional method through which Hawthorne and Melville make a transcendent order a real possibility in their novels. But if they do not suppress romance, they do not succumb to it either" (202, 203). They dramatize the interpenetration of and opposition between theological and psychological visions with each paying obeisance to the other, illuminating the gap between them where the human condition exists most fully, seeking no final explanation but the process of seeking itself.

By the time he wrote *The School of Hawthorne* (1986), Brodhead was not only exploring the institution of literature as both a public and economic cultural phenomenon but also meant to "trace the artistic legacy of Hawthorne . . . in later American fiction" (ix) to such writers as James, Faulkner, and Flannery O'Connor: "Hawthorne is the only American fiction writer never to have lived in the limbo of the non-elect, [and] he is also the only such writer whose work has always incited and guided others' practice" (11). He also "was the first author to have to contend with the canonical stature of Hawthorne" (70), elevated as he was to classical status very quickly by a growing literary establishment desperate to mark out an American literary tradition as different from the British. He had to deal with and was very much aware of his canonization in his own lifetime.

In regard to Hawthorne's legacy, Brodhead spells out what he sees as the true attributes of his fiction and, therefore, of American romance. First, Brodhead elaborates on his earlier idea about the "playing out" of the romance form, of its openness as a form that suggests a "primal state of undifferentiated possibility" (193), producing oppositions, contradictions, reciprocal ambiguities, and the clash of the actual and the imaginary, "such apparent opposites [are] commingling and reciprocally generated" (191). Second, he says that public manners mask private emotions in romance generally as well as specifically in Hawthorne's fiction; unlike literary realism, "human passion is prior to the particularized social context in which it appears" (165). Third, the design of the romance is in Brodhead's view highly stylized and ritualized like a formal ceremony, structured out of "obtrusive symmetries . . . its dancelike pairings and re-pairings of couples . . . [its] catechistical rites" (187) and its scaffold epiphanies. Finally, the romance suggests a parable with its "stark embodiments of ultimate mysteries, or of experience pressed toward the purity of ultimate states" (185).

Brodhead also singles out the monomaniacal natures of many of Hawthorne's characters with their obsessive self-projections upon the world, which he calls "daimonization," "the process by which an ordinary self gets seized by an imperious will, becoming the witness, through this mastery, to a reality ordinary realty denies . . . a kind of fate, an irresistible process whose sources remain obscure" (36, 37). This analysis of the process of daimonization reveals the psychological forces and compulsions within the use of allegory as a form of self-expression, such as Chillingworth's demonic commitment to and being singularly possessed by revenge in *The Scarlet Letter*. Brodhead's idea of how obsession can appear as demonic possession paves the way for similar critical insights regarding the fiction of William Faulkner and Toni Morrison, among others, including such radically different writers as William Styron, Joyce Carol Oates, and Paul Theroux. His vision of a "school of Hawthorne" also establishes the existent and power of the romance genre in American fiction.

In *The Shape of Hawthorne's Career* (1976), Nina Baym traces his development as a writer, emphasizing the fact that he constantly toyed with different personae, styles, and approaches and that the stories we read today were canonically determined by the "creation of Freudian criticism after 1950" (181). She maintains that before 1850 Hawthorne could not be considered a romantic or an anti-romantic and divides his career into different phases or periods. These phases include Hawthorne's early gothic mode, which also encompasses his moralized fictions and sketches that satirize society's values, and the major phase with his four romances, which expanded and explored such themes as individual passions in conflict with a repressive society in *The Scarlet Letter*, a more comprehensively detailed look at the operation of the emerging capitalistic society of the 1850s in *The House of the Seven Gables*, the veiled tyrannies of individuals in conflict with communal values in *The Blithedale Romance*, and finally the moral and cultural weight of art and history in the Rome of *The Marble Faun*. Baym also suggests, in quoting Edgar Dryden, that the several definitions of the romance in Hawthorne's day were so broad and inconsistent that "any attempt to fix [the meaning of the term] is a creative rather than a descriptive activity" (Dryden's *Form* 223).

For Baym, Hawthorne's career can be viewed as "a series of tentative solutions to the question of the social significance of the artist" (275) that also involved the recognition of female sexuality, a process that fascinated but also troubled him. Hester returns to Boston at the end of the romance to lead a celibate life, wearing her scarlet letter; Zenobia commits suicide when Hollingsworth rejects her; Miriam remains isolated and alone while Donatello goes to prison. The "cherished stereotypes" of the Genteel Tradition — Phoebe, Priscilla, and Hilda — all end up married, however wounded and self-denying. "A man's liberation and fulfillment require his accepting a more fully sexual image of woman than the culture allows,"

Baym insists. "The woman's sexuality (she is a secondary being in a patri-archal system) is suppressed in society as a means of inhibiting the male; both sexes suffer" (191). Although Hawthorne buys into the reign of the genteel maiden, he is, in Baym's view, nevertheless "strongly sympathetic" toward feminist ideas (199). I will discuss Baym's feminist position more specifically in chapter 7.

Waggoner's reaction to Baym's book is typical of the New Critics' reaction to such criticism. He objected to her view that Hester is wholly admirable, viewing her as a more complex combination of good and evil, a position that would support his own neo-orthodox views but also Hawthorne's own contradictory attitudes toward her. Waggoner upbraided Baym for "her operative vocabulary: *drives, repression, inhibition; oppres-sion, authority, patriarchy*" (121), recognizing in this the influences of feminism, Freud, and Marx, which he viewed as products of the late 1970s. "Hawthorne's real subject was always imagination," he insists, "(that is, in effect, his own art) and the artist's relation to society . . . the same as that of many of the novelists typical of the 1970s" (125–26).

The polarization at the heart of Hawthorne's fiction appealed to the New Critics because of their fascination with mythic and psychological patterns, with neo-orthodoxy and the Cold War paradigm, with allegory, religion, paradox, and Oedipal conflicts. In the 1960s psychological criti-cism viewed the religious perspective of good versus evil as products of the splintered psyche in Hawthorne's particular vision of the human condition in general. Hawthorne's American romance became the generic name for the vaguely supernatural and shadowy "neutral territory" where such dual-isms could stalk, infiltrate, and confront one another, freed from the social realism that British novelists in particular seemed to favor. This delicately interwoven tapestry of textual unity, psychological truths, and entangling alliances began to fray, however, as deconstruction, in its own way as for-malistic as the New Criticism, entered the critical arena in the late 1960s and 1970s, and the linguistic turn it championed shattered the New Critical complacency that had ruled the literary landscape for so long.

6: Doubting Dualisms: The Strategies of Hawthorne's Romance

W E BEGIN TO SEE in the literary criticism of the late 1960s and 1970s the "linguistic turn" and the deconstructionist perspective that originated at that time in the criticism of French philosophers and social critics such as Jacques Derrida, Roland Barthes, Michel Foucault, and Jean-Francois Lyotard and was explored by critics such as Paul de Man and J. Hillis Miller. While Derrida dealt explicitly with language and texts and Lyotard with the demise of metanarraritives, those overarching cultural myths of progress and value, Barthes dismantled and deconstructed the idea that an author's intentions could be discovered in a text (in proclaiming the death of the author), Foucault undermined hierarchical concepts of power (he saw power dispersed everywhere and in everyone, even in discourse itself), while de Man and Miller refined Derrida's original ideas. Each of these critics, whom we can label "deconstructionist" in opposition to the more traditional critics with their New Critical perspectives and backgrounds, attacked conventional concepts such as language's transparency and connection to the world at large, the author's individual intentions in regard to her text, and power as a simple hierarchy to which individuals are subject as citizens to states.

From the deconstructionist point of view, everything becomes a text, a discourse. All the symbolic, psychological, and mythic patterns that the New Critics championed are the creation of language, which in many ways becomes, in Fredric Jameson's phrase, its own prison house, its own code that is separated from the world at large. All dualisms and polarities break down and collapse inward upon themselves as if into a black hole. Representation becomes suspect; words feed only upon themselves in their sense of difference and deferral and do not lead the reader to any world beyond the text. Everything becomes a signifier of something else, never a signified. All is metonymy, parts of an imagined but forever deferred nonexistent whole. We can know only disruption, dispersion, and disconnection, however much language tries to convince us otherwise. Language speaks us rather than the other way around, and we are victims of such cultural codes and conventions as we become aware of such linguistic structures and patterns and how they operate within and around us. As we become more aware of such conventions, we recognize more clearly our own victimization in relation to them.

The gap that Hawthorne recognized between imagination and actual physical objects becomes from the deconstructionist perspective a permanent unfathomable abyss, and the bridge of language on which we try to cross over it remains flimsy, frail, and faulty. Words themselves become the sites for ideological struggles: To whom do they belong? Who has the power to use them? Who gets to frame the critical discourse in which we find ourselves entrenched? There are no absolute beginnings, no teleological ends, except death, only chatter, signs, scrawls, semiotic systems, and historical contexts. No two texts are separate; each exists in relation to each. Each is entangled with the other. In this we begin to see the stirrings of postmodernism, with its emphasis on flux, difference, and anxieties associated with representation at all levels. (I can't help but notice that this more fluid, origin-less view corresponds to the invisible, inaccessible, irreducible quantum flux of quantum theory, from which entanglement emerges as a metaphor for the cosmic condition. We become our own ghosts, trapped in language that can only remain baffled and stunned at the ways and wonders of the subatomic world. We are entangled in texts and our own carefully crafted experiments, and thus no original relation to the world is ever possible.) The darker aspects of this vision coincide all too easily with Hawthorne's fiction, and if the New Criticism helped revive his fortunes, the "linguistic turn" has spawned a new era of criticism that both delights and chills.

As part of this "turn" or perhaps because of it, several critics affirmed the validity and distinctive qualities of the American romance, as Hawthorne tried to define it, by exploring it from the vantage point of several literary and stylistic strategies that helped create it. These include such critics as Kenneth Dauber (1977), J. Hillis Miller (1991), Edgar A. Dryden (1977 and 1988), John Carlos Rowe (1982), Evan Carton (1985), Gordon Hutner, Darrel Abel (both 1988), Richard Millington (1992), John Dolis (1993), and Clark Davis (2005). Other critics, such as Michael Davitt Bell (1971 and 1980), Neal Frank Doubleday (1972), George Dekker (1987), and Elissa Greenwald (1989), approached the romance form from more traditional points of view in terms of literary conventions, forerunners, and genres. Before examining the deconstruction-minded critics from Dauber to Davis, we will first turn our attention to the more traditional group of critics from Bell to Greenwald as a background to the new developments that culminated in G. R. Thompson and Eric Carl Link's book, *Neutral Ground: New Traditionalism and the American Romance Controversy* (1999), which we will discuss below. One outspoken dissenter from the belief in the worth and triumph of the romance form, William Ellis, assaulted the very notion of its being a special genre that these critics tried to fathom, describing it as "failed writing" with its "inferior novelistic qualities" (167, 125), but the majority disagreed.

The New Traditionalism

In *Hawthorne and the Historical Romance of New England* (1971) Michael Davitt Bell takes a look at what writers in the nineteenth century meant when they called themselves romancers. He does so after first examining Hawthorne's myth of decline from the "integrity and manhood" (22) of the Calvinist Founding Fathers to their more gloomy and fanatical sons, focusing upon "how the noble intolerance of the fathers became the superstitious intolerance of the sons" (156), in a way that subverted, with its tension between liberty and tyranny, the American belief in the linear and steady trajectory of progress. Here we see a more cultural and historical description of the term "romancer": the romancer "admitted or proclaimed what the 'novelist' strives to conceal or deny: that his fiction was a figment of imagination . . . [a] highly self-conscious experimental fictional tradition that transcended solipsism by exploiting and investigating an analogous self-consciousness in the national experiment of which it was a part" (xiii). In *The Development of American Romance* (1980) Bell links the idea of the romance in America to Scottish Common Sense thought, and thus it was always split between the imaginative and the actual, never sacrificing its relation to the real world but accommodating that world. As the Scottish Common Sense philosophers would have it, Hawthorne's neutral territory was "a moral or psychological battlefield" (16) that as a form suggested more reconciliation than disconnection. This theory of romance relied upon "associationist aesthetics and ultimately on American 'reality' [and] was finally a theory of realism, of rational mimesis" (19) as opposed to more fanciful romancers like Poe, writers of science fiction, and others who would create their own gothic or futuristic worlds.

To choose to be a romancer, as Bell suggests, was to choose a deviant career because the romancer, in effect, was announcing to a hostile society that imagination was just as or more powerful than that society's reality. Hawthorne chose always to distance himself from his work in an attempt to assure both himself and his society that he was not some wild romantic, that he had his feet firmly planted on the ground. In his fiction, for example, he excoriated his male characters/allegorists for imagining and assuming that their abstract categories revealed the truth of the world to them, whereas, according to Bell, Hawthorne is drawn to "allegory observed. Not allegory imagined" (134).

Bell maintains that "the idea that abstract notions violate life is itself, after all, an abstract notion. An anti-allegorical allegory is still an allegory — self-reflexive but not expressive" (136). To allegorize is to mask other truths, and that masking and unmasking clearly inhabit and create the romancer's territory. Thus the polarities rule once more, revealing "the neurotic dualism of romance — the tension between language and impulse, form and suggestion, repression and expression" (19), allegorical signs and the subjective dreams and compulsions that underlie them. That Bell views this strategy in terms of the cultural demands of Hawthorne's era expands the notion of the romancer so that it takes on a definite historical and developmental identity.

Neal Frank Doubleday in *Hawthorne's Early Tales: A Critical Study* (1972) makes a very strong case for Hawthorne having looked at how Washington Irving and Sir Walter Scott wrote romances, particularly Irving's reliance on American materials (even though "Rip Van Winkle" and "The Legend of Sleepy Hollow" relied on German folklore in terms of their plots and characters; Irving had spent several profitable days with Scott learning about Scott's use of national Scottish materials in his fiction). For Doubleday, the promotion of literary nationalism provides "a vigorous theory ahead of practice" (120, 18) as seen in Irving's *Sketch Book* (1819–20), James Fenimore Cooper's *The Spy* (1821), and William Cullen Bryant's *Poems* (1821).

Doubleday also explains how difficult it was for American writers to establish an American literary tradition, since by 1830 only 40 percent of books published were American. The other 60 percent were British, due to a lack of copyright laws, which allowed British books to be pirated and published at will. Doubleday makes much of Hawthorne's early attempts at connected stories such as "Seven Tales of My Native Land," "Provincial Tales," and "Legends of the Province House." He notes that Scott pointed American writers in this direction, and they readily followed. George E. Woodberry had noticed the touch of Scott in Hawthorne's work as early as 1902, in particular Hawthorne's use of "'the figure-grouping, the high speeches . . . and especially in the use of set scenes individually elaborated to give the high lights and to advance the story'" (Woodberry 126 qtd. in Doubleday 42).

Doubleday also states that Hawthorne chose to leave many of the darker tales that delight and confound us today — "Roger Malvin's Burial" (1831), "My Kinsman, Major Molineux" (1831), "Young Goodman Brown" (1835) — out of the first volume of *Twice-Told Tales* (1837). "Brown" didn't appear until *Mosses from an Old Manse* in 1846. "Molineux" wasn't published until *The Snow-Image* volume in 1851, although in 1837 Hawthorne did collect three stories from 1835: "The Minister's Black Veil," "The Maypole of Merry Mount," and "Wakefield." Perhaps, as Doubleday suggests, Hawthorne decided that for his first volume he should serve up more sentimental and conventional fare to the public and exclude the darker stories.

Doubleday's critical acumen is none too sharp. He finds the conclusion of "Roger Malvin's Burial" muddled and unclear, Hawthorne having taken "a wrong narrative track" (197), whereas most other contemporary critics find it purposely ambiguous in terms of Reuben Bourne's religious sense of guilt and expiation and the stark fact that he has killed his son.

Referring to "Young Goodman Brown," Doubleday attributes contemporary interpretations of the story in terms of Brown's own difficulties with sexuality, perception, and judgment to the "inability of readers to follow the tale as an exercise of the historical imagination" (201). Doubleday finds "My Kinsman, Major Molineux" "too complex an attempt and not completely in Hawthorne's control" (245), particularly in terms of its "territory of lunacy" (232), whereas most New Critics, who almost single-handedly "re-discovered" this tale in the 1950s, found it brilliantly ambiguous when it comes to Hawthorne's presentation of colonial Boston just before the Revolution and Robin Molineux's transformation from "shrewd" youth to willing participant in the major's disgrace. Doubleday does allow for Hawthorne's "residue of mystery" (47) and "multiple allusiveness" (56) as part of the gothic literary convention and decides that "clearly his work is strongest when it most depends upon the tradition he devised from what he had at hand" (252).

George Dekker in *The American Historical Romance* (1987) examines Henry Fielding's and Horace Walpole's analyses of the romance form as a product of medieval superstitions and fantastic doings coupled with "psychological realism" (19) to bring them up to date and make them more palpable for a contemporary audience. He lists several polarities that the romance builds upon, viewing the Romantic Revival as "ordering reality in terms of one or more sets of binary oppositions" (47) — jollity and gloom, men and women, history and myth, light and dark, poetry and prose — and locates Hawthorne midway between respect for and an assault on American Puritans. Hawthorne wished to have it both ways "to apotheosize the Puritans as founders and liberators while interjecting ironic notes . . . that remind us of their acts of destruction and confinement" (148).

Such a polarized view strikes me as simplistic and overly dualistic, especially when Dekker attacks Michael Colacurcio, whose book, *The Province of Piety: Moral History in Hawthorne's Early Tales* (1984), pioneered the view of Hawthorne as a self-confirmed moral historian when it came to exploring and judging the historical eras he wrote about. Doubleday described Colacurcio's Hawthorne as "a conspiratorial figure, a kind of good wizard engaged in subverting that idolatrous civil religion which Jacksonian ideologues were rearing on the foundations of the New England Covenant" (151), elsewhere charging that Colacurcio's view of Hawthorne's hidden 'subversive' agenda [becomes] too programmatic and cunning by half . . ." (149). Dekker's is certainly too programmatic by half, reducing *The Scarlet Letter* to a presentation of Puritanism as a regression to Old Testament values and patriarchy in its attempt to eradicate the more matriarchal values of the Catholic church. He does, however, accurately describe the hypocrisy and paranoia generated by Calvinism in "The Minister's Black Veil" as a way of life that promoted ineradicable personal and private guilt as well as the compulsion to appear "pure" in public.

In *Realism and the Romance* (1989), Elissa Greenwald links Hawthorne and Henry James as writers who rely in the structure of their fiction on the interrelation between romance and realism in equal measure. Each is a mode of perception, a way of seeing, and no reality exists outside or beyond our representation of it. The projection of inner states of mind generates plots, which both authors shape in terms of tableaux, epiphanies, emblems, icons, and impenetrable mystery. The process of desire reveals a reality thoroughly transformed and permeated by consciousness, wherein public spectacle arises from private reveries.

From the depths of his haunted mind, Greenwald's Hawthorne created self-consciously fictive tales in his struggle to find meaning, made his presence visible in his fiction in pursuit of this quest, plumbed the deep psychology of his characters' and his own often contradictory speculations, produced various symbols and images to encapsulate his vision, recognized how society could manipulate such symbols and images for its own sake, and strove to create his neutral territory where fact and fancy, the present and the past, dream and actuality could fight it out. The logic of the unconscious perpetually undermines conventional cause and effect, artworks within his fiction often mirror the story's actions, and the reader is seduced into participating in the entire process. The narrative thus springs from the characters' private reveries, the upshot being that "the public sphere is virtually dissolved, revealed as a construct or representation which no longer expresses the desires of the people, the 'truth of the human heart'" (49). However bald this description of romance, Greenwald does manage to explore the mechanics of the genre and at the same time indicate the atmosphere of mystery that Hawthorne is able to create, for instance, in the way he manages to suggest that the scarlet "A" "signifies the web of moral intrigue in which his characters are enmeshed" (31).

Greenwald discusses the similarities and differences between *The Scarlet Letter* and *The Portrait of a Lady*. Hawthorne's pictorial process becomes James's more dramatic use of the portrait, as tableaux become more dramatically activated. Hawthorne undermines the romantic elements in *The Blithedale Romance* with his use of mesmerism as a virtually naked will to power that parodies and eviscerates the romantic quest for meaning and significance. At the last she decides perceptively that Hawthorne "often ironizes romance by showing it as susceptible to being overpowered by reality. For James, though, romance is present in reality. Romance is found within, not outside of, daily experience. Consciousness so fully shapes reality that desire becomes a mode of knowing" (149).

All this discussion of the romance form comes to a head in Thompson and Link's *Neutral Ground* (1999) as a way to try and answer all the issues that deconstruction had evoked in terms of textual indeterminacies. They argue that romance was always seen as a "generic transgression" with its indeterminate style and structure that it transformed psychological notions into epistemological themes, and that there never has been one single form of romance but multiple forms throughout its literary existence. Hawthorne's neutral territory reflects romance's neutral ground, a place to explore prior assumptions, "dialogically negotiate" various claims concerning perception, encourage a plurality of voices, keep things open-ended, and never approach any ultimate synthesis (18). The perspective of each character and each reader will always suggest multiple meanings.

Thompson and Link trace the analyses of the American romance from F. O. Matthiessen's *American Renaissance: Art and Expression in the Age of Emerson and Whitman* (1941) to Charles Feidelson, Jr.'s *Symbolism and American Literature* (1953), which celebrates the multiple meanings of symbolism at the expense of the more static form of allegory, and from R. W. B. Lewis's *The American Adam: Innocence, Tragedy, and Tradition in the Nineteenth Century* (1955) and Richard Chase's *The American Novel and Its Tradition* (1957) to Donald Pease's *Visionary Compacts: American Renaissance Writings in Cultural Context* (1987), which speaks to the division between aesthetics and politics in the New Criticism as affected by the Cold War and insists that such a liberal consensus, limiting dissent to the private realm, disguises the basically conservative and reactionary points of view like Chase's. According to Pease, the resulting political consensus not only represses the relationship between politics and aesthetics but disenfranchises certain groups within that consensus such as African Americans and women. Thompson and Link charge Pease with moral presumption insofar as he claims to speak for marginalized others with "his certain possession of a higher truth" (46).

Thompson and Link, however, often set up "straw critics" to attack. They clearly come down on the side of the traditionalists in terms of form and culture such as Matthiessen, Trilling, Feidelson, Lewis, and Chase and deride the "New Americanists" such as Baym, Pease, Budick, and others as returning us to the Parrington era "of over-generalized sociological criticism" (9). Despite this willful critical blindness, Thompson and Link do construct a strong case for the age and scope of the romance form: "Poe, Hawthorne, and Melville were to raise this psychological notion of romance to an epistemological *theme* and magnify the art of the psychological romance to the status of epistemological romance" (emphasis in original, 121). They do acknowledge that "there is no single form of the American romance" (158) and then decide that "the privileged status of Hawthorne, James, Melville and company would not seem to be an innate *function* of the romance form. Is it possible that male dominance in nineteenth-century romance is an *accident* of American literary history?" (emphasis in original, 185).

Which leaves us at this point in this chapter with William Ellis. In *The Theory of American Romance: An Ideology in America Intellectual History* (1989), he declares that novels rose from class conflict, that they should stick to that social conflict and analyze it, and that there is no exceptional American novel tradition, only weak fictions that "could not sustain the substantiality of European novels" (15). We exceptionalists may set out to define and examine the romance tradition; Ellis sees only failed novels.

American novels do not belong to a different genre from European novels, Ellis insists. Their concerns are the same, so those of us who subscribe to the romance tradition are really trying to make yet another case for American exceptionalism, which is based on the false notion, "the thesis of consensus history" (35), that no cultural tensions exist between classes. Trilling, Chase, and others have led us down the garden path. Trilling was also convinced that class did not determine culture in the United States, for he subscribed to the single ideology of liberalism that we had reached an essentially non-ideological point of view. This may have been true in the 1950s, says Ellis, but it fails to take into account the real class struggle that is on display in the literary-cultural criticism by Parrington and other progressives who recognized the social conflicts that are inherent in capitalism and later critics who participated in the same struggles. Trilling was very much a man of his time, but being decidedly unexceptional myself, I will have to leave it up to others whether or not to buy Ellis's pointed argument.

Ellis attacks the supposed American romance with a vengeance: its characters are too abstract and therefore insubstantial, and this abstraction "is a substitute for satire and criticism of American life . . . [an] evasion or overwrought response in the context of traditional novels" (204). The romance is too melodramatic, too symbolic in its technique, too metaphysical in its meaning, too obsessed with mythic archetypes, and, therefore, decidedly inferior in other, more novelistic qualities: "Hawthorne's fancies and conceits are a substitute for sustained, critical and imaginative observation . . . The difference is that where American novels are merely metaphysical and symbolic, European novels are usually metaphysical, symbolic *and* substantial" (emphasis in original, 125, 178). Differences lie in quality, not genre. The American novels that Ellis champions are, therefore, *The Bostonians* and *The Adventures of Huckleberry Finn* because they "achieve the poise of the great European novels, and offer us a substantial, critical, and satirical analysis of American manners, ideas, passions, and follies" (202). Hawthorne loved Trollope, and I presume so would Ellis, but there is more than one definition of "substantiality."

The Deconstructive Turn

The "linguistic turn" that deconstruction effected and pursued, as mentioned at the beginning of this chapter, shattered the New Critical complacency of the 1960s and led to studies of Hawthorne that emphasized his rhetorical strategies and the linguistic indeterminacy of his fiction. Such approaches opened Hawthorne's work to more conflicting interpretations than those that had focused on its aspects of religious allegory and psychological patterning. Deconstruction recognized and expanded the entanglement between readers and texts, scrutinizing the fragility of all representation and undermining once and for all the "unity" that New Critics had sought and found in Hawthorne's texts. Such Hawthorne scholarship, thanks to the likes of Kenneth Dauber and Edgar A. Dryden, continues to this day.

One of the breakthrough books that focuses on the "linguistic turn" was Dauber's aptly named *Rediscovering Hawthorne* (1977) in which he dismissed the New Criticism's emphasis on unity and wholeness and sought to explore Hawthorne's attitude toward his work in terms of its purpose "beyond communication of a message" (10). From a proto-structuralist and deconstructionist position, he explained that language and genres often "write" the author, that "the forms of fiction impose themselves . . . To write is to repeat what has already been written. [Hawthorne's] work exists as a cultural imposition before he begins. It is a tyranny he cannot resist" (41). For Dauber, one's culture dictates what can be written and automatically circumscribes what can be said about it, but this "death-of-the-author" interpretation, however fashionable at the time, strikes me as unbalanced and rigid, as if all that single authors can accomplish is to mirror the world that surrounds them.

Dauber's book, often opaque and hard to follow, focuses on the unresolved contradictions and oppositions in Hawthorne's work, such as in "Rappaccini's Daughter," which, according to Dauber, can be seen as a tale about an innocent girl destroyed by a faithless love and/or a dangerous woman enticing an innocent boy (31). For Dauber both themes are present but are in no way integrated. In respect to the first theme, the negative characters are Baglioni and Giovanni; in respect to the second they are Beatrice and her father. When asked by his wife Sophia, while he was writing the story, whether Beatrice would turn out to be an angel or a devil, Hawthorne replied that he didn't know. What the New Critics described as a unified example of ambiguity, Dauber sees as Hawthorne's typical "process of oscillation . . . He presents himself divided against himself, mocking one half with the other . . . It is the attempt, by authorially affirming opposite interpretations of the same fiction, by linking in a single printed text two contradictory stories, to create a fiction that affirms itself" (34–35). Such affirmation raises more questions than it answers, unless fiction from Dauber's point of view must always remain indefinite and contradictory.

Dauber sees division as a strategy in place of unification, a calculated assault on the New Critics' obsession with the supposed unity found in all successful texts. There is no synthesis: "Hawthorne's works are structures that contain no vision . . . [they are] forms without subjects [that pursue] the unity of integral structures that are the printed work's component parts" (23). The various "subjects," such as Hawthorne's Puritanism, religious impulses, moral values, and Christian typology, are just the sporadic effects and results of these divisions. It is up to the reader to provide a center in the form of his interpretation of it, since Hawthorne's use of allegory is "so undirected the reader may overcome it with any number of explications of his own. [The reader] works his will on the text" (16–17).

New Critics like Waggoner in *The Presence of Hawthorne* responded to Dauber's interpretation by suggesting that he was mistaken to reject all past Hawthorne criticism, to advocate the idea that many readers create many different texts, and to assert that "a text is really only a gesture, an action" (123). His deconstruction of Hawthorne's fictions "by intuition alone . . . leads him into extravagances too private to be shared" (123, 127). Waggoner misunderstands, however, Dauber's attempt to overcome the traditionally thematic analysis of Hawthorne's work in order to examine it in terms of its peculiar structure and its central contradictions.

For Dauber, *The Scarlet Letter* collapses into allegory at the end; the fragmented story becomes "thoroughly dislocated . . . remarkably unhinged" (97) as Hawthorne's process of oscillation rigidifies and curdles. The virtue and failure of *The House of the Seven Gables* culminate in a pictorial stasis that goes nowhere. No single image pattern triumphs. Such a perspective with its emphasis on deconstructing the supposed unity of Hawthorne's fictions, as opposed to the New Critics' celebration of such unity, paved the way to the many deconstructive analyses that followed in Dauber's wake.

In the last two romances, according to Dauber, Hawthorne's disengagement with the romance form shows. In *The Blithedale Romance*, for example, "romance is converted to realism," so much so that gothic conventions reveal their sexual aspect, all is demystified and mechanized, nothing is concealed, and reality, freed from subjective interpretations, is unmasked as empty and valueless (184). Hawthorne's attitude toward his art mirrors Coverdale's and Westervelt's toward mesmerism: each reflects a will to power for its own sake. There are no elemental truths, just veils upon veils and sleights of hand. In *The Marble Faun* Hawthorne becomes a mere tour guide, trapped in a kind of "sterile hermeneutics" (196), in which geography and ruins replace action, sequence, and causality (217). The narrator interprets everything on the spot, and everything is repeated and replicated as Kenyon "alternates between elaborate interpretation and confession of the poverty of interpretation" (202). Miriam and Hilda reach a standoff, interpreting different aspects of the Fortunate Fall; Miriam suggests it; Hilda dismisses it: "The point between them is vacant. But Hawthorne, once again through iteration, pretends it is full. By positioning the opposites side by side and then repeating the position a number of times, he makes opposition come to stand for relation" (216–17).

Dauber's book opened up new perspectives on Hawthorne's fiction and pointed to new directions beyond the New Criticism. If Dauber's own work suggests "sterile hermeneutics" at times, it did provide other critics different ways of grappling with texts to see how they actually function. Dauber's view of romance as mutual coercion with a bristling, often confused, often disunited center of pure possibility ushered in a new era of Hawthorne criticism.

Perhaps one of the best examples of deconstruction in relation to Hawthorne's work is J. Hillis Miller's *Hawthorne and History* (1991), in which he discusses "The Minister's Black Veil" as "the unveiling of the possibility of the impossibility of unveiling" (51). For deconstructionists, words and the images they create remain enigmatic and indecipherable, a veil of a veil of a veil in which "the text offers neither confirmation nor disconfirmation of any speculative formulation about its meaning" (106). Whether the story reads as an allegory or as a realistic fiction, the sign of the black veil remains unfathomable and inaccessible to any logical explanation based on cause and effect. The story's meaning, therefore, remains indeterminate. In fact, as Miller puts it, "nothing happens except the proffering of an enigmatic sign" (118), which can only deface, distort, and disrupt a meaning that does not exist.

Miller makes a strong case for the tale's indeterminacy, but that indeterminacy is not ultimately complete. If anything it suggests several "decidable" interpretations, all of which occupy the same analytical space, and none of which takes precedence over the others. I would also suggest that the people in the village and the Reverend Mr. Hooper are so Calvinistically cornered that they can only view the veil in the bleakest and darkest of terms as an emblem of sin, crime, sexual indiscretion, insanity, or murder. Each invests the veil with incredible powers since it becomes a kind of icon of a vision of a darkly Calvinist realm. Hawthorne creates a kind of mesmeric ceremony, I maintain, in which the veil grows in stature and power and hypnotizes the entire populace, so much so that the title of the tale and the last phrase in it are exactly the same.

Such power necessarily eludes linguistic "fixes," hence Miller's deconstructive analysis of it: "The veil is the type and symbol of the fact that all signs are potentially unreadable" (97). However true this is, and I think it is true, the veil can nevertheless be worshipped and glorified as it shifts in the tale from black cloth to a powerful icon. As Miller admits, "The most successful allegorical signs are those, like the black veil, that resist successfully any conceptual formulation of their meaning" (120). Imprisoned in the code of language, and viewing most things as linguistic signs, deconstructionists may miss other possibilities inherent in such a tale, which does elude "conceptual formulation" but is not, therefore, completely uninterpretable, however indeterminate in its several, often conflicting interpretations.

The Romance as a Particular Genre

With the romance form having been resurrected, defined, explored, and analyzed by the likes of Chase, Brodhead, Baym, and others, later critics took up the clarion call and continued to extend and expand the exploration into the nature of this particular and peculiar American genre. Edgar A. Dryden in *Nathaniel Hawthorne: The Poetics of Enchantment* (1977) builds upon the dualisms and polarities established in previous criticism. Whereas Male, Fogle, and Waggoner generated symbolic, Crews psychoanalytical, and Normand psychopoetic readings of Hawthorne's texts, Dryden located their focus in a Keatsian dialectic between dream and reality, enchantment and disenchantment that always ends in loss: "The dialectic of enchantment and disenchantment, possession and dispossession that governs the forms of the relationship of the self and the other is seen to be the result of a myth of origin which posits an original unity lost to the lonely wanderer now but destined to be regained at some point in the future. Once that myth is identified and rejected the idea of romance loses its validity" (171). As a result, according to Dryden, "dreams and reality are unable to coexist as one always seeks to invade and transform the other" (138).

Origins in Hawthorne always seem far away and long ago, a yearning in the present for the loss of such origins in a distant past, as if recognizing that one can only sense the full impact of one's childhood, for example, after one has lost it. Consequently his characters try to make up for that abiding loss, according to Dryden, through various "enchantments" that eventually fail. The enchantment of distance rescues one from the desires and the "infinite, shivering solitude" (34) of the present. The enchantment of the other sets culture in opposition to nature, a momentary at-homeness with history and the past that also suggests an aggressive will to power, a battle of wills between the self and the other. Love provides another enchantment, but however desired it eventually fades.

Beyond the enchantments that Dryden discovers in Hawthorne's fiction lies the additional enchantment of reading it, a position undermined by Derrida's notions of eminent deferral and disruption. The writer may cast his spell over the reader, but it must always end. Dryden suggests that Hawthorne's use of mystery encourages the reader's commitment to the text in the form of attempts to understand the story and fathom the psychological depths not only of the characters but of Hawthorne's ultimate design and vision. Hawthorne also reveals the artifice of his texts to disorient the reader who lurches between fascination and interpretation. He thus initiates a strategy of hidden things, creating an aura of mystery crafted to seduce and lure the reader into participating in all the text's various poses and perspectives, which always remain elusive and out of reach. Riddles, secrets, mysterious backgrounds, and compulsive quests suggest even more possibilities, the romance vision of the open-ended text that continues indefinitely, that enchants and mesmerizes, that is not only itself a veil but that has several other veils behind it. Analogies breed endless analogies; interpretations breed other interpretations, but "no matter how interpretations proliferate . . . something will always remain hidden" (134). Representation, therefore, becomes "the expression of rather than the solution to a mystery" (129). With his description of this process, Dryden suggests perhaps better than any other critics what Hawthorne as a romancer was up to.

The final enchantment in Dryden's book speaks directly to these issues, since it involves origins; the idea that in our present state of acknowledged exile, we long for a return to some original place, state, or condition, but that that is only a nostalgic myth, a yearning bred of American discontinuity, disruption, and infinite deferral. Writing can suggest the presence of something hidden, of desire to roam free unmolested, but finally in Hawthorne "the metaphor of the web of fiction . . . demystifies the myth of origins by suggesting the extent to which narrative or story is the product of will and desire rather than a reconstruction of tradition or a representation of qualities that lie beyond the senses" (171). There is no center, there is no origin, and language itself incarnates the ultimate veil of consciousness in all its fragmented and disconnected state of being. Disenchantment will always win out in the end. The enchantment of possible unity, therefore, remains an illusion for which the romance searches. Each, however, participates in that "lurid intermixture" of Hawthornian romance: the illusion of enchantment and the reality of disenchantment continue their dialectical dance as "one alternates between a world of dreams and the cold hillside of reality" (137).

In 1988, in *The Form of American Romance*, Dryden extends his dialectic to discuss the continuous conflict between a story's entertaining spell and its search for a moral or significance. The enchantment of romance cannot be sustained, but it can make "the experience of reading explicit in a way that disturbs and blurs the distinction between creative and interpretive acts and raises the question of its own relationship to history and tradition" (212), a result in part of deconstruction's pervasive perspective: "It is unclear whether the notion of narrative derives from human history or whether the very idea or 'fiction' of history is the product of an impulse to understand human events as narrative" (29).

For Dryden *The Marble Faun* reveals the limits of romance, burdened as it is with the ruins of Rome, absences, decay, fragments, structural discontinuities, and insubstantial characters such as Miriam's model. The disenchantment of separation and disconnection overwhelms the enchanted search in which objects signify that some form of ultimate identity and individuality is possible over time and through the wreckage. A sylvan dance, like art, can only function "as a mystified defensive strategy that seeks to offer an escape from the destructive effects of time" (44). This is probably true of all art, but Hawthorne's last published fiction reveals its cracks and fissures more visibly. Its fragmentary epiphanies seem to be the only insights left of Hawthorne's vision. The gaps were always there, but Dryden sees them as gaping ruins, casting a spell that is now only malignant (59).

Other critics continued to rely on various polarities. Rita K. Gollin in *Nathaniel Hawthorne and the Truth of Dreams* (1979) considers dreams in opposition to the thought of the Scottish Common Sense philosophers who were forever suspicious of the imagination and stressed clear-eyed logic and self-knowledge, the kind of philosophy Hawthorne would have imbibed at Bowdoin. For him, says Gollin, dreams enacted a kind of romantic reverie, however nightmarish and gothic; "for him, composing fiction was a form of dreaming" (221). For Gollin, "My Kinsman, Major Molineux" is "dreamlike in its transformations, condensations, and elliptical communications . . . it takes place in a series of curious half-lights" (116) in a kind of spiritual and physical wilderness, but in *The Marble Faun*, "symbols and transformations characteristic of dreams recur without the necessary leading idea to unify them" (196).

The title of John Carlos Rowe's book, *Through the Custom-House: Nineteenth-Century American Fiction and Modern Theory* (1982), reveals his critical intentions in his application of contemporary theory to the examination of nineteenth-century American fiction. He also believed that contradictions have always shaped the best and most characteristic American fiction, that language itself contains the textures and issues of modernity, so modernity is not being imposed upon it — "modernity lurks as a possibility in every utterance" (xii) — and that therefore "the scientific claims of structural linguistics . . . seem to strike a death blow to the modernist's desperate effort to preserve the integrity of an authorial consciousness" (173). Modernity reveals a self-reflexivity in all writing and representation but at the same time always represses certain ideas or emotions.

Both Freud and Derrida would agree with Rowe that "writing is unthinkable without repression," that it persistently uses its "power to suppress its own divided structure" (17), thereby suppressing division and contradiction while leaving traces of such suppression in the writing itself. The intertextuality of all texts is always present in them, but according to Rowe, it is "the intertextuality of romance and realism [that] is the distinguishing mark of Hawthorne's literary production, and it necessitates a perpetual renewal of the confrontation . . . from the romantic synthesis of *The Scarlet Letter* to the clash of conflicting interests in *Blithedale*" (24).

Rowe is particularly perceptive when he applies his critical acumen to *The Blithedale Romance*. There he finds three competing narratives: the popular romance, which offers "wizards and devils, dark and fair ladies, hidden origins, secret compacts, mesmeric machinations [and] mistaken identities," and the desire of Zenobia, Priscilla, Westervelt and Old Moodie "to enchant and possess others"; Hollingsworth's project, which conflicts with the Blithedale experiment; and Coverdale's struggle to untangle the first two narratives (58). Rowe asserts that "Coverdale learns not only how fanciful all conceptions in reality are but how they disguise our most ego-tistical drives" (66), except possibly his own. Rowe employs Sartre's idea of imagination versus perception; whereas the latter is never complete and always open, the former, however similar, relies upon the absence of actual objects in order to conjure up its own mental images. It depends upon the absence of sensory objects but also excludes and negates them. Both are essentially veils, as is consciousness itself, and therefore no character can escape that "lurid intermixture" of imagination and perception, of the conceptual and the sensory that fuel that consciousness. Confusing the actual with the imagined lies at the heart of Hawthorne's fiction and of his characters' grapplings with one another as revealed in *Blithedale*: "The truth of the romance lurks in its capacity to employ the imagination in order to reflect upon the process of consciousness itself . . . to enable us to make consciousness itself an object of reflection" (68).

Rowe tends to give Coverdale too much of the benefit of the doubt, but his general critical overview of Hawthorne's third romance and his romances in general strikes me as right on target. He recognizes the very romantic conception that consciousness, imagination, and perception are all kindred aspects of the subjective point of view that English Romantics from Blake to Shelley wrestled with in their poetry and Coleridge explored in philosophical detail (with substantial help from the German Romantics). Without this conviction about the nature of human consciousness, only the "mute and meaningless substance of the world" exists. We can never satisfy our desires in and for that world, but "Hawthorne himself seems to affirm desire as the structural principle of human consciousness, the very element that distinguishes man" (74).

Unsatisfiable desire at the heart and structure of consciousness, Rowe insists, plagues all the characters in *Blithedale* and cripples each of them, especially when reduced to the manipulations of mesmerists and would-be reformers. Coverdale in his tepid efforts to unscramble the mysteries of his friends and enemies recognizes that "man's fundamental estrangement from the world and his primary desire to overcome such alienation" (82) will never be resolved or fulfilled, particularly in his own case where self-comfort and self-absorption almost totally blind him from his own prurient compulsions and muddled musings. At least he does in certain moments recognize his kinship to Westervelt, his own will to power as egotism replaces love in this third romance of Hawthorne's, and alienation rules the day.

In *The Rhetoric of American Romance: Dialectic and Identity in Emerson, Dickinson, Poe, and Hawthorne* (1985), Evan Carton sees the romance form as a cluster of particular structures and strategies, built upon the by-now-familiar dialectical relations, dualisms, and polarities. Redemption and alienation fight it out in all of Hawthorne's romances, "and there is no avoiding such doubleness, since it informs the self's every attempt to make contact with what is external to it" (125). Language supplies both instrument for and impediment to such a vision, as Carton quotes Jonathan Arac's contention from "Reading the Letter" (1979) that Hawthorne's fiction "'frustrates mimetic reading, refuses to yield a fet-ishized, objective product' but insists on sustaining 'human activity'" (157). Rhetoric supplies the romancer's performance as he navigates the well-trod path between reverie and fact, presence and absence: "Romance is the literary art that sets itself the task of illuminating language's enter-prise" (20).

Both Gordon Hutner in *Secrets and Sympathy: Forms of Disclosure in Hawthorne's Novels* and Darrel Abel in *The Moral Picturesque: Studies in Hawthorne's Fiction* (both 1988) focus on the indeterminacy of experience that they find at the core of Hawthorne's fiction, the same indeterminacy that deconstruction locates in all texts, an idea that strikes me as more critically useful and helpful than the more apocalyptic notion of "undecid-ability." For Hutner, Hawthorne's use of secrets not only generates mys-tery and casts a spell but is also at the heart, or should be, of sympathy among the characters and between them and the reader. We should learn to recognize and accept the existence of secrets, the mystery of others, and in so doing make it the basis of our sympathy for them. The world is intrin-sically mysterious, and therefore "the writer creates fictions, interpretive acts of conjecture [in] a world of intrinsic mystery" (168). Absolute knowledge can never be possible, but sympathy should be, for just as "secrets . . . propel the plots of Hawthorne's novels . . . their compromised articulation intensifies the reader's sympathetic involvement" (89). For his part, Abel insists that "Hawthorne's fictions are what Robert Frost called 'tentatives,'" and thus involve "various grasps at an ultimately ungraspable beyond" (21). The moral picturesque reveals various human patterns in a cosmic drama, for Hawthorne's favorite words include "*mystery, phantas-magoria, hieroglyphics, chaos, labyrinth, vicissitude* and *riddle*. . . . The only certainties are subjective and imperfectly communicable. . . . His fondness for such participles as *glimmering* and *flitting* indicates the mistrust of the reality of objective evidence" (20). In both Hutner's and Abel's books, what Abel calls "distancing as a strategy of perception" (72) suggests both spiritual possibilities and the arbitrariness of all explanations. Revelation remains a riddle, and, as Hutner puts it, no amount of "premeditated observation" will ever solve anything (159).

As Nina Baym traced Hawthorne's development of in terms of his attitudes toward the imagination and women, so Richard Millington in *Practicing Romance* (1992) tracks what he calls narrative form and cultural engagement in Hawthorne's fiction, broadening the idea and practice of romance as both a narrative and cultural strategy. He depicts a savvy and strategically adept Hawthorne who examines the American self as a cultural product. Hawthorne's tales can be seen as warnings, as tragic examples of what not to do. Thus for Millington, Hawthorne's "series of experiments in fictive strategy . . . [his] narrative tactics . . . can replicate or parody the operations of cultural authority" (6–7). Romance creates that neutral territory where, unlike real experience, the imagination and the actual meet as mutual combatants and equals and can intermingle with and affect one another "with the capacity to overturn customary and conventional ways of seeing" (53). There can be "no such thing as absolute property in one's self" (139) in such a realm, since Hawthorne probes, subverts, and upends the American myth of self-reliance and self-possession.

Millington admires and builds upon the work of several critics who were rethinking Hawthorne in the 1970s, such as Crews, Baym, Brodhead, Dryden, Hutner, and Dauber. For him, Dauber finds that "an attempt to establish intimacy with the reader is the animating purpose of Hawthorne's writing." Dryden celebrates "Hawthorne's strategy of self-presentation," but Millington suggests that Hawthorne also always keeps something in reserve; and Hutner sees "a complex dynamic of incomplete self-revelation as the animating principle of Hawthorne's work" (213). As cultural critic Hawthorne explores all facets of American identity and will to power, and as fictional strategist he juggles various perspectives, so that the reader will constantly question all forms of authority.

It is true, allows Millington, that romance may be "less a 'form' than a condition of mind" (53), and it can become solipsistic and self-enclosing, seeking refuge in a self-distancing analysis that may reflect the very kind of authority that Judge Pyncheon embodies in *The House of the Seven Gables*. On the other hand "the freedom from interpretive coercion that [Hawthorne] allows his reader puts his work extraordinarily at risk" (49) in that the reader is given no guidance as to which interpretations carry the most weight: "To write romance, for Hawthorne, is to risk invention by the reader" (50). He manages to walk a very narrow tightrope in this regard, but his attacks on various careerists, such as the Reverend Mr. Hooper, Wakefield, Aylmer, Young Goodman Brown, and Ethan Brand for their determination to impose meaning on the world around them, isolate themselves, and exercise their will to power underscores one of the major centers of his art.

According to Millington each major romance foregrounds a different aspect of Hawthorne's perspective and cultural strategy. In *The Scarlet Letter* Millington identifies the theme of "romance as revision" in which the various acts of interpretation of the letter reveal "the communal function of romance" (99). Characters' choices and limitations are constantly revised and reinterpreted within the Puritan milieu, with Hester and Pearl growing as individuals and the narcissistic Dimmesdale and Chillingworth shrinking. *The House of the Seven Gables* reflects the "romance as engagement" from its cultural center, as three opening narrators — the writer as public man, as genial historian, and as scoffing author — compete with one another in an effort to express how the American cultural system operates. Romance goes on the attack in *The Blithedale Romance*, revealing the self as one more commodity in the market economy, a self that is plagued by fears of domination, penetration, and manipulation. According to Millington, "the notion of the self's permeability to others — the central hope of sentimental ideology — is simply becoming too frightening" (170). And in *The Marble Faun* romance goes down to defeat, overwhelmed by the genteel authority of the rigidly puritanical Hilda. Millington sees the romance as "narrative combat" between Miriam and Hilda, leading to "the moment of interpretive demand characteristic of Hawthorne's fiction — the moment when the reader is left alone to interpret without or in opposition to the confirmation of narrative authority . . . [which] creates an interpretive problem" (200). Do we choose sides, remain unconvinced by either side, or finally assume that the romance itself generates more calculated confusion than comprehension?

Conscious narrative strategies loom within most of the Hawthornian criticism of the 1970s and beyond, conjuring up an author who knows exactly what he is up to in terms of structure and technique and who continuously experiments with different perspectives and authorial positions, the kind of experimentation that lies at the heart of the form of the romance. John Dolis in *The Style of Hawthorne's Gaze: Regarding Subjectivity* (1993) revels in these different perspectives as facets of an overall subjective gaze as Hawthorne wrestles with the entire perceptual situation, undermining the static, fixed, and rigid poses of daguerreotypes with their black and white contrasts in order to explore the "synecdochic oscillations" (66) of the kinds of gazes that isolate objects against a background of darkness, transform them into images that defy any strict allegorical framework, and merge with the dream mode of Hawthorne's fiction. Hawthorne's situation is itself an act of perception, which he constantly explores and examines, substituting a gestalt field for the usual static frame one finds bordering black-and-white daguerreotypes. Romance plumbs that inner space in his sequences of close-ups, tight shots, panoramic perspectives, and obsessively-focused details, converting consciousness into a more open experience of the world around and within it that actual daguerreotypes cannot possibly reveal.

For Dolis, images emerge out of darkness as consciousness selects and exposes them. Objects become icons as they "function expressively" and shape the narrative (67). Subjects and objects participate in one another, thus creating a new field of vision that is neither subjective expression nor objective description but creates a new vision, a spell (86, 85). For Dolis this new image or icon reveals "a primordial coherence between subject and object," a pre-objective structure of perception that the perceiver participates in (57): "Hawthorne's description transforms the transparency of an objective world 'without' into the ambiguous opacity of an interior space" (58). The object the gaze selects automatically excludes others, which then recede into the obscurity of the background. Thus darkness haunts Hawthorne's narrative background with its atmosphere of the guilt and will to power that inhabit every human heart. The mind remains forever haunted by such a presence, in psychological terms akin to the unconscious, and for Heidegger, upon whose philosophical perspective Dolis relies, the state of being itself.

Hawthorne, then, according to Dolis, however much he relies on forms of allegory, must forever violate and defy them, undermine them and create the more fluid process of perception in motion, constantly shifting, shaping, and re-seeing experience as it occurs: "Textuality transforms an original object whose (in)significance is fixed (factual) into a beginning intention (to mean) whose significance is open and multiple (fictive) . . . The text itself inaugurates its own authority. There's no origin, just the process of narrative with its intentional beginnings" (180, 181). Dolis affirmingly quotes Heidegger's statement from "What Are Poets For?" that "the interior of uncustomary [i.e., unconventional] consciousness remains the inner space in which everything is for us beyond the arithmetic of calculation, and free of such boundaries" (258). Such a space not only mirrors the "neutral territory" of Hawthorne's American romance but also supports the depths of its psychological truths and imaginative undermining of conventional fictional boundaries.

Clark Davis adds in *Hawthorne's Shyness: Ethics, Politics, and the Question of Engagement* (2005) that Hawthorne's manner was as much a personal strategy as it was a literary one, used to create distance in order to see more clearly the various ethical positions his characters find themselves in. Akin to Levinas's idea of ethical engagement, to recognize the other as an "other" requires distance. To engage with others is to recognize one's separation from them. For Davis, Hawthorne's outlook involves "a passive but ethical skepticism, wary of ideas, attuned to the local" (44). Davis himself is wary of ideological criticism that reduces the individual to a cultural and historical product and attempts to link Hawthorne's political quietism and conservatism to a more solidly ethical stance that undermines all totalities of thought, but in any case Hawthorne's requirement for distance in both his personal affairs and in the romance form adds to our comprehension of how that particular form works and how we are all "strangely connected," which Davis takes to be "the summation of Hawthorne's thoughts on human relationships" (158). In so doing he restores the discussion of substantive ethical issues that he locates in Hawthorne's fiction.

Of course, Hawthorne criticism since the 1960s has not been merely linguistic. For instance the explosion of approaches involving feminism, race, gender roles, Queer Theory, politics, and cultural studies has revealed how much Hawthorne was both a part of and a critic of his place and times. The stereotypical image of the isolated aesthete, cocooned in solitude and alienation, steeped only in Calvinist doubt and puritanical terror, has been undermined by the criticism of the last forty years. Deconstruction helped to undermine the New Critics' isolation of the texts, which had spawned the isolated Hawthorne as much as the texts themselves had, and opened them to social, historical, and cultural concerns. It is these concerns, which have expanded our awareness of Hawthorne as author and cultural critic, to which we will now turn.

7: Ideological Contexts: Deconstruction, Feminism, the New Historicism, Race, and Entanglement

From the New Criticism to Ideological Criticism

IN THE 1960s AND 1970s DECONSTRUCTION, which undermined not only the various dualisms that seemed permanently attached to the nineteenth- and early twentieth-century critical approaches to Hawthorne as man and artist but also the assumptions and strategies of the New Criticism and psychological approaches of the mid-twentieth century, was not the only critical revolution that occurred. Feminist criticism also flourished, as did other perspectives that included those of African American writers and critics and those of Marxist critics with their concerns of class and ideology. In general these can be seen as part of a tendency toward a thorough exploration of the traditional American literary canon and how it was constructed. The roles seen to have been played by women in Hawthorne's life — Sophia Peabody Hawthorne, Elizabeth Palmer Peabody, Elizabeth Hawthorne, Margaret Fuller and others — underwent a significant shift from spouse and/or acquaintance to collaborator and subject. The New Critical obeisance to unity broke down, as texts revealed fissures and inconsistencies, as well as traces from previous texts. Cultural compulsions were unearthed and exposed that shaped Hawthorne's idea of women, African Americans, the male role in a capitalist society, and the stratification of class both of the Puritan era and of Hawthorne's own.

The overall difference in critical approaches to Hawthorne's work emerges most clearly when we compare Lionel Trilling's famous essay of 1964, "Our Hawthorne," to Gordon Hutner's "Whose Hawthorne?" of 2004. Trilling's essay all but announces the end of the New Critical era. He upbraids Henry James for denying "the darkness of Hawthorne's mind" (431) and at the same time praises Hawthorne's strategy of ambiguity as the core of humanity's moral nature. He recognizes that Hawthorne's rise as the subject of critical study coincided with the rise of the New Criticism influenced as it was by T. S. Eliot's notion that literature casts primal spells and is itself "an expression of belief in the magical force and authority of words and their arrangement" (436). Perhaps criticism had gotten too much in the way of our ability to enjoy Hawthorne's stylistic charms that James and others praised so readily; Trilling believed that "for us today, none of Hawthorne's stories surpasses in interest 'My Kinsman, Major Molineux.' James does not mention this great story" (443). Trilling also compares Hawthorne to Kafka, who expresses the contemporary mood and reality in his vision of the "radical incompatibility of world and mankind" (446), whereas Hawthorne himself, according to Trilling, remains trapped in and by the actual world; it forever weighs upon his flights of fancy and his imaginative outlook: "Over Hawthorne's imagination, the literal actuality of the world always maintains its dominion" (451). He reveals "no great tyrant-dream in which we can take refuge" (457) but insists on the world's intractability and its persistent power over our imaginations. Therefore Hawthorne "is, in Nietzsche's phrase, one of the spirits of yesterday — and the day after tomorrow" (458).

For Trilling, Hawthorne was the perfect American classical writer to criticize, recognizing as he did "our Hawthorne" as a creature largely spawned by the New Criticism. While Trilling had already decided that it was time to move away from the New Criticism, he recognized that it had revealed a darker, more psychologically ambiguous Hawthorne, in such tales as "My Kinsman, Major Molineux," which went all but unnoticed in the nineteenth century. He admired Hawthorne's ambiguities — ambiguity was the singular touchstone of the New Criticism — but for him the era of the New Criticism was over. It was, therefore, necessary in his view to relegate Hawthorne to the past and move on to more modern writers such as Kafka. For Trilling public intellectual discourse should be exploring writers like Kafka with their "tyrant dreams" and not Hawthorne with his cultural and historical limitations.

Forty years after Trilling, in "Whose Hawthorne?" Hutner retraces several critical perspectives on Hawthorne from James to Trilling and decides that in 1964 "Hawthorne was read for his power of endorsing the era's liberal consensus even as he was asked to give it the depths of his tragic awareness" (254). As contextual criticism appeared in the 1970s from feminist and other perspectives, he became "a chilling model of the dead white male of European origin . . . perhaps only Hemingway rivals Hawthorne in the degree to which his canonical status has been challenged" (259). Thus Hutner carves out a space for a new but diminished Hawthorne, describing him in terms of Hawthorne's own racist and anti-feminist leanings, taking him to task for not wrestling with the great political and cultural issues of his day such as slavery, race, women's rights, and rapacious capitalism. From Hutner's perspective in 2004, Hawthorne's limits as a writer were "even too apparent" (262) as the historicist and context-driven criticism of the previous thirty years or so had revealed his complicity in his era's conventional values, despite or because of the entan-

gled ambiguities of his fiction. Interestingly enough, such criticism as
Hutner's has created a more interesting Hawthorne in terms of the nineteenth century and his ambivalent relationship to it. Far from dismember-
ing him, it has produced a more nuanced writer in terms of social and
political realities, even though, as Hutner acknowledges, "Hawthorne's
magnitude has been revised downward to more manageable proportions
than [in] previous generations," even as he recognizes that "part of that is
the general devaluation of authorship that has occurred in the last twenty-
five years" (262).

The volume *Ideology and Classic American Literature* (1986), edited
by Sacvan Bercovitch and Myra Jehlen, brought together a series of essays
that foreground ideology and politics and summarize many of the critical
strands that had emerged from the 1960s onwards. First of all, the volume's introduction contends that more attention must be paid to race,
gender, and class in literature. (Nowadays we would add sexual orientation
as well.) Second, it points out that much of the newer criticism is based on
"European theories of culture including a complex tradition of ideological
theory" (1). Ideology, according to the editors, can be seen as positive,
negative, or neutral, but its presence in all facets of life in repressing social
and class differences masks the will to power of the dominating social class
and embodies a false consciousness that tries to portray such power politics
as natural and eternal. Politics inhabits and inhibits language itself, which
is viewed as a system that establishes power and control where even the use
of individual words can become the site of ideological warfare.

In his afterword, Bercovitch, writing from a Marxist perspective, links
ideology not only to a particular social system but also views it as a tool of
the ruling classes to keep that system intact. Bercovitch's overview of ideology in general emphasizes particular ideologies from feminism to New
Historicism. A given ideology may appear to be "natural," but that is only
the result of the status quo asserting its sense of privilege to make it appear
that way. Hawthorne's political appointments, for example, reveal how
carefully he could work the system through a kind of white male network
and find paying positions to support himself and his family.

At the same time Bercovitch insists that "every ideology . . . breeds its
own opposition, every culture its own counterculture" (431) and thus supports his case that conventional society, which in Hawthorne's day was
becoming increasingly capitalistic, could co-opt various ideological positions as part of the ongoing trajectory of American culture. In fact for
Bercovitch one of the purposes of ideology is not only to create an opposition but also to co-opt every attempt at opposition.

The American form of this ideological trap turns "potential conflict
into a debate about fusion and fragmentation — in effect [turning] what
might have been a confrontation of alternatives into the alternation of
opposites . . . to absorb the very terms of opposition into the promise of

the New . . ." (438). The polarities of opposition and contradiction, bina-
ries of either/or and neither/nor result in the dynamic dialect of both/
and, which easily morphs into a synthesis of the status quo: "Multiplicity
is not necessarily opposite to hegemony; the two may simply be different
sides of the same coin" (437). One can see how this analysis could easily
be applied to the entangled ambiguities of Hawthorne's art, where the
deeper the critic delves into his characters' psyches, the more he or she
might be diverted from a critique of conventional society, thus leaving the
status quo intact.

In his controversial *The Office of the Scarlet Letter* (1991) Bercovitch
explains how ideology plays out in Hester's returning to Boston.
Determined to replace the old polarities of critical argument, he treats the
events of the novel as subject to further development, seeking an ultimate
synthesis, which is, however, relegated to some future time. For Bercovitch,
therefore, symbolic polarities become mutually sustaining, not internally
conflicted, promising an ultimate reciprocity and consensus (23): such is
the liberal faith in American pluralism. Hester's return becomes "a parable
of reconciliation — reconciliation, complementarity, and compromise are
the keys to Hawthorne's art" (113). Things may appear dark in the
present, but in the future all will be resolved, a liberal belief that maintains
itself whether or not that future ever actually occurs.

Part of what Hawthorne "tells us" may involve the loss of moral
certainty, however prejudiced, persecutorial, and perverse, but I have
long disagreed with Bercovitch's hungering for synthesis or at least his
criticizing Hawthorne's works for being conceived so as to imply a future
synthesis. Hawthorne's fiction with all of its dualities and contradictions
for me conjures up a dark entanglement of self and world that can neither
be fathomed nor comprehended. It is the "dark necessity" of this ultimate mystery, a negative synthesis, a lack of all possible reconciliation that
lies at the heart of such romances as *The Scarlet Letter*. Bercovitch disre-
gards present tragedy in his diagnosis of the cultural possibility of a
brighter future that it supposedly allows for, thus riding roughshod over
the actual experience of reading *The Scarlet Letter*, which surely includes
reflection upon the gloom and doom of its major characters. Their dark
necessity is not the same as Chillingworth's conscious campaign of
revenge, but it is the result of the entanglement of many contradictory
forces — cultural, historical, spiritual, physical — that congregate and
smolder in the human heart.

Bercovitch, therefore, all too easily empties out the tragic, the entangled, the urgently contradictory and conflicted forces and characters in
Hawthorne's first romance in order to uphold his diagnosis of "a rhetoric
of reconciliation that was rooted both in the ambiguities of legal language
and in a providential sense of mission" (66). In doing so he sees Hawthorne
as maintaining that very providential sense of the American mission that

Hawthorne questions, subverts, probes, and undermines. Hester is not simply "the dissenter as agent of socialization, a self-professed sinner self-transformed into a herald of progress" (159), as Bercovitch has it. She does not merely "re-form herself, voluntarily, as the vehicle of social order" (15). She returns to the scene of her passion, her "crime," and her very existence because it has become a part of her and always will be. Arthur is still there, and so will she be.

In his essay in the Bercovitch and Jehlen volume, "The Politics of *The Scarlet Letter*," Jonathan Arac either politicizes the power plays inherent in Hawthorne's entangled view of the world and the self or unearths the politics already present in the language and the plots that Hawthorne uses, depending on one's view. Hawthorne's indeterminacy and openness, Arac insists, reflect the political stasis of the 1850s, the attempt to avoid civil war at all costs. Thus character analysis and political personalities on the public stage replace political action. Such indeterminacy upholds the fragile status quo: "Action is intolerable; character takes its place" (255). *The House of the Seven Gables* performs the same sleight of hand: "The point of the plot . . . is to erase and undo all action" (254). Arac builds on Bercovitch's analysis that all contradictions are denied or blurred, strategically made ambiguous in order that they can be swallowed up by the liberal consensus, reducing dissent to a continuing dialogue within a notion of inherent historical progress. Thus Hawthorne's persistent skepticism about all fundamentally absolute ideas in his fiction accomplishes no more than upholding the conservative politics of the moment.

From such a perspective Hawthorne also becomes an apologist for middle-class values and the creation of the middle-class family. According to Joel Pfister in *The Production of Personal Life: Class, Gender & the Psychological in Hawthorne's Fiction* (1991), the middle class envisioned the home as the sanctuary from the increasingly industrial world with its ruthless divisions between capital and labor but at the same time supported and undergirded that world by viewing itself as a kind of retreat from it: time off for good behavior. According to Pfister, the construction of middle-class gender roles, which rigidly define the female as mother and wife at the hearth and the male as the one who must go forth and make money, consistently supported the emerging capitalist world, in effect reproducing the hierarchical relationship between manager and worker as husband and wife. In Pfister's view, "we need to theorize and historicize the political relationship between the emergence of a rigidly gendered, somewhat privatized, psychologized nineteenth-century consciousness and the determinative process of class formation" (183, 184).

Thus the subjective qualities of psychology become, for Pfister, a socially constructed reflection of middle-class formation, a way for that class to describe and envision itself. Sexuality as the essence of subjectivity becomes the touchstone of that vision and underscores all social conditions or helps create them. Therefore "the social construction of psychological codes and the emergence of the 'psychological' as a category produced within the middle class" (17) occur as the class concept of self develops. Such a production of a subjective self masks a will to power and tries to submerge class, racial, and gender antagonisms. The Hawthornes were both victims and producers of this middle-class strategy or vision, and thus performed anxiously within it as presented in great detail in T. Walter Herbert's 1993 biography.

Hawthorne, says Pfister, recognized the will to power that inhabits the construction of allegory, that "produces and extends stereotypes as he both uses and deconstructs it" (42). He certainly saw how this played out in his male characters who, when the world fails to materialize in the guise of the strict and rigid codes that they wish to live by, create and face their own self-destruction. For Hawthorne the allegorical method produced the very content he felt ambivalent about, producing "the masculine obsession to stereotype how women read themselves" (45). Understandably, then, according to Pfister, Hawthorne implies that "gender roles . . . can be like lived allegories" (47). The reason he calls attention to the artifice of his stories is to undercut the allegorical authority of his male characters and of himself, wanting "his readers to catch the narrator in the act to focus on narrative sleights of hand" (179). Thus is he "a product, agent, and critic of an emerging middle-class interiority" (183), a decidedly subtle strategy that Pfister explains well. Hawthorne's narrative techniques exist, therefore, "both to inscribe resisting female characters and to contain their resistance" (162). Sin may educate and help to subvert "the middle-class ideology of feminization as cultural redemption" (180), but Hawthorne, as in everything else, could never be entirely sure, and went on to dramatize that psychological as well as middle-class ambivalence.

Feminist Criticism

Feminist criticism emerged in the late 1960s and early 1970s and continues to explore both the role of women in Hawthorne's fiction, his relationship to the women in his life, such as Margaret Fuller and Elizabeth Palmer Peabody, and his texts as viewed from a feminist perspective. Nina Baym in 1976 and Emily Miller Budick in 1994, in particular, stand out for the way they relate Hawthorne's ideas about the romance to women in general, thereby "engendering" the romance tradition, and the way they summarize the ideologically feminist criticism that preceded them.

A good example and summary of feminist criticism in its earlier stages would be Louise DeSalvo's *Nathaniel Hawthorne* (1987) — "Hawthorne *never* supports the feminist efforts of these characters, but rather always criticizes them" (4) — as though any element of criticism automatically undermines support of any kind. She briefly covers the feminist critics who have preceded her, those who exposed "the misogynist implications of Hawthorne's works," those like Baym, Gloria C. Erlich, and T. Walter Herbert who explored Hawthorne's treatment of women both in his art and life, those like Baym, Jonathan Auerbach, and Carolyn Heilbrun who read the fiction "as a demonstration of women's power," those like Judith Fryer, Sandra Gilbert, Susan Gubar, and Herbert who placed Hawthorne's fictional women "within the context of the prevailing mythology of his times," and others from various perspectives (25). DeSalvo clearly aims to expose in Hawthorne the misogynistic patriarchal view that idealizes women in an attempt to veil the deep hostility toward them and believes that for Hawthorne, "grief and suffering, rather than being destructive to a woman, is, in fact, ennobling, so long as she does not become a social reformer as a result of it" (65). For her, each one of Hawthorne's novels leaves the reader "trapped within a misogynist point of view . . . with . . . women submerged by the reigning forces of the patriarchy" (120).

At times misogyny seems to be the only psychological and cultural attitude that DeSalvo acknowledges, a reductionist view that seems more primal scream than literary criticism. She reveals the patriarchal argument but does not go much beyond it. Coverdale, for example, in *The Blithedale Romance*, is described as "a psychopathic murderous misogynist" (118), and DeSalvo suggests that he might have killed Zenobia. Finally she admits to disliking the form of romance that Hawthorne writes, "which blunts the realism of the events, and obscures the moral or ethical conclusions . . . the destitute circumstances of the women portrayed [in *The Blithedale Romance*] get lost in a language which either obfuscates or deliberately distorts what has happened to them" (120). Romance, thus, blunts, obscures, obfuscates, and distorts, especially since the narrator reveals himself as possessing "the consciousness of a murderous maniac" (120).

Laura E. Tanner takes a different tack in "Speaking with 'Hands at Our Throats': The Struggle for Artistic Voice in *The Blithedale Romance*." She describes both Zenobia and Coverdale as artists, struggling for their artistic voice. Yes, Coverdale is guilty of all his sentimental psychologizing and patriarchal condescension — he indicts Zenobia for sacrificing her feminist ideals to her love for Hollingsworth, a position Tanner exposes as Coverdale's manipulating his narration in order to make it so — and, yes, in writing the stirring passage about Zenobia's suicide he might very well be, as Tanner suggests, "guilty of narrative necrophilia" (15), but his indictment of Zenobia is matched by her own ability at playing various roles, taunting him with her asides and assaults — "Zenobia becomes a self-conscious artist experimenting with rhetoric and disguise rather than a romantic artist intent on defining a stable poetic identity"

(Tanner 6) — as her "apparent humility is merely a guise which she adopts in order to expose the tactics of her oppressors" (Tanner 12). Coverdale controls the narrative and creates his own Zenobia to fit his misogynistic message, but as for Hawthorne's novel itself, "rather than embracing Coverdale's misogyny, [it] traces the way in which the artist's destruction of the self-conscious female voice within also destroys the possibility for creation" (18), a perspective both Baym and Budick would agree with. DeSalvo's book captures the simplistically ideological feminist view of Hawthorne, but Tanner, it seems to me, produces the more thoughtful critical analysis.

DeSalvo's view has never really vanished from the critical scene. Jamie Barlowe in *The Scarlet Mob of Scribblers: Rereading Hester Prynne* (2000) complains that Hawthorne finally subjects Hester to male judgment and self-punishment, silencing her once and for all, and that not enough feminist critics have pointed out within the mainstream of Hawthorne criticism that ideological flaw. This strikes me as willfully one-dimensional and old-fashioned in terms of what critics like Nina Baym, Myra Jehlen, Rita Gollin, Melinda Ponder, Millicent Bell, Alison Easton, and others have brought to the table. True, many of these critics may not be "pure" feminists, in the sense that they don't restrict themselves solely to gender issues but branch out to consider wider social, historical, and cultural phenomena (within which gender plays a central role), but neither is Hester "purely" silenced and incarcerated, as the more simplistic applications of feminist theory — such as DeSalvo's and Barlowe's — would have it. Seeing Hester in such a fashion strikes me as simplistic as viewing her as a romantic rebel against the Calvinist establishment. There lurks a bit of both in her in her entangled self and role, neither of which is either explicitly one thing or the other.

It may help the cause of a particular feminist outlook, suggests Barlowe, to praise the Demi Moore film of *The Scarlet Letter* in which Demi-Hester speaks her mind, transcends Lillian Gish's portrayal, in the 1926 film version, of the girl-woman who participates "in the cultural conditioning of women to accept all responsibility and blame and then to redeem men" (93), and is finally along with Arthur rescued from the scaffold by Indians, thus politically correctly giving them a more prominent role in the tale. I agree that "the film represents the historical and sexual excesses that a Hawthornian semiotics tries to contain" (81), but do such excesses honestly free us from cultural repression in *The Scarlet Letter*? Is containment in its "attempt to hide the failures of cultural repression" (81) so explicitly gendered? Historically this has been true, but if Barlowe is saying that women scholars should destabilize and disrupt mainstream (male) positions without dispensing with them, I'm not sure what that accomplishes. If we must transcend functioning "in terms of Othering," how exactly are we to accomplish this?

Nina Baym has made it very clear that she sees Hawthorne as a femi-nist writer. She, therefore, opposes the patriarchal idea of Crews, Male, and many other New Critics who believed that Dimmesdale is the central char-acter of *The Scarlet Letter*. For her, Hester embodies all the human passion and self-expressing self-reliance that the Calvinist authorities work to restrict, contain, and dismiss.

In her 2005 essay, "Revisiting Hawthorne's Feminism," Baym begins: "In this essay I swim against the tide to argue — again — for Hawthorne as a feminist writer from *The Scarlet Letter* onward. I argued this in essays published throughout the 1970s and 1980s, as well as in *The Shape of Hawthorne's Career* (1976)" (541). She confronts all the popular issues: in the rough-and-tumble Jacksonian era, men had to reject, ignore, and silence women's voices as Jamie Barlowe suggests. Women for Hawthorne supposedly are nothing more than bourgeois puppets on the capitalist game board. "To suggest a feminist Hawthorne in the face of all this criticism," says Baym, "is foolhardy" (548), but she nevertheless charges ahead to show how Hawthorne leaves space for feminist analysis in his romances, how Hester's flaws and failures do not automatically invalidate her ideas and perceptions, and how "to say that Hawthorne's women have more heart than his men does not imply that they have less brain" (553). Both Zenobia and Miriam, for instance, Baym considers smarter than Hollingsworth, Coverdale, and Kenyon. In doing so she maintains her major revision of the basic view of Hawthorne in regard to gender. Hawthorne's romances, Baym concludes, "place transgressing women at the center, insist on women's equality with men, and deny the universal applicability of domestic ideals" (557).

Emily Miller Budick in *Engendering Romance: Women Writers and the Hawthorne Tradition, 1850–1990* (1994) agrees with Baym's assessment of the proto-feminist vision in Hawthorne's fiction, since she maintains that his romances rely on a radical skepticism that offers questions but no answers, a strategy that she clearly associates with feminist rather than patriarchal perspectives. Such a position in Hawthorne's fiction automati-cally reveals his aversion to all conformist ideas and conventional values, which have been persistently patriarchal. Hester's role, for instance, forever engages in a dynamic dialectic with the community around her, and that engagement continues throughout the book. Hester, in fact, "engenders uncertainty" (18) in the face of the Puritan patriarchal tradition, which has marked her as an outlaw.

The female romance tradition, embodied in the work of Carson McCullers and Flannery O'Connor, is directed according to Budick "toward family and community, reconstructed and redefined . . . It com-poses itself as a multiphonic, many-voiced text, representing not an inde-terminate or decentered text but a multifaceted consciousness" (161), which Budick identifies with the feminist perspective as opposed to the celebrated self-autonomy and rigid routines of patriarchy. She expands similar concepts in order to analyze the more distinctly feminist African American romances of Toni Morrison: "Like the romance tradition generally, the African American romance raises fundamental questions about perception. It proposes as a response to doubt the acknowledgment and affirmation of family and community" (184). For Morrison, conversation supplies the instrument for that goal. The feminist position, unlike the patriarchal one, knows implicitly that "there is no transcendental place for Faith, Hope, and Grace, no world of wholly autonomous, mutually independent capitalized selves" (245).

In 1990, Monika Elbert adopted a similar strategy in *Encoding the Letter "A": Gender and Authority in Hawthorne's Early Fiction*. For Elbert, the feminist perspective automatically assumes that all perspectives are subjective and shifting. It rejects the absolutist polarities of the patriarchal society: male/female, black/white, etc. The bifurcation of all things is a "male-induced construct" that falsifies life and experience. In Hawthorne's earlier stories, men like Reuben Bourne, Robin Molineux, and Young Goodman Brown are so transfixed by these "arbitrary polarities," such as good and evil, angels and demons, that they cannot act beyond them and end up upholding the patriarchal vision (12). Women remain "passive bystanders" in these early tales (12).

According to Elbert, Hawthorne constructs a vision where he explores all sides to an issue or character and chooses none: "He has no place to stand outside the fleeting perception of the persona whom he portrays at any given moment"; "Hawthorne's vision encompasses all and nothing" (235, 243). Elbert insists that Hawthorne's "final word is doubt" (20) and that "the narrator [in *The Scarlet Letter*] does not imply that one mode of perception is superior to the other" (212). It is Hester as woman and mother who with her defiant silence opposes the power plays of the theologically rigid Dimmesdale and the scientifically objective Chillingworth, each of whom become so self-absorbed either with guilt or revenge that they betray their public roles. For Elbert, Hester's silence reveals not a woman silenced but a person choosing silence so as not to participate in the pervasive male discourse of Boston. However plagued by doubt and uncertainty, she remains true to her self — raising Pearl, helping others, administering to the sick — within the limited role that Calvinist society allows, without acknowledging the limits of that role.

Robert S. Levine in his 2005 essay reveals how *The Scarlet Letter* was received by antebellum feminists, a part of the story of the book's critical reception long ignored by all critics, and discovers, for instance, that in 1850 Jane Grey Swisshelm, "a major voice in women's rights, antislavery, and temperance reform" (276), praised Hester as "a woman who, in a world of timorous and judgmental men, bravely acts on her romantic and sexual desires" (278). Swisshelm recognized Hawthorne's attraction to his heroine and "his desire to contain her" (279) but celebrated her subversive powers and "poetic imagination and inventive genius" (278). Many women reviewers, finds Levine, appreciated "an imaginative writer who, despite his possible containment strategies, was responsive to feminist issues of the time, and thus could be read in the context of their own political projects . . ." (290). Levine recognizes the precarious uncertainty of Hester's position in regard to her Puritan community.

In *Hawthorne, Gender, and Death: Christianity and Its Discontents* (2008), Roberta Weldon combines and integrates psychological and feminist positions, specifically in terms of socially constructed gender roles, with cultural and social issues, convinced that "the way we imagine death is determined by our culture" (1). For her the middle class in Hawthorne's time attempted to deny death, to evade and avoid it, and for men this meant reducing women to materialist, mortal bodies as opposed to their own quests to achieve transcendence beyond them. The male sovereign self, in fashioning itself, reduced women to "self-sacrificing sufferers" (4), says Weldon, not a new critical position but one that Weldon links to the patriarchal culture of Christianity. In refusing to accept death, men are doomed to embody "the logic of melancholy," an idea she borrows from Freud's "Mourning and Melancholy," which insists that "until melancholy becomes mourning, the melancholic is doomed to be unhappy" (105). Thus Hawthorne's melancholy men — Dimmesdale, Chillingworth, Old Moodie, Coverdale, and others — try to re-establish their patriarchal power over women like Hester and Zenobia and must sacrifice them to that power. For Hawthorne all systems are "arbitrary," "corrupt," and "despotic" (141), and thus the patriarchal yearning for domination and submission can lead only to melancholy and wasted lives, buttressed by a Christian culture that fosters "a patriarchal religion with an authoritarian structure and . . . [sacrifice]" (143). The men strut publicly with their authority; the women, therefore, must be sacrificed to this ancient order.

Masculinist Criticism

David Leverenz in *Manhood and the American Renaissance* (1989) stresses the developing pressures on men to maintain their authority in the burgeoning new world of a capitalist economy with its resulting class struggle among the patrician colonial elite, the artisans who trumpet the pride in their craft, and the new entrepreneurial males who bring with them "a new middle-class ideology of competitive individualism" (3). Domination or humiliation become the fear and creed of the day, which often parallel Hawthorne's fictional world of masters and slaves, caught in the dynamic dialectic of the ongoing battle between them. "Humiliation . . . is the real terror of the entrepreneurial marketplace" (24) in which men work and from which women retreat to the sanctity of their domestic sanctuaries. For Leverenz gender issues blur these very real class distinctions.

Hawthorne, caught in the marketplace web, sees the position of a self-declared romancer, according to Leverenz, as a strategy created to distance himself from these Jacksonian masculine ideologies, destabilizing narratives and at the same time trying to create a new perspective out of his own alienation. Leverenz quotes Baym's description of Hawthorne's and Melville's fictions as "melodramas of beset manhood" (17), a half-facetious remark that acknowledges the rule of women in writing novels in the mid-nineteenth century and the lack of social status that came with a man's writing fiction. Part of Hawthorne's literary strategy, Leverenz suggests, views "manhood as demonic possession" (239) and tries to undermine such characters as Chillingworth, Rappaccini, Judge Pyncheon, Westervelt, Baglioni, and others as well as the plots that they dominate. Leverenz's approach involves "'un-Manning' such a man, or such a man in himself" (244), Leverenz's pun on Hawthorne's Uncle Robert Manning with his bookkeeper's mentality and business acumen. The upshot in Hawthorne's fiction is "a fascination with male dominance and humiliation [that] displaces a potentially feminist vision of patriarchy" (272).

On the other hand, in *Aesthetic Headaches: Women and a Masculine Poetics in Poe, Melville, and Hawthorne* (1988) Leland S. Person makes the case that Hawthorne was really "exploring the possibility of identifying his own creative power with a woman — not with a feminized, narcissistic self-image, but with an autonomous female other" (16). Person recognizes that men have always treated women as art objects, framed by the insistent male gaze — especially in the aggressive and self-reliant era of Jacksonian democracy — but sees Hawthorne as attempting, in his "deep reluctance to objectify women," to resist that deterministic form, struggling in the romance toward more "open literary forms" (16). True, his male characters continue their crusade to encapsulate and embalm women in what they see as their "natural" or stereotypical roles, but Person presses his case for Hawthorne's having created strong women whose creative powers, rejected by men, cripple these men. Dimmesdale's reconciliation with Hester in the forest leads to his terrific Election Sermon, thus indicating that "relationship is essential to selfhood" (130). Person also says that Hawthorne "uses Phoebe, as he had used Hester, to test the 'reading' ability of his male characters" (140) and that in Zenobia and Miriam, both artists, he emphasizes their "desire to define and create" themselves (161), especially with Zenobia's challenge to Coverdale to transcend "all available linguistic and literary forms and to achieve, at least in the manner of her discourse, the ideal kind of 'gushing out' that Hawthorne had defined in his love letter" to Sophia (150).

Hawthorne did, however, according to Person, also contain women within the male gaze: "If, as I have argued, Hawthorne embodied his deepest creative impulse in his strongest female characters, he also destined each of them for a life of frustrated seeking for that perfect reader" (172). In any case Person insists that Hawthorne does finally attack the macho masculinity of the Jacksonian era by having his female characters disrupt, deconstruct, and undermine that "male hegemony in his fiction" (175).

In Florence on June 9, 1858, Hawthorne commented in his notebook on nine-year-old Robert "Penny" Browning, the son of Robert and Elizabeth Barrett Browning:

> I never saw such a boy as this before . . . so slender, fragile, and sprite-like . . . He seems . . . less manly than would befit that age. I should not quite like to be the father of such a boy . . . I wonder what is to become of him: — whether he will ever grow to be a man — whether it is desirable that he should. (Notebooks 300)

Hawthorne never knew his father, of course, so his experience of that masculine role began with its absence and an awareness that his Uncle Robert, however authoritative and helpful, could not legitimately fill that space. He also chose a profession in which women were successful and popular and, in effect, cursed himself in "The Custom-House" from the perspective of his Calvinist ancestors: what would they think to have produced a storyteller in the family? Why, that's almost as bad as being a fiddler! In mid-nineteenth-century America men were supposed to be up and doing, making money, carrying their weight in society, a position that Hawthorne longed for, reduced, as he was to having to accept political appointments to feed his family.

In his *Men Beyond Desire: Manhood, Sex, and Violation in American Literature* (2005), David Greven, building upon David Leverenz's critique of American manhood, undertakes an exploration of the construction and development of the middle-class masculine role from homosocial and homoerotic perspectives, especially since Hawthorne was extraordinarily handsome, Elizabeth Palmer Peabody having proclaimed him more handsome than the notorious Lord Byron when she first met him. The American male, the self-sovereign "isolato," was somehow to remain inviolate, above the fray of sexual intrigue and desire, somehow pure and intact, an image we continue to see in many American novels. Greven's analysis partakes of a Masculinist and Queer Studies approach and opens wide the doors to a more thorough look at just what it meant to be male in Hawthorne's day. Greven even goes so far to suggest that Dimmesdale must die: "faced with the impossibility of making a choice between Woman and Male Friendship, the only option is death" (123). As Philip Weinstein in his book on Faulkner suggests, "this male quest for immolation is at heart a lust for virginity, a desire to transform (by discipline or abuse) one's own motley body into a self-owned space that would fantastically command or refuse all trace of the Other" (125).

Several scholars continue to produce excellent work on women in relation to Hawthorne's life and work, especially Patricia Dunlavy Valenti's ongoing, two-volume biography of Sophia, *Sophia Peabody Hawthorne: A Life,* the first volume of which appeared in 2004, and Megan Marshall's superb study of all three Peabody sisters, *The Peabody Sisters: Three Women Who Ignited American Romanticism* (2005). Jana Argersinger is currently at work on editing Sophia's *Cuba Journal.* John Idol and Melinda Ponder have published a full-bodied series of essays entitled *Hawthorne and Women: Engendering and Expanding the Hawthorne Tradition* (1999), including Valenti on Rose (Valenti also published a biography on Rose Hawthorne Lathrop in 1991), Rita Gollin on Annie Fields, Luanne Jenkins Hurst on Sophia, Claudia Durst Johnson on Louisa May Alcott, and others of Hawthorne's literary neighbors. The feminist agenda, however shifting in its strategies and approaches, continues in full force, upholding Margaret Fuller's idea that men and women contain both masculine and feminine characteristics, that neither one is purely one or the other, and that both are immersed in the fluidity and entanglement of gender roles, which American society, both in Hawthorne's day and in our own, seeks to render rigid, undeviating, and intransigent.

New Historicist Criticism

Jane Tompkins declared in her 1985 book, *Sensational Designs: The Cultural Work of American Fiction, 1790–1860,* that every text "is engaged in solving a problem or a set of problems specific to the time in which it was written, and that therefore the way to identify its purposes is not to compare it to other examples of the genre, but to relate it to the historical circumstances and the contemporary cultural discourse to which it seems most closely linked" (38). She was throwing down the gauntlet in favor of the New Historicist approach to literature, an approach that was already underway at the time, and focused on Hawthorne in her chapter, "Masterpiece Theater: The Politics of Hawthorne's Literary Reputation." "It seems to me," suggests Pierre Walker in his "Why We Still Read Hawthorne 150 Years Later" (2010) "that the return to history in Hawthorne interpretation reflects just how fundamentally contested our own American history has been for at least the last twenty-five years" (8). The relationship between literary texts and their historical eras opened up a whole new way of exploring the historical and cultural contexts within which they had been written. From Michael J. Colacurcio's perspective, Hawthorne was really examining and exploring in his fiction the moral history and culture of the Calvinist era, while other self-declared New Historicists related Hawthorne's work more explicitly to his own times.

Colacurcio's monumental *The Province of Piety: Moral History in Hawthorne's Early Tales* (1984) expands the range and scope of Hawthorne's fiction by regarding him as a moral historian, a writer determined "to expose the moral premises which shaped the experience of the past" (162). Hawthorne's tales deal with the psychology of characters that are shaped within historical Calvinist boundaries. Thus the Reverend Mr. Hooper re-enacts the practices and beliefs of the Great Awakening, just as Young Goodman Brown, as a third-century Puritan, is a victim of the belief in and power of spectral evidence. Colacurcio dismisses generalized psychological approaches as inadequate and reductionist, thus restoring Hawthorne's very real interests in the cultural and religious history of his region as "a writer of psychohistorical fiction" (306). His is "a plausibly unfolding attempt to discover the moral significance of America's Puritan exception-alism [by] investigating America's self-created moral peculiarities" (28, 35), and the critic, rather than seeking in a positivist fashion Hawthorne's sources and historical allusions for their own sake and thereby overwhelm-ing the texts by exegesis as Perry Miller did, must recognize Hawthorne's moral intent, although at one point, Colacurcio early on exclaims, "My God — Hawthorne *is* Perry Miller" (1).

Colacurcio exposes the various literary camps that have preceded him. The James camp, which included Brooks, Parrington, and Winters, focuses too much on art for art's sake, on Hawthorne's work as merely fanciful, obscure, or unreal, and therefore misses the very real moral issues and questions that Calvinism has raised. The Melville camp, with its emphasis on the aspects of guilt and self-doubt at the Calvinist core, includes Lawrence's notions of diabolical symbolism, Austin Warren's combination of guilt and sin, Matthiessen's sense of tragedy, and Waggoner's vision of a distinctly Christian dimension but has created a more ahistorical and generalized picture of Hawthorne's vision. Crews, of course, in his first Freudian outing, reduced Hawthorne's works all too schematically to identifiable Oedipal conflicts in their plots, even though he recanted later on. Deconstruction, says Colacurcio, "tiresomely locates the placement of natural images within the visual shape of the spatial text but resists examination of the historical semantics" (127). "Hawthorne repeatedly allowed the Puritan language of diabolical simulation and, more generally of the 'invisible world' to control the limits of his own psychological investigations" (285).

In his elaborate and brilliantly thorough analyses of such tales as "Roger Malvin's Burial," "My Kinsman, Major Molineux," "The Gentle Boy," "The May-Pole of Merry Mount," "Young Goodman Brown," and "The Minister's Black Veil," Colacurcio examines all of them from the historical and cultural Calvinist perspective that is revealed within them. He also analyzes Hawthorne's investigation of those historical and cultural perspectives that have warped and limited his characters' points of view.

Puritan self-analysis discovers a sinful self that must perpetually re-examine itself to see where it stands. Such a process creates not only the possibility of individual salvation but also a self-absorption so intense that the world at large can only reflect it. Colacurcio's discussion raises several questions: Can consciousness itself be sinful? Was original sin the recognition of one's own self-consciousness? Does this obsessive quest for a self only recognize that there is none, that there is only a black hole where a self should be, an absence that can only be compensated for by continual self-examination *ad nauseum*? Is this the legacy with which Calvinism has left us? The liberal can discover only "intolerable contradictions," the ironist "powerful but unstable resolutions" (61).

The tales Colacurcio probes reveal complex and often contradictory views. For instance in "My Kinsman, Major Molineux" he meticulously separates Robin's growing up from the beginnings of revolution that surround him in Boston at midnight. Robin's maturation, if that is indeed what is happening, is not merely the psychological underpinnings of revolution, an Oedipal "answer" to why revolutions occur in the first place, as Crews suggested. In relation to the Boston mob, "*His* story is not *theirs*. *His* story is, quite simply, the discovery that they do indeed have one . . . grown-ups have a story which boys do not know" (153). The psychological progression of childhood to adulthood does not merely reflect the horrible circumstances of political conspiracy and mob violence. Colacurcio makes a strong case that Hawthorne meant for the revolution to be understood as the historical one and not just some allegorical element.

For Colacurcio the dichotomy between jollity and gloom in "The May-Pole of Merry Mount" represents a Puritan allegory that John Endicott and his kind had already imposed upon actual history before Hawthorne wrote his story. Endicott may have originally cut down the maypole as a symbolic Calvinist action, thereby reducing history to the Calvinist allegory of good versus evil or youthful pleasure versus adult realities. Thus Hawthorne exposes Endicott's allegorical performance for what it is, both in its historical incarnation and in its inability to deal with the real complexities of the world, as revealed in Hawthorne's story, in which Edith and Edgar's experience of the complex depths of love for one another has already transcended the simplistic jollity-versus-gloom scenario before Endicott in the story even arrives on the scene. "But if man cannot live by allegory alone," Colacurcio declares, "apparently Puritan historiography cannot live without it" (266).

Colacurcio's situating of Hawthorne's tales in actual history, seeing Hawthorne's role as a way of examining and subverting the Calvinist culture from within, broadened Hawthorne criticism and helped provide the historical and cultural context that had long been neglected or underplayed by the New Critics and the linguistic and deconstructionist speculators. In this way the use of history came to play a greater role in the 1980s and beyond, particularly in terms of cultural studies approaches. Deconstruction seemed to self-destruct as wider frameworks of historical circumstance and cultural contexts rose to take its place. Much of this we owe to Colacurcio's work, which has influenced much of the criticism that followed.

In her books *Fiction and Historical Consciousness: The American Romance Tradition* (1989) and *Engendering Romance: Women Writers and the Hawthorne Tradition* (1994), Emily Miller Budick discusses historical consciousness as a kind of limit to American self-absorption and self-reliance and extends the Hawthorne tradition of skepticism that "facilitates the reexperiencing of doubt . . . living with and through what cannot be known . . . to create and sustain together a world of human manufacture" (*Engendering* 5). She also expands Hawthorne's fascination with the romance of the family, which involves Christian patriarchy and the desire to control female reproduction and power. Having studied with Colacurcio, Budick makes a very strong case for the historical basis of the American belief in the myth of self-reliance and independence, based as it is on "a dangerously egocentric, ahistorical imagination that seemed . . . to reach far back into America's past" (xiii). She maintains that that myth must be grounded within a more historical sensibility to counteract the flight from history contained in that myth. Obsessed with Biblical history, Hawthorne's characters "act out an American tendency to prefer grand, mythic reenactments of sacred events to the limited human actions that bespeak moral commitment and responsibility" (*Fiction* 62). One thinks immediately of male characters such as Ethan Brand, Dimmesdale, Hollingsworth, Hooper, and Reuben Bourne.

For Budick, "Hawthorne's historical romantic art establishes the independent existences of the world and the self and sets the stage on which mutuality and independent perception occur" (*Fiction* 135), which strikes me as an elegant way not of getting away from the vision of polarities but of performing them in an interactive manner that helps blunt their rigid and categorical distinctions. Young Goodman Brown can, therefore, be seen as a creature of a particular historical context, not only seeing himself as separate and different from everyone else around him but also relying on the devil's sweeping indictment of humanity, which may be no more than the spectral evidence that surfaces in his own imagination. Brown allegorizes the world because his Calvinist community does so. Hooper's hiding behind the black veil is just another example of Calvinist allegory at work and places his self-absorption in a historical and cultural context. Budick quotes Stanley Cavell, whom she acknowledges as an influence along with Sacvan Bercovitch, as having stated that "men will mythologize their forces, as they always have, project them into demigods, and then serve their projections" (*Fiction* 131).

In her *Engendering Romance*, Budick insists that Hester returns to Boston both to accuse and resist the community of which she will always be a part: "Hester's A establishes that the issue between her and the Puritans is, as Cavell says about Emerson, always joined, never settled, in an unending argument between them" (8). The battle remains unfinished, still engaged and open-ended, like romance itself, that "antimimetic mode of representation [that challenges] the reader to enter into an interpretive relationship with it [in the attempt to discover] whether and what we can know" (4). For Hawthorne, because of his cultural background, matriarchy remains more perilous than patriarchy, and, therefore, he must reintegrate the mother-figure, Hester Prynne, within the patriarchal community, at the same time preserving his doubts about such a position.

In *European Revolutions and the American Literary Renaissance* (1988) Larry J. Reynolds sees Hawthorne as betraying a "strong reactionary spirit" (81) that is opposed to revolution and the mobs they spawn. He also reveals Hawthorne's awareness of the revolutions in Europe in 1848, probably through the letters that Margaret Fuller wrote from Italy for the *New York Tribune*. He points out that the Bloody June Days of 1848 in France brought back memories of the Reign of Terror during the French Revolution and that in Puritan times, the structure used for hangings was called the gallows, never the scaffold. But Hawthorne used that word in *The Scarlet Letter*: "The word *scaffold* served as a synecdoche for a public beheading — by the executioner's axe or the guillotine" (84). Reynolds notes also that the romance is set from May 1642 to May 1649, during the English Civil War. Charles I was beheaded on January 30, 1649, which Hawthorne would have read about in Lamartine's *History of the Girondists*, in which a chilling description of the beheading occurs in almost the exact center of the narrative: "'The plank sunk, the blade glided, the head fell'" (88).

Once again historical events have influenced Hawthorne's work and perspective as opposed to his merely occupying the fanciful territory of a "morbid" imagination. Reynolds goes on to suggest that Hawthorne treats Hester sympathetically as he might have treated Charles I and Louis XIV, as the aristocrat condemned by the masses, but when she begins to speculate about overthrowing society, "she loses the narrator's sympathies" (92).

In *American Romanticism and the Marketplace* (1985) Michael T. Gilmore specifically links the artist's role to the rise of the capitalist marketplace in the antebellum period. Using Marx's idea that in a capitalist economy, the concrete material object becomes a commodity to buy and sell, thus acquiring an exchange value that may have nothing to do with the functional worth of the object at all, he sees this essential split reflected in the American romance's pursuit of symbolic values for concrete reality, a proto-allegorical approach that necessarily separates it from later "realist" fiction. Thus Hester standing in the marketplace at the beginning of *The Scarlet Letter* occupies a role in a society intent on "seeing and being seen" (72), in which the very nature of language's ability to represent anything is called into question as the "exchange value" of the letter shifts and changes. Dimmesdale's private guilt when expressed in public comes out a lie — he never actually admits that he is Pearl's father but allegorizes himself as a generic sinner — as if public speech will always falsify whatever private intentions or origins exist.

Gilmore also takes Hawthorne to task for the happy ending of *The House of The Seven Gables*, viewing him as having created it to make his second romance more marketable — and it did sell more copies at first than *The Scarlet Letter*. Quoting phrases that occur in *Seven Gables*, Gilmore says that Holgrave, who takes a daguerreotype of Judge Pyncheon's corpse, "corresponds to the seer whose 'sadly gifted eye' detects the corpse within, 'the true emblem' of the man's soul. But this truth, which is also the truth of Hawthorne's art, has been characterized throughout the book as private and unsalable" (109). Gilmore charges Hawthorne with hypocrisy akin to the judge's. In the book's conclusion, he says, Hawthorne "follows the example of Judge Pyncheon manufacturing a sunny exterior to win the favor of the public. Passages that denounce the villain for hypocrisy become ironically self-accusing when considered in relation to the novel's ending . . . Hawthorne has become like the character whom he hated most in all his fiction" (110, 111). The ending, therefore, has always struck me as false and sentimentally forced.

American society, with its concern for the weakening of its myths of the Revolution and on the brink of Civil War, desperately sought a new myth, a new sense of community to hold it together, suggests Donald Pease in *Visionary Compacts: American Renaissance Writings in Cultural Context* (1987). Hawthorne helped construct that sense of community with his ideas about the past and memory, however complex and contradictory. As Pease puts it: "romance performed a necessary cultural task" (81), not in the strictly oppositional pattern of us versus them of the Cold War period, which welcomed the New Critics' assessment of Hawthorne's work, but in terms of the particular historical challenges of the 1840s and 1850s. Hawthorne helped to restore a sense of community in the antebellum period of growing capitalism, viewing his characters in terms of their social roles: "In *The Scarlet Letter*, none of the characters are [*sic*] independent of the positions they occupy in the communal narratives" (97). The past, however guilt-ridden, provides cultural memory, as "Hawthorne reminded his readers of their continuing relationship with the ancestral agreements upon which the nation was founded" (274), thus supplying America with newer myths to help sustain itself.

In *The Anatomy of National Fantasy: Hawthorne, Utopia, and Everyday Life* (1991), Lauren Berlant argues that Hawthorne was not as interested in providing America with a new national myth or sense of itself as he was in creating "diverse sites of identity, knowledge, and practice [to] provide a kind of antidote to American monomania" (208). For Berlant, Hawthorne also fully realized that "there is no natural anything that is not also fully textualized according to some prior author; finally, it requires that the subject's body and sensuality be central to the construction of a self-conscious collective subjectivity" (51), a challenge Berlant explores particularly in regard to *The Scarlet Letter*. She also describes how Hawthorne's work also "reveals the incredible hope behind . . . political faith, including the willingness to forget, in advance, its betrayal in the national public sphere" (217).

Since the idea or myth of America already exists, the artist in America may find himself or herself automatically in conflict with it, since he or she in creating his or her own artistic vision must compete with that concept, suggests Myra Jehlen in *American Incarnation: The Individual, the Nation, and the Continent* (1986). America is already a work of art, a fiction, and is, therefore, "immanently transcendent" (10), or as Jehlen quotes Thomas Jefferson as having suggested, "The land is the agent of its own transformation" (57). From such a perspective, artists can be viewed as rebels and subversives, since they may create alternative visions to the American ideology of liberal democracy in which no radical reform is ever necessary since change is automatically built into the American ideal of progress and evolution. The romancer, therefore, tries to avoid the confrontation between fiction/art and the world/reality by establishing multiple points of view and investigating questions of identity. Fiction necessarily already prioritizes conflict in its plots and in doing so may undermine the conventional mythic vision of the creation and evolution of America.

Jehlen re-envisions the Miriam-Hilda polarity in *The Marble Faun*, for example, by describing a hopeless opposition between Kenyon, with his belief in a universal piety and faith in a benevolent design that exists beyond history, and Donatello, immersed as he is in crime, remorse, and the consequences of his own historical actions. For Hilda to help Miriam would be to sink from her pious point of view to the level of blasphemy, but in order to cling to her belief in a divine design, her abandonment of Miriam "amounts to a rejection of story as such" (174). The telling of stories generates conflict, and Hilda wishes not to recognize it. Thus according to Jehlen, "this novel ends in a negation of the terms that made it possible. It is as if Hawthorne had shocked *himself* beyond words" (184). In order to maintain faith in an ideal America and a Protestant view of a benevolent deity, Hawthorne must reject history, says Jehlen, and in doing so reject the possibilities of fiction.

Hawthorne may reject the generic idea of history in *The Marble Faun*, but Peter West in *The Arbiters of Reality: Hawthorne, Melville, and the Rise of Mass Information Culture* (2008) explores another facet of Hawthorne's era, thus adding to the overall vision of Colacurcio, Budick, Gilmore, and Pease (among others) connecting him to his period. The romancer saw himself as a privileged seer within the growing mass culture of newspapers and magazines, as "the figure who redefines reality in the face of the fictionalizing threat of the marketplace" (64), and attempted "to recast the authentic as that which resists linguistic and verbal representation, as the defining achievements of autonomous, uncompromised selfhood" (x). The romance, therefore, existed as a reaction against "the fictionalizing forces of modernization by redefining the real as that which eludes specific technologies and modes of consumption" (8). Such a narrative strategy interrogates the reality that exists beneath the surfaces of mass culture and attempts "to philosophically exploit the instability of . . . truth and fiction at a particular moment in time" (12–13). As a New Historicist, West defines reality "as a category constantly being shaped by social, economic, and psychological conditions" (17) and thus views Hawthorne as implicated in the new marketplace of magazines and the "penny press" — how could he not be? By attempting to write about the truth of the human condition that will always remain too complex and elusive for newspaper narratives, addressing his vision of that truth by way of his self-conscious storytelling in an effort to subvert the daily fodder of spectacle and sensationalism that pretends to "an unmediated relationship with reality." David S. Reynolds would agree in *Beneath the American Renaissance: The Subversive Imagination in the Age of Emerson and Melville* (1988), in which he meticulously exposes how writers such as Hawthorne reacted to daily spectacles such as were made of murders and other crimes and "ironized" and subverted their straightforward narratives.

Reynolds attacks the notion that writers such as Hawthorne and Melville were isolated from the surrounding culture, that they were marginalized and alienated by their lofty literary pursuits. He views them as very much products of their times, wrestling with the same themes and ideas that filled popular fiction and potboilers — from murder and mayhem to repressed sexuality and melodrama. For Reynolds our classic authors concentrated on subjects that were very popular at the time they were writing — from socialist communities to whaling, middle-class manners, race — but complicated them by means of paradox, irony, and ambiguity. In a sense he applies New Critical qualities to their fictions while placing their works squarely within the arena of popular culture. They celebrated ultimate mystery in their often self-conscious and open-ended art as opposed to the melodramatic resolutions of popular fiction such as celebrating the many secrets and unresolved contradictions and conspiracies of *The Scarlet Letter* instead of conjuring up the final, airtight solutions of a book like *The Da Vinci Code*.

Racial Criticism

The New Historicism provided historical and cultural contexts for Hawthorne's fiction that had been all but avoided by the New Critics and the practitioners of psychological and myth-based criticism. New Historical critics rooted Hawthorne's work in historical soil as opposed to the more "transcendental" and trans-historical tools of previous critics. As just mentioned in Reynolds's case, particularly in the 1990s, they also began to tackle issues of race, which had been marginalized and ignored for years, probably because, however present race was in Hawthorne's fiction, he too had marginalized it.

When it comes to critical approaches to race in Hawthorne's fiction, the lines have been carefully drawn. Jean Fagan Yellin in 1989 argued that Hawthorne employs a "strategy of avoidance and denial," since the "link between . . . metaphorical slavery and the literal enslavement of blacks is conspicuously absent" in his fiction (88, 97). Like Bercovitch and Arac Yellin applies New Historicist approaches to expose Hawthorne's conservatism and his failure to support abolition. On the other hand, Leland Person argued in 2001 that Hawthorne intended to undermine the feminist argument that not only slaves but also white women were enslaved, thus critiquing "the conflation in nineteenth-century victimology of white mothers and slave mothers" (664). Person believes that Hawthorne was aware of the false presumption that equated "the identification of black and white women's experiences and politics" (669), which blurred the distinct differences between them.

Hawthorne was aware of slavery as the most pressing political issue of the time. In "Chiefly About War Matters" he mentions that the *Mayflower*, which brought white English colonists to the New World, was also used to bring slaves, "a monstrous birth." Teresa A. Goddu shows convincingly in her *Gothic America: Narrative, History, and the Nation* (1997) that all of Hawthorne's jobs in various customs houses and consulates were intimately involved with the slave trade, which lay at the heart of much commercial traffic at sea: "To enter international commerce meant taking part in the slave trade" (64) as Salem had for years. His editing — some would say complete re-writing — of his friend Horatio Bridge's *Journal of an African Cruiser* reveals how aware he was of the trade: "I really do consider the shooting of these niggers a matter of very questionable propriety; and am glad, upon the whole, that you bagged no game [i. e., killed or captured no Africans] on either of those days . . . In one point of view, these warlike occurrences [the battles that involved the slave trade] are very fortunate — that is, in supplying matter for the journal" (56). In arguing for these occurrences as fortunate for Bridge's narrative, Hawthorne also reveals a much more callous attitude toward Africans and slaves than just being aware of the slave trade in general. Goddu goes on to suggest that Hawthorne generally considered his editing work more commercial, while acknowledging that his role as a writer of imaginative fiction was far less popular in the sense of being far less commercial. She maintains, however, that writing romances could be considered a "more liberal form of editing" (57) and that editing and writing were not as oppositional as he tried to make them appear. Perhaps as an editor of Bridge's text and as a writer of Franklin Pierce's campaign biography, he felt less bound by a responsibility to deal with slavery from a more personal point of view.

David Anthony's "Class, Culture, and the Trouble with White Skin in Hawthorne's *The House of the Seven Gables*" (1999) tackles the issue of race head on, exploring Hawthorne's use of it as a way to deal with class distinctions and the rise of mass culture in a similar manner to the way in which Leverenz suggests he may have used gender to avoid those same issues. Anthony presents a very strong case that Hawthorne used race as a way of commenting on class divisions, so that a character like the artisan Matthew Maule, in talking with "black Scipio" in Holgrave's tale of Alice Pyncheon, could claim "to look black like yourself" in an effort to share the black's sense of victimization and oppression: "There is simply no more powerful metaphor for pain, abjection, and dispossession in antebellum culture" (456). The working class often appeared dirty and unhygienic to Hawthorne, and by making references to African blood and the like he could use race as a metaphor for such appearances in order to obscure the very real developing class divisions he may have been afraid of. According to Anthony, however, "Hawthorne's repeated efforts to displace class difference onto racial difference" ultimately failed (459).

Anthony goes on to point out how Hawthorne relies on black stereotypes, a visible irony in that he failed to see that such stereotypes were the products of the very mass culture he claimed to despise or at least be repelled by. Hepzibah's selling Jim Crow cookies and the white pale aesthete Clifford looking out the arched window onto the Italian organ grinder and his dancing monkey only confirm Hawthorne's use of such blatantly prejudicial images of blackness without his apparent awareness that he was doing so. "Class decline and racial degeneracy" in *The House of the Seven Gables,* says Anthony, were all too easily clothed in then-current African American stereotypes. In fact, as Anthony concludes, "Hawthorne appears to have found himself reliant upon fantasies of race produced within a mass culture [Anthony investigates several of them] which itself worked consistently (if not always intentionally) to undermine the stability of race as a category." Hawthorne seemed to fail to realize "that race could not be used as a reliable means of waging conflicts of class and culture, in particular because 'race' was itself a fiction frequently manipulated by the very people and texts from whom and from which he sought to distance himself" (256). The paleness of Judge Pyncheon's corpse may even suggest, says Anthony, the final overthrow of "the conception of white racial

purity which the protective walls of high culture have been erected to protect" (458).

As Philip Roth wrote in *The Human Stain* in 2000, it may be to
Hawthorne's credit that he alerted us to the "persecuting spirit, [to that]
ecstasy of sanctimony [and] the stringent rituals of purification" in
American culture (2), but in recent years Hawthorne's politics and their
intersection with his opinions on race have come under careful scrutiny,
most recently by Arthur Riss and Larry Reynolds. For instance, while
David Anthony had explained that "the black bodies" in *The House of the
Seven Gables* "refuse to adhere to a depth model of the self" (444), Riss
argues that many whites had difficulty with even thinking of a black body
as a self.

"Where once Hawthorne had no politics, now it seems that all he has
are bad politics," writes Riss in *Race, Slavery, and Liberalism in Nineteenth-
Century American Literature* (2006), quoting Jonathan Arac's description
of Hawthorne's politics as "a politics of issueless patience" (17). Riss goes
on to examine in detail the nineteenth-century obsession with the Negro
slave as a person: *was* a slave a person? Could he or she ever be? For Riss
the idea of a "person" becomes an effect, not a being deserving of individual human rights in terms of how we think of such issues today. He,
therefore, attacks the kind of political liberalism, which Bercovitch also
critiques in *The Office of the Scarlet Letter*, that can engulf and absorb all
differences as it looks toward a future of ultimate reconciliation.
Consequently it remains a politics of process that does its best to avoid
specific problems, initiating a strategy of pluralism that remains indefinitely
and probably infinitely open to everyone. It pursues an open-ended conti-
nuity of various procedures as opposed to content: as Riss puts it,
"Liberalism offers only a set of formal principles rather than a particular or
predetermined interpretation" (123). It thus evades the whole question of
the Negro in the nineteenth century, whether or not the slave can be considered a person at all. As Riss suggests, "Liberalism . . . brands any specific
meaning or identity as arbitrary and contingent and thus attempts to transcend such particularism" (123), as Hawthorne does in writing about the
"A" in *The Scarlet Letter*.

In Riss's view, Hawthorne shared in the "Negrophobia" of all his
white friends and neighbors. For Riss Hawthorne "is not critiquing racist
hierarchies; he is critiquing the materialist logic on which such hierarchies
have been conventionally predicated" (147). Hawthorne attacks the use of
skin color as an ontological category and the pseudo-scientific analyses that
marked African Americans as an inferior race as the basis for racial distinctions "without ever doubting the legitimacy of racial hierarchies" (149).
(The Swiss naturalist, Louis Agassiz, was both convinced about and
appalled by their inferiority.) Since the Negro, in Riss's conception of
Hawthorne's view, has no real self or at least displays an unstable self, the

Negro can therefore be seen as an aesthetic object, threatening "the very premises of citizenship and personhood" (161).

Riss sees Donatello and Miriam Schaefer as the "dark couple" in *The Marble Faun* and as an example of the havoc that can be caused by such "racist" possibilities. Riss's argument may be a bit tortuous and circular at times, but he produces many worthwhile insights. For instance, "because the Negro's essential character is to lack a materially stable character, the Negro can never be transformed into a citizen of the United States" (161). Thus Hilda, rejecting the aesthetics of Rome as well as what she sees as Miriam's attempts to aestheticize the murder of the model by Donatello, makes the right choice in doing so and abandons the old city with her husband-to-be Kenyon.

In *Devils and Rebels: The Making of Hawthorne's Damned Politics* (2008), Larry J. Reynolds deliberately places Hawthorne front and center amid the politics of his day with its blatant racism, providing thorough and excellent accounts of presidential politics, the Cotton Whigs of Boston and the Conscience Whigs of Salem, John Brown's martyrdom and murder, the annexation of Texas and the spread of slavery, and the escalating violence of the 1850s that would eventually erupt in civil war. He also makes it clear that Emerson, Thoreau, Theodore Parker, and other ardent abolitionists were as racist as Hawthorne but that because they came down hard on the necessity for violence to preserve the union and Hawthorne did not, Hawthorne has been castigated for this human failing while they have not been as closely cross-examined about their ideas about race as they should be.

Reynolds describes Hawthorne's politics as based on pacifism, but it seems to me that Hawthorne was more opposed to self-righteous violence than he was an outright and self-declared pacifist. Reynolds insists that Hawthorne "drew upon images of revolutionary violence and witchcraft hysteria to shape and explore contemporary political issues" (229); linking witchcraft, rebellion, and the obsessively-focused rage and violence of the abolitionists against the South, Hawthorne despised false accusations, the fanaticism of leaders, and the readiness of the people to submit to their fears and superstitions (52). It is Hawthorne's critique of "the notion of righteous violence" (203) that marks his vision and his work, which may or may not be described as pacifism, depending on one's perspective.

Reynolds forces many aspects of Hawthorne's romances into his politically astute thesis — Does Phoebe really represent the electorate? Is Donatello actually made demonic by murdering the model? Does a deeply felt Christian heroism really lurk at the center of *The Marble Faun?* — but his overall vision strikes me as right on target. Race and politics appear as the flip sides of the same sordid coin, and no matter how many times Hawthorne praised Franklin Pierce's pro-Union position (even though it was in opposition to his own more separatist and regional approach), he could not have avoided the realization of how pro-Southern that position actually was by Pierce's supporting the status quo.

As is pointed out by Hawthorne biographer, Brenda Wineapple, in her 2005 essay, "Nathaniel Hawthorne Writer; or, The Fleeing of the Biographied," the current climate in academia "is moralistic in tone and aim, despite pretensions to the contrary [and] critics less overtly psycho-analytic now travel a different and presumably 'historical' road, upbraid-ing Hawthorne for what he did not write rather than looking at whom he knew and what he did" (188–89). In this context she raises the issue of race:

> To take one case, consider the recent books that flay Hawthorne for *not* mentioning race in his stories or novels, even though race plays a part in such diverse writings as "Old News," "A Select Party," and "Sunday at Home," as well as *The House of the Seven Gables* and *The Marble Faun*. In truth, race was very much on Hawthorne's mind, early and late, particularly in his unfinished "Elixir of Life" manu-scripts, where the main character, Septimius, is descended from both Indians and Africans. Septimius is a "hybrid" (*CE* XIII, 40): Hawthorne's term is not used in its current fashion as something salutary. "The mixture of race is a crime against nature," Hawthorne writes in his notes to himself, [and] "therefore pernicious" (*CE* XIII, 40, 246).
>
> That Hawthorne writes about racial issues directly, forcefully, or unpleasantly is no discovery . . . (189)

Reynolds contends that Hawthorne was suspicious of reformers, of partisans in any guise, at least in theory, but in terms of the spoils system and the political landscape, he played his cards well in order to secure the job at the custom house in Salem until he was fired for "signing off on the corrupt practices within the customhouse" (161). He held to one of his most primary beliefs that in trying to achieve good in the world, humanity always overlooks the unforeseen consequences that result from its actions. Reynolds quotes Hawthorne's statement that it would always be the folly of man to think "that he can ever be of any importance to the welfare of the world; or that any settled plan of his, to be carried on through a length of time, could be successful." "Such a humbling thought," Reynolds maintains, "lies at the heart of Hawthorne's politics" and infuriated the abolitionists (qtd. in Reynolds 124).

The flip side of this essential vision demonizes the enemy, a nasty American trait that seems built into the Calvinist cosmos in all its exclusive racist, gendered, class-conscious, and exclusive myths. Virtually all of Hawthorne's major male characters suffer from this, whether demonizing the Native American and the African American or, as Michael Rogin sug-gests in terms of other American "demons," "the papal whore of Babylon

. . . the demon rum, the bomb-throwing anarchist, the many-tentacled Communist conspiracy, the agents of international terrorism." All of this reveals "a consistent, repressed feature of American sociopolitical history" (qtd. in Reynolds, 79), which in Hawthorne's time as in our own, I also explored in my *Paradigms of Paranoia: The Culture of Conspiracy in Contemporary American Fiction* (2005). Hawthorne easily made the connection between repressed fantasies and violence, recognizing his own complicity in such things. As Saidiya V. Hartman asks, quoted in a footnote in Reynolds's book, "Is the act of 'witnessing' a kind of looking no less *entangled* with the wielding of power and the extraction of enjoyment?" (263, emphasis added). Such a position may have been shared by Hawthorne in his awareness of what he called "the tendency of putting ice into the blood" (241), always keeping a sharp eye on the events around him, thus serving and maintaining the tragic entanglement of all human issues and desires.

The bicentennial of Hawthorne's birth in 2005 gave rise to several commentaries and reassessments of Hawthorne's works. In her introduction to the volume of essays *Hawthorne and the Real* (2005), Millicent Bell makes clear that "our" Hawthorne was very aware of social realities and "the objective common conditions and public issues of his day" (viii). Therefore in this volume we find several essays continuing to discuss and wrestle with politics, feminism, slavery, race, and other pertinent and very real issues of Hawthorne's day and our own. Trilling's Hawthorne may have been "more the moral allegorist than the historian" (vii), but "ours" is not. For Bell, Hawthorne's concern with the relationship between the imagination and actuality is as much a problem of the nature of that actuality as it is of imagination.

Many contemporary works have opened up even further territories to be explored in Hawthorne scholarship. In *The Half-Vanished Structure: Hawthorne's Allegorical Dialectics* (2001), Magnus Ullen relates Hawthorne's use of allegory to his Christian faith and begins to recover the role that religion or at least Hawthorne's religious speculations played in his life and art. Allegory, says Ullen, allows for distance between the material and the spiritual, making room for the necessity of mediation in the romance. At one point Ullen suggests that "the concept of mediation is central to all dialectical thinking, [and therefore] the mediating function of Christ in Hawthorne is relocated to the very medium through which he attempts 'to open an intercourse with the world:' the romance." For Hawthorne, art doesn't replace religion, "rather, it replicates it. Hawthorne relies upon the romance to perform the role once occupied by Christ" (100). However at the same time he recognizes that mediation is not itself a matter of salvation and deliverance; "interpretive freedom is not depicted as a desired *telos* [since] it marks rather the existential state that the individual is condemned to as a consequence of the Fall." The very necessity to rely on allegory and thus subject ourselves "to a conception of the world as a system of meanings" reveals how much we have fallen from religious faith and vision (71). It is this precarious equilibrium that the best of Hawthorne's art achieves, a perilous symmetry that can shatter at any moment, a consistently dark entanglement that is not to be denied.

The title of Jason Courtmanche's 2008 book, *How Nathaniel Hawthorne's Narratives Are Shaped by Sin: His Use of Biblical Typology in His Four Major Works,* reveals its trajectory. Since typology is virtually ignored in the academy these days and completely unknown to most undergraduates, Courtmanche's book comes at a necessary time, revealing the biblical tradition that Hawthorne was raised in and worked with. Hawthorne's own "blasted allegories," whether blasted because he cursed them or blasted in the sense of being consciously shattered, incorporated that biblical tradition, and Courtmanche prowls through the major romances to explore how Hawthorne both uses and undermines it, in some ways similar to Emily Dickinson's use of biblical rhetoric.

Leland S. Person in his essay, "Nathaniel Hawthorne" in *Prospects for the Study of American Literature* (2009), has suggested future avenues for scholarly work. These would include a reassessment of the unfinished manuscripts, which have always been dismissed; the editing and publishing of Sophia Hawthorne's *Cuba Journal, 1833–1835,* which is being undertaken at this very moment; a new critical edition of Hawthorne's eight *American Notebooks;* raising "Chiefly About War Matters" to the ranks of Hawthorne's finest essays; more work on Hawthorne's reputation abroad, especially in places like Japan, where devoted Hawthorne scholars continue to thrive; providing a critical edition of Horatio Bridge's *Journal of An African Cruiser;* and studying more comprehensively the 1828–1850 period of Hawthorne's career. Person also notes how much Hawthorne was assaulted in the 1980s and 1990s for his conservative views on race and gender and suggests that perhaps it is time to move on and consider him as an analyst of such issues, not merely the product or victim of them.

Many issues remain to be explored. For instance Hawthorne's view of the self as elusive and enigmatic anticipates similar visions in the contemporary fiction of Joan Didion, Don DeLillo, Thomas Pynchon, Joyce Carol Oates, and Tim O'Brien, among others, as well as in that of modernists such as Faulkner, Styron, and Roth. John Updike, in fact, wrote a series of three novels, each of which focuses on one of the three adult characters in *The Scarlet Letter: A Month of Sundays* (1975, on Dimmesdale), *Roger's Version* (1986, on Chillingworth), and *S.* (1988, on Hester). Hawthorne's use of a series of clauses to undermine preceding statements in his fiction, a kind of deconstructive action within his texts, suggests a proto-postmodernist style that we often see in all of the authors just mentioned above. His awareness of how history can be used by various cultural and social authorities also reveals his interest in it as narrative, as a fictional construct. His skepticism tackles all absolutes, whether religious, cultural, or otherwise, and thus leaves open the continuing debate on such issues. His exploration of the uneasy alliance between violence and American identity, war and American "exceptionalism," remain ongoing concerns, as does his penetrating representation of the clash between the individual and the state, what the British writer Anthony Burgess defined as the greatest theme in our contemporary world. Hawthorne's concerns in terms of reformers and scientists continue to underscore our own uncertainties about the blessings and horrors of technology, and his interest in genetics and ancestry both preceded and anticipated Darwin as evolution continues to be a much-debated topic. Hawthorne's perspective on capitalism and its problems still haunts us today.

Dualisms and polarization continue to inhabit Hawthorne criticism as they have his fiction in various forms of multiple choice, alternative interpretations, New Critical ambiguities, paradoxes and contradictions, and the ongoing analysis of whether he relied on types or tropes in telling his tales. For an example all we need do is look at the various explanations he sets up in regard to Dimmesdale's confession at the end of *The Scarlet Letter*, whether it is honest, false, fraudulent, spiritually enlightening, or just plain self-justifying. Whereas the nineteenth century puzzled over his Augustan style vs. his morbid content, the nature of Calvinism in his work (aesthetic or religious vision?), the head vs. the heart, his penchant for allegory vs. what he called his "blasted allegories," his New England regionalism vs. the possibilities of his becoming a more nationally-recognized "classical" author, and whether or not he wrote romances or novels, twentieth- and twenty-first-century critics have grappled with psychological puzzles such as conscious control vs. unconscious compulsions in terms of his writing and his characters, middle-class manners vs. psychological depths, Hawthorne as proto-feminist vs. misogynist, political "innocent" vs. racist politico, and whether he was totally in control of his material and had a definite literary strategy or was just a pawn and victim of the literary and cultural dilemmas of his own era. For me the quantum notion of entanglement helps describe this polarization in many ways.

Manjit Kumar in *Quantum: Einstein, Bohr, and the Great Debate about the Nature of Reality* has defined entanglement in the subatomic realm as a theory "in which two or more particles remain inexorably linked no matter how far apart they are" (378). At first they appear to be separate and mutually exclusive, but experiments have revealed that they are, in fact, permanently entwined and ultimately complimentary. Each invades and subverts the other. Each appears as one side of the same coin. None stands alone and absolute. Hawthorne in his fiction stages this dilemma, marking his territory between polarities, aware of their existence as part of a kind of allegorical "hangover" within New England culture and the Calvinist tradition. Looked at in this way, I think we can in some sense transcend the dualistic perspective, however deeply rooted in his texts, the critical responses to them and our own American perspective, and carve out a new landscape for Hawthorne's romances.

Of course critics must be wary of every theoretical approach, since Hawthorne's fiction structurally and stylistically doesn't allow itself to be entirely explained or defined by any one of them. Like Coverdale in *The Blithedale Romance,* we must be aware that when we isolate certain passages and patterns to support our theories, we are, in effect, disconnecting them from the intricacies of the text and illuminating them in ways that can deform and distort them. This has always been the critic's problem, but with Hawthorne we must be even more on our guard.

It is interesting that in view of Hawthorne's interest in management and labor issues, complicated by race and gender in his own times, he still carries formidable clout in strictly economic terms in contemporary culture. For instance, Christie's recently auctioned off the corrected proofs of *The Scarlet Letter,* discovered in 2004 in a drawer at the Natick, Massachusetts Historical Society, to an anonymous bidder for $545,000. Thus it seems we are still entangled in Hawthorne's work and the cultural roles and aesthetic values he continues to embody.

Works Cited

Abbott, Anne W. "*The Scarlet Letter.*" *North American Review* 71, no. 148 (July 1850): 135–38. In Idol/Jones, 127–32.

Abbott, John S. C. "Bowdoin College — Nathaniel Hawthorne." 1875. In Bosco/Murphy, 156–60.

Abel, Darrel. *The Moral Picturesque: Studies in Hawthorne's Fiction.* West Lafayette: Purdue UP, 1988.

Anthony, David. "Class, Culture, and the Trouble with White Skin in Hawthorne's *The House of the Seven Gables.*" In *The House of the Seven Gables*, ed. Robert S. Levine, 438–59. New York: Norton, 2006.

Arac, Jonathan. "The Politics of *The Scarlet Letter.*" In *Ideology and Classic American Literature*, ed. Sacvan Bercovitch and Myra Jehlen, 247–66. New York: Cambridge UP, 1986.

Argersinger, Jana L., and Leland S. Person, eds. *Hawthorne and Melville: Writing a Relationship.* Athens: The U of Georgia P, 2008.

Arvin, Newton. *Hawthorne.* 1929. Rpt., New York: Russell & Russell, 1961.

Auerbach, Jonathan. *The Romance of Failure: First-Person Fictions of Poe, Hawthorne, and James.* New York: Oxford UP, 1989.

Auster, Paul. "A Life in Books: My Five Most Important Books." *Newsweek*, 9 February 2009, 17.

Barlowe, Jamie. *The Scarlet Mob of Scribblers: Rereading Hester Prynne.* Carbondale: Southern Illinois UP, 2000.

Bates, Katherine Lee, ed. and introduction. *The Works of Nathaniel Hawthorne*, 14 vols. New York: Crowell, 1902.

Baym, Nina. "Revisiting Hawthorne's Feminism." In *Hawthorne and the Real: Bicentennial Essays*, ed. Millicent Bell, 107–24.

———. *The Shape of Hawthorne's Career.* Ithaca: Cornell UP, 1976.

Bell, Michael Davitt. *The Development of American Romance: The Sacrifice of Relation.* Chicago: The U of Chicago P, 1980.

———. *Hawthorne and the Historical Romance of New England.* Princeton: Princeton UP, 1971.

Bell, Millicent, ed. *Hawthorne and the Real: Bicentennial Essays.* Columbus: Ohio State UP, 2005.

———. *Hawthorne's View of the Artist.* New York: SUNY Press, 1962.

————, ed. *New Essays on Hawthorne's Major Tales*. New York: Cambridge UP, 1993.

————. "The Prophecy of Hester Prynne." *The New York Times Book Review*, June 11, 2000, 9.

Bellis, Peter J. *Writing Revolution: Aesthetics and Politics in Hawthorne, Whitman, and Thoreau*. Athens: The U of Georgia P, 2003.

Bensick, Carol Marie. *A Nouvelle Beatrice: Renaissance and Romance in "Rappaccini's Daughter."* New Brunswick: Rutgers UP, 1985.

Benson, Eugene. "Poe and Hawthorne." *The Galaxy*, vi, December 1868, 742–48. In Crowley, 432–39. In Idol/Jones, 466–70.

Bercovitch, Sacvan. *The Office of The Scarlet Letter*. Baltimore: The Johns Hopkins UP, 1991.

————. "*The Scarlet Letter*: A Twice-Told Tale." *Nathaniel Hawthorne Review* 22, no. 2 (fall 1996): 1–20.

Bercovitch, Sacvan, and Myra Jehlen, eds. *Ideology and Classic American Literature*. Cambridge: Cambridge UP, 1986.

Berlant, Lauren. *The Anatomy of National Fantasy: Hawthorne, Utopia, and Everyday Life*. Chicago: U of Chicago P, 1991.

————. "Fantasies of Utopia in *The Blithedale Romance*." *American Literary History* 1, 1989: 30–63.

Blomfield, John. "Branded with the 'Scarlet U': From Manhattan Commutes to Morning School Drop-off Rituals: It's Not Easy Adjusting to Unemployed Life." *Newsweek*, 3 March 2009, 22.

"Book Notices." *Portland Transcript*, 13, no. 50 (30 March 1850): 3. In Idol/Jones, 121.

Bosco, Ronald A., and Jillmarie Murphy, eds. *Hawthorne in His Own Time*. Iowa City: U of Iowa P, 2007. In text as Bosco/Murphy.

Brickhouse, Anna C. "'I Do Abhor an Indian Story': Hawthorne and the Allegorization of Racial 'Commixture.'" *Emerson Society Quarterly* 42 (1996): 233–53.

Bridge, Horatio. *Journal of an African Cruiser*, ed. Nathaniel Hawthorne. New York: Wiley and Putnam, 1845.

————. *Personal Recollections of Nathaniel Hawthorne*. New York: Harper and Brothers, 1893.

————. "*Twice-Told Tales*." *Age* 6, no. 17 (5 April 1837): 3. In Idol/Jones, 21–22.

Bright, Henry Arthur. "On First Meeting Hawthorne in America, 1852." In Bosco/Murphy, 59–61.

"A British Objection to Hawthorne and his Audience, from an unsigned essay, 'Modern Novelists — Great and Small.'" *Blackwood's Magazine*, May 1835, lxxvii, 562–66. In Crowley, 310–13.

Brodhead, Richard. *Hawthorne, Melville, and the Novel.* Chicago: The U of Chicago P, 1976.

———. *The School of Hawthorne.* New York: Oxford UP, 1986.

Brook, Thomas. *Cross-Examinations of Law and Literature: Cooper, Hawthorne, Stowe and Melville.* Cambridge: Cambridge UP, 1987.

Brooks, Van Wyck. *The Flowering of New England, 1815–1865.* New York: E. P. Dutton, 1940.

———. *New England: Indian Summer.* New York: E. P. Dutton, 1940.

Brownson, Orestes. From a review in the *Boston Quarterly Review*, April 1842, v, 251–52. In Crowley, 86–87.

———. From a review in *Brownson's Quarterly Review*, October 1850, n.s., v, 528–32. In Crowley, 175–79.

Budick, Emily Miller. *Engendering Romance: Women Writers and the Hawthorne Tradition, 1850–1990.* New Haven: Yale UP, 1994.

———. *Fiction and Historical Consciousness: The American Romance Tradition.* New Haven: Yale UP, 1989.

Buell, Lawrence. *New England Literary Culture: From Revolution through Renaissance.* Cambridge: Cambridge UP, 1986.

Burton, Richard. *Literary Leaders of America: A Class Book on American Literature.* Boston: Lothrop Publishing Company, 1904.

Byrnes, P. Cartoon in *The New Yorker*, 8 and 15 June 2009, 66.

Cady, Edwin H. "'The Wizard Hand': Hawthorne, 1864–1900." In *Hawthorne Centenary Essays*, ed. Roy Harvey Pearce, 317–66. Columbus: Ohio State UP, 1964.

Cameron, Sharon. *The Corporeal Self: Allegories of the Body in Melville and Hawthorne.* New York: Columbia UP, 1981.

Canedy, Dana. "Florida 'Scarlet Letter' Law Is Repealed by Gov. Bush." *The New York Times*, 31 May 2003. Accessed 23 February 2011. http://www.nytimes.com/2003/05/31/us/florida-scarlet-letter-law-is-repealed-by-gov-bush.html.

Cantwell, Robert. *Nathaniel Hawthorne: The American Years.* 1948; rpt., New York: Octagon Books, 1971.

Carlson, Jane. "Readers Responding to 'Rappaccini's Daughter.'" *The English Journal* 77, no. 1 (January 1988): 49–53.

Carton, Evan. *The Rhetoric of American Romance: Dialectic and Identity in Emerson, Dickinson, Poe, and Hawthorne.* Baltimore: The Johns Hopkins UP, 1985.

Cella, Lorraine. "Reading the Complex World: Students Approach *The Scarlet Letter* from Multiple Perspectives." *The English Journal* 91, no. 6 (July 2002): 77–82.

Chai, Leon. *The Romantic Foundations of the American Renaissance*. Ithaca: Cornell UP, 1987.

Chase, Richard. *The American Novel and Its Tradition*. Garden City, NY: Doubleday Anchor Books, 1957.

Chorley, Henry Fothergill. From a review in the *Athenaeum*, 23 August 1845, 830–31. In Crowley, 95–96.

———. "Nathaniel Hawthorne." *Athenaeum* [England], 11 June 1864, 808. In Idol/Jones, 437–38.

———. "*The Scarlet Letter*: A Romance." *Athenaeum*, 15 June 1850, 634. In Idol/Jones, 126–27.

Clark, C. E. Frazer, Jr. *Nathaniel Hawthorne: A Descriptive Bibliography*. Pittsburgh: U of Pittsburgh P, 1978.

Clark, Lewis Gaylord. "*The Scarlet Letter*." *Knickerbocker* 35, no. 5 (May 1850): 451–52. In Idol/Jones, 125–26.

Clarke, Sarah Ann. Quoted in Bosco in his "Introduction," xxxviii. From "Sarah Clarke's Reminiscences of the Peabodys and Hawthorne," by Joel Myerson. *The Nathaniel Hawthorne Journal*, 1973, 131–32.

Coale, Samuel Chase. *In Hawthorne's Shadow: American Romance from Melville to Mailer*. Lexington: The UP of Kentucky, 1985.

———. *Mesmerism and Hawthorne: Mediums of American Romance*. Tuscaloosa: The U of Alabama P, 1998.

———. *Paradigms of Paranoia: The Culture of Conspiracy in Contemporary American Fiction*. Tuscaloosa: The U of Alabama P, 2005.

Cohen, B. Bernard, ed. *The Recognition of Nathaniel Hawthorne*. Ann Arbor: The U of Michigan P, 1969.

Cohen, Nancy. "Nathaniel Hawthorne, Family Reunited in Grave." *NPR*, 27 June 2006. Accessed 23 February 2011. http://www.npr.org/templates/story/story.php?storyId=5516305.

Colacurcio, Michael J., ed. *New Essays on* The Scarlet Letter. New York: Cambridge UP, 1985.

———. *The Province of Piety: Moral History in Hawthorne's Early Tales*. Cambridge: Harvard UP, 1984.

"Contemporary Literature in America." *The Westminster Review*, October 1852, lviii, 592–98. In Crowley, 259–64.

Conway, Moncure D. *Life of Nathaniel Hawthorne*. London: Walter Scott, 1890.

Courtmanche, Jason Charles. *How Nathaniel Hawthorne's Narratives are Shaped by Sin: His User of Biblical Typology in His Four Major Works*. Lewiston, NY: The Edwin Mellen P, 2008.

Cowley, Malcolm. "Hawthorne in Solitude." (1948) In Cowley, *New England Writers and Writing,* edited and with an introduction by Donald W. Faulkner, 3–27. Hanover: UP of New England, 1996.

———. "The Hawthornes in Paradise." (1958) In Cowley, *New England Writers and Writing,* edited and with an introduction by Donald W. Faulkner, 28–43. Hanover: UP of New England, 1996.

Coxe, Arthur Cleveland. "The Writings of Hawthorne." *Church Review and Ecclesiastical Register* 3, no. 4 (January 1851): 489–511. In Idol/Jones, 146–52.

Crews, Frederick. *The Sins of the Fathers: Hawthorne's Psychological Themes.* Berkeley: U of California P, 1966.

———. *Skeptical Engagements.* New York: Oxford UP, 1986.

Crowley, J. Donald, ed. *Hawthorne: The Critical Heritage.* London: Routledge and Kegan Paul, 1970. In text as Crowley.

Curtis, George William. "Editor's Easy Chair." *Harper's Monthly* 66 (March 1883): 629–31. In Idol/Jones, 410–13.

———. "Hawthorne." In *Homes of American Authors.* New York: G. P. Putnam, 1853, 291–313. In Bosco/Murphy, 64–78.

———. "Hawthorne, the Salem Recluse." From an unsigned review in the *North American Review* 99, no. 205 (October 1864): 539–57. In Crowley, 412–21.

Daniels, Bruce. "Bad Movie/Worse History: The 1995 Unmaking of *The Scarlet Letter.*" *Journal of Popular Culture* 32.4 (Spring 1999): 1–11.

Dauber, Kenneth. *Rediscovering Hawthorne.* Princeton: Princeton UP, 1977.

Davidson, Edward Hutchins. *Hawthorne's Last Phase.* New Haven: Yale UP, 1949.

Davis, Clark. *Hawthorne's Shyness: Ethics, Politics, and the Question of Engagement.* Baltimore: The Johns Hopkins UP, 2005.

Davis, Rebecca Harding. "Memories of the Hawthornes at the Wayside in 1862," "A Little Gossip," *Scribner's Magazine* 28, November 1900, 562–66, 568–70. In Bosco/Murphy, 102–9.

"Dead Letter." *Denver Westword,* 30 March 1994. Accessed 29 December 2008. http://www.westword.com/1994-03-30/culture/dead-letter/.

Dekker, George. *The American Historical Romance.* Cambridge: Cambridge UP, 1987.

Deming, Richard. *Listening on All Sides: Toward an Emersonian Ethics of Reading.* Stanford: Stanford UP, 2007.

DeSalvo, Louise. *Nathaniel Hawthorne.* Brighton: The Harvester Press, 1987.

Dirda, Michael. "Spellbound." Review of *Man in the Dark* by Paul Auster. *The New York Review of Books,* 4 December 2008, 36–38.

Dolis, John. *The Style of Hawthorne's Gaze: Regarding Subjectivity.* Tuscaloosa: The U of Alabama P, 1993.

Donohue, Agnes McNeill. *A Casebook on the Hawthorne Question.* New York: Crowell, 1963.

———. *Hawthorne: Calvin's Ironic Stepchild.* Kent, OH: The Kent State UP, 1985.

Doubleday, Neal Frank. *Hawthorne's Early Tales: A Critical Study.* Durham: Duke UP, 1972.

Dryden, Edgar A. *The Form of American Romance.* Baltimore: The Johns Hopkins UP, 1988.

———. *Nathaniel Hawthorne: The Poetics of Enchantment.* Ithaca: Cornell UP, 1977.

Dutton, Samuel W. S. "Hawthorne and the natural style, from 'Nathaniel Hawthorne.'" *The New Englander,* January 1847, v. 56–69. In Crowley, 135–40.

Duyckinck, Evert A. From a review in the *Literary World*, viii, 26 April 1851, 334–35. In Crowley, 192–94.

———. "Hawthorne as an Established Writer, from an unsigned essay, 'Nathaniel Hawthorne.'" *The Democratic Review,* April 1845, xvi, 376–84. In Crowley, 96–100.

———. "Hawthorne's Early Work, from an unsigned essay, 'Nathaniel Hawthorne.'" *Arcturus,* May 1841, I, 330–37. In Crowley, 74–78.

———. "The Loiterer: Hawthorne's *Twice-Told Tales.*" *Arcturus* 3, no. 17 (April 1842): 394. In Idol/Jones, 59.

———. "Nathaniel Hawthorne." *Arcturus* 1, no. 6 (May 1941): 330–37. In Idol/Jones, 417–19.

———. "*The Scarlet Letter.*" *Literary World* 6, 30 March 1850, 323–25. In Idol/Jones, 121–22. In Crowley, 155–57.

Easton, Alison. *The Making of the Hawthorne Subject.* Columbia: U of Missouri P, 1996.

Elbert, Monika M. *Encoding the Letter "A": Gender and Authority in Hawthorne's Early Fiction.* Frankfurt am Main: Haag & Herchen, 1990.

———. "Hester on the Scaffold, Dimmesdale in the Closet: Hawthorne's Seven-Year Itch." *Essays in Literature* 16 (1989): 234–55.

———. "Hester's Maternity: Stigma or Weapon?" *Emerson Society Quarterly: A Journal of the American Renaissance* 36 (1990): 175–208.

Ellis, William. *The Theory of the American Romance: An Ideology in American Intellectual History.* Ann Arbor: UMI Research Press, 1989.

Erlich, Gloria C. *Family Themes and Hawthorne's Fiction: The Tenacious Web.* New Brunswick: Rutgers UP, 1984.

"*Fanshawe.*" *Boston Daily Advertiser*, 12 November 1828, 2. In Idol/Jones, 3–5.

Feidelson, Charles, Jr. *Symbolism and American Literature*. Chicago: The U of Chicago P, 1953.

Fessenden, Thomas Green. "A Valuable Book." *New England Farmer, and Gardener's Journal* 15, no. 37 (15 March 1837): 88. In Idol/Jones, 20–21.

Fields, James T. *Yesterdays with Authors*. Boston: Houghton Mifflin, 1871.

Fogle, Richard Harter. *Hawthorne's Fiction: The Light & The Dark*. 1952; rpt., Norman: U of Oklahoma P, 1964.

Foote, Caleb. "*The Scarlet Letter.*" *Salem Gazette*, 19 March 1850, 2. In Idol/Jones, 119.

"From an unsigned review." *The American Whig Review*, November 1852, xvi, 417–24. In Idol/Jones, 267–71.

Frye, Northrop. *The Anatomy of Criticism: Four Essays*. Princeton: Princeton UP, 1957.

Fuller, Randall. *Emerson's Ghosts: Literature, Politics, and the Making of Americanists*. Oxford: Oxford UP, 2007.

Gilder, Louise. *The Age of Entanglement: When Quantum Physics Was Reborn*. New York: Knopf, 2008.

Gilmore, Michael T. *American Romanticism and the Marketplace*. Chicago: The U of Chicago P, 1985.

Goddu, Teresa. *Gothic America: Narrative, History, and Nation*. New York: Columbia UP, 1997.

Gollin, Rita K. *Nathaniel Hawthorne and the Truth of Dreams*. Baton Rouge: Louisiana State UP, 1979.

———. *Portraits of Nathaniel Hawthorne: An Iconography*. DeKalb: Northern Illinois UP, 1983.

Greenwald, Elissa. *Realism and the Romance: Nathaniel Hawthorne, Henry James, and American Fiction*. Ann Arbor: UMI Research Press, 1989.

Greven, David. *Men Beyond Desire: Manhood, Sex, and Violation in American Literature*. New York: Palgrave/Macmillan, 2005.

Hale, Nathan, Jr. From a review in the *Boston Miscellany*, February 1842, I, 92. In Crowley, 79–80.

Hale, Sarah Josepha. From a review in the *Ladies' Magazine*, November 1828, I, 526–27. In Crowley, 42.

Harris, Kenneth Marc. *Hypocrisy and Self-Deception in Hawthorne's Fiction*. Charlottesville: UP of Virginia, 1988.

Hawthorne, Elizabeth Manning. "Reminiscences of My Brother from His Childhood through the 1830s." 1870–71. In Bosco/Murphy, 2–12.

Hawthorne, Hildegarde. *Romantic Rebel: The Story of Nathaniel Hawthorne*. New York: The Century Company, 1932.

Hawthorne, Julian. *Nathaniel Hawthorne and His Wife*. Boston: Houghton Mifflin, 1884.

Hawthorne, Nathaniel. *The Centenary Edition of the Works of Nathaniel Hawthorne*. Ed. William Chavat et al. 23 volumes. Columbus: Ohio State UP, 1962–97. In text as *CE*.

———. "Chiefly About War Matters by a Peaceable Man." *The Atlantic Monthly*, July 1862.

———. *Life of Franklin Pierce*. Boston: Ticknor, Reed, and Fields, 1852.

———. *Our Old Home*. Amsterdam: Fredonia Books, 2002.

———. "*Twice-Told Tales*: Preface to the 1851 Edition." 11 January 1851. *Centenary Edition* 9: 3–7. In Crowley, 226–29.

"Hawthorne as the favourite of the British, from an unsigned essay." *North British Review*, November 1853, xx, 81–99. In Crowley, 299–303.

Hazeltine, Mayo Williamson. "Some New Books." [New York] *Sun*, 24 December 1882, 2. In Idol/Jones, 397–400.

Herbert, T. Walter. *Dearest Beloved: The Hawthornes and the Making of the Middle-Class Family*. Berkeley: U of California P, 1993.

Holmes, Oliver Wendell. "Hawthorne." *Atlantic Monthly* 14, July 1864, 98–101. In Bosco/Murphy, 125–29.

Howe, Desson. "The Scarlet Letter: R." *The Washington Post*, 13 October 1995.

Howells, William Dean. Review of *Hawthorne* by Henry James. *The Atlantic Monthly*, 1880.

Hull, Raymona E. *Nathaniel Hawthorne: The English Experience, 1853–1864*. Pittsburgh: U of Pittsburgh P, 1980.

Hutner, Gordon. *Secrets and Sympathy: Forms of Disclosure in Hawthorne's Novels*. Athens: The U of Georgia P, 1988.

———. "Whose Hawthorne?" In *The Cambridge Companion to Nathaniel Hawthorne*, ed. Richard H. Millington, 251–65. Cambridge: Cambridge UP, 2004.

Hutton, Richard Holt. "Hawthorne and the Calvinist Imagination, from an unsigned essay, 'Nathaniel Hawthorne.'" *National Review*, October 1860, xi, 453–81. In Idol/Jones, 366–87.

———. "Hawthorne, the 'Ghost of New England,' from an unsigned essay, 'Nathaniel Hawthorne.'" *The Spectator*, 18 July 1864, xxxvii, 705–6. In Crowley, 407–12.

———. "Mr. Hawthorne's Last Fragment." *The Spectator* [England] 37, 17 September 1864, 1075–6. In Idol/Jones, 300–303.

———. "Nathaniel Hawthorne." *The Spectator* [England] 37, 18 July 1864, 705–6. In Idol/Jones, 439–42.

Idol, John T., and Buford Jones, Jr., eds. *Nathaniel Hawthorne: The Contemporary Reviews.* Cambridge: Cambridge UP, 1994. In text as Idol/Jones.

Idol, John T., and Melinda M. Ponder, eds. *Hawthorne and Women: Engendering and Expanding the Hawthorne Tradition.* Amherst: U of Massachusetts P, 1999.

Irwin, John T. *American Hieroglyphics: The Symbol of the Egyptian Hieroglyphics in the American Renaissance.* New Haven: Yale UP, 1980.

James, Caryn. "*The Scarlet Letter* (1995): Film Review: Passion, Nudity, Puritans, and, Oh, Yes, That Scarlet Letter 'A.'" *The New York Times,* 13 October 1995. Accessed 23 February 2011. http://movies.nytimes.com/movie/review?res=990ce7da1538f930a25753c1a963958260.

James, Henry. *Hawthorne.* 1879; rpt., Ithaca: Cornell UP, 1997.

———. "Hawthorne." A letter in commemoration of the One Hundredth Anniversary of the Birth of Nathaniel Hawthorne. 10 June 1904. Salem, MA, Essex Institute. Accessed 22 February 2011. http://www.hawthorneinsalem.org/mirror_eldritch/hj04.html.

———. "Hawthorne's French and Italian Journals." *Nation* 14, 14 March 1872, 172–73. In Idol/Jones, 355–58.

———. "Nathaniel Hawthorne." In *The Library of the World's Best Literature Ancient and Modern,* vol. 18, ed. Charles Dudley Warner, 7053–61. New York: International Society, 1897. Google Books.

Japp, Alexander P. "Nathaniel Hawthorne's Life and Writings." *London Quarterly Review* 37, October 1871, 48–78. In Idol/Jones, 482–87.

Jehlen, Myra. *American Incarnation: The Individual, the Nation, and the Continent.* Cambridge: Harvard UP, 1986.

Johnson, Claudia. *The Productive Tension of Hawthorne's Art.* University: The U of Alabama P, 1981.

Kaul, A. N., ed. *Hawthorne: A Collection of Critical Essays.* Englewood Cliffs: Prentice-Hall, 1966.

Kazin, Alfred. *An American Procession: The Major American Writers from 1830 to 1930: The Crucial Century.* New York: Knopf, 1984.

———. *God and the American Writer.* New York: Knopf, 1997.

———. "Hawthorne: The Artist of New England." *The Atlantic Monthly,* December 1966.

Kumar, Manjit. *Quantum: Einstein, Bohr, and the Great Debate about the Nature of Reality.* New York: Norton, 2010.

Lahiri, Jhumpa. *Unaccustomed Earth.* New York: Knopf, 2008.

Lathrop, George Parsons. *A Study of Hawthorne*. Boston: Houghton Mifflin, 1876.

Lathrop, Rose Hawthorne. *Memories of Hawthorne*. Boston: Houghton Mifflin, 1897.

Lawrence, D. H. *Studies in Classic American Literature*. 1923; rpt. London: Penguin, 1977.

Leggett, William. "Fanshawe." *Critic: A Weekly Review of Literature, Fine Arts, and the Drama* 1, no. 4 (22 November 1828): 53–55. In Idol/Jones, 5–7.

Leverenz, David. *Manhood and the American Renaissance*. Ithaca: Cornell UP, 1989.

Levin, Harry. *The Power of Blackness: Hawthorne, Poe, Melville*. 1958; rpt., New York: Vintage Books, 1960.

Levine, Robert S. "Antebellum Feminists on Hawthorne: Reconsidering the Reception of *The Scarlet Letter*." In *The Scarlet Letter and Other Writings*, edited by Leland S. Person, 274–90. New York: Norton, 2005.

———. *Conspiracy and Romance: Studies in Brockden Brown, Cooper, Hawthorne, and Melville*. New York: Cambridge UP, 1989.

———, ed. *The House of the Seven Gables*. New York: Norton, 2006.

Lewis, R. W. B. *The American Adam: Innocence, Tragedy, and Tradition in the Nineteenth Century*. Chicago: The U of Chicago P, 1955.

Libby, Dorville. "Hawthorne and the supernatural, from 'The Supernatural in Hawthorne." *The Overland Monthly*, February 1869, ii, 138–43. In Crowley, 453–60.

Loggins, Vernon. *The Hawthornes: The Story of Seven Generations of an American Family*. New York: Columbia UP, 1951.

Longfellow, Henry Wadsworth. From a review in the *North American Review* 45, no. 96 (July 1837): 59–73. In Crowley, 55–59.

———. Review in the *North American Review* 56 no. 119 (April 1842): 496–99. In Crowley, 80–83.

"Lori Laitman's Opera *The Scarlet Letter* World Premiere: *The Scarlet Letter*." 6 November 2008. Accessed 22 February 2011. http://newswire.scena.org/2008/08/lori-laitmans-opera-scarlet-letter.html.

Loring, George Bailey. From a review in the *Massachusetts Quarterly Review* 3, no. 12, September 1850, iii, 484–500. In Crowley, 168–75. In Idol/Jones, 133–43.

———. "Nathaniel Hawthorne." In *Papyrus Leaves*, ed. William Fearing Gill, 250–62, 266–68. New York: Worthington, 1880. In Bosco/Murphy, 187–94.

Lowell, James Russell. "Hawthorne." In "A Fable for Critics." New York: G. P. Putnam, 1848.

———. "The Marble Faun, by Nathaniel Hawthorne." *The Atlantic Monthly*, April 1860. Accessed 22 February 2011. http://www.theatlantic.com/past/docs/unbound/classrev/marblefa.htm.

Lowell, Robert. *The Old Glory.* New York: Farrar, Straus & Giroux, 1965.

Luedtke, Luther S. *Nathaniel Hawthorne and the Romance of the Orient.* Bloomington: Indiana UP, 1989.

Magee, Richard. "Food Puritanism and Food Pornography: The Gourmet Semiotics of Martha and Nigella." *Americana: The Journal of American Popular Culture 1900 to the Present* 6.2 (Fall 2007). Accessed 22 February 2011. http://www.americanpopularculture.com/journal/articles/fall_2007/magee.htm.

Maguire, Ken. "Hawthorne Joined by Kin in Final Plot." *USA Today*, 26 June 2006. Accessed 22 February 2011. http://www.usatoday.com/news/nation/2006-06-26-hawthorne-burial_x.htm.

Mailloux, Steven. *Reception Histories: Rhetoric, Pragmatism, and American Cultural Politics.* Ithaca: Cornell UP, 1998.

Male, Roy R. *Hawthorne's Tragic Vision.* New York: Norton, 1957.

Mann, Louise. E-mail to the author. 16 September 2010.

Marshall, Megan. *The Peabody Sisters: Three Women Who Ignited American Romanticism.* Boston: Houghton Mifflin, 2005.

Marx, Leo. *The Machine in the Garden: Technology and the Pastoral Idea in America.* New York: Oxford UP, 1964.

Mather, Edward. *Nathaniel Hawthorne: A Modest Man.* New York: Thomas Y. Crowell, 1940.

Matthews, Brader. *Introduction to American Literature.* New York: American Book Company, 1896.

Matthiessen, F. O. *American Renaissance: Art and Expression in the Age of Emerson and Whitman.* London: Oxford UP, 1941.

McDonnell, Claudia. "Hawthorne Dominicans Bring Remains of Founder's Mother, Sister Home." *Catholic News Service*, 29 June 2006. Accessed 23 February 2011. http://www.catholicnews.com/data/stories/cns/0603741.htm.

McFarland, Philip. *Hawthorne in Concord.* New York: Grove Press, 2004.

McWilliams, John P., Jr. *Hawthorne, Melville, and the American Character: A Looking-Glass Business.* Cambridge: Cambridge UP, 1984.

Melville, Herman. "Hawthorne and His Mosses. By a Virginian Spending His Summer in Vermont." *Literary World*, 17 and 24 August 1859, vii, 125–27, 145–47. In Crowley, 111–26. In Idol/Jones, 194–215.

Mellow, James R. *Nathaniel Hawthorne in His Times.* Boston: Houghton Mifflin, 1980.

Mieszowski, Katharine. "A Scarlet Letter for Sex Offenders?" *Broadsheet*, 6 November 2006. Accessed 23 February 2011. http://www.salon.com/ life/broadsheet/2006/11/06/shirt.

Miller, Edwin Haviland. *Salem is My Dwelling Place: A Life of Nathaniel Hawthorne*. Iowa City: U of Iowa P, 1991.

Miller, J. Hillis. *Hawthorne and History*. Cambridge: Basil Blackwell, 1991.

Miller, Louise. "*The House of the Seven Gables* as Literature for Secondary Schools." *The School Review* 17.1 (January 1909): 495–97. Google Books. Accessed 23 February 2011.

Millington, Richard H., ed. *The Cambridge Companion to Nathaniel Hawthorne*. New York: Cambridge UP, 2004.

———. *Practicing Romance: Narrative Form and Cultural Engagement*. Princeton: Princeton UP, 1992.

Mishra, Raja, and Sally Heaney. "Hawthornes to be Reunited: Wife's Remains to be Returned from UK." *The Boston Globe*, 1 June 2006. Accessed 23 February 2011. http://www.boston.com/news/local/articles/2006/ 06/01/hawthornes_to_be_reunited/.

Mitchell, Thomas R. *Hawthorne's Fuller Mystery*. Amherst: U of Massachusetts P, 1998.

Moore, Margaret B. *The Salem World of Nathaniel Hawthorne*. Columbia: U of Missouri P, 1998.

Moore, Thomas R. *A Thick and Darksome Veil: The Rhetoric of Hawthorne's Sketches, Prefaces, and Essays*. Boston: Northeastern UP, 1994.

More, Paul Elmore. "The Solitude of Nathaniel Hawthorne." *The Atlantic Monthly*, November 1901. Google Books. Accessed 22 February 2011.

Morris, Lloyd. *The Rebellious Puritan: Portrait of Mr. Hawthorne*. New York: Harcourt, Brace, 1927.

Morrison, Toni. "Blacks, Modernism, and the American South: An Interview with Toni Morrison." By Carolyn C. Denard. 1998. In *Toni Morrison Conversations*, ed. Carolyn C. Denard, 178–95. Jackson: U of Mississippi P, 2008.

———. "I Will Always Be a Writer." Interview by Jessica Harris. 1976. In *Toni Morrison Conversations*, ed. Carolyn C. Denard, 3–9. Jackson: U of Mississippi P, 2008.

Mukherjee, Baharti. *The Holder of the World*. New York: Fawcett Books, 1993.

Mumford, Lewis. *The Golden Day: A Study in American Experience and Culture*. New York: Boni and Liveright, 1926.

"Nathaniel Hawthorne." *North British Review* 49 (September 1868): 173–208. In Idol/Jones, 442–66.

"Nathaniel Hawthorne's Last Work." *London Review* 10 (September 1864): 300–1. In Idol/Jones, 298–99.

"Notices of New Books." *United States Magazine and Democratic Review*, 28 May, 1851, 478. In Idol/Jones, 164.

Newman, Lea Bertani Vozar. "One-Hundred-and-Fifty Years of Looking At, Into, Through, Behind, Beyond, and Around 'The Minister's Black Veil.'" *The Nathaniel Hawthorne Review* xiii, no. 2 (Fall 1987): 5–12.

Normand, Jean. *Nathaniel Hawthorne: An Approach to the Analysis of Artistic Creation*. Cleveland: The P of Case Western Reserve U, 1970.

Oerter, Robert. *The Theory of Almost Everything: The Standard Model, the Unsung Triumph of Modern Physics*. New York: Pi Press, 2006.

O'Malley, Sheila. "The Books: *The Scarlet Letter* (Nathaniel Hawthorne)," *The Sheila Variations*, 5 November 2007. Accessed 23 February 2011. http://www.sheilaomalley.com/?p=7212.

Parks, Suzan-Lori. *The Red Letter Plays*. New York: Theatre Communications Group, 2001.

Parrington, Vernon Louis. *The Beginnings of Critical Realism in America: 1860–1920*. Volume 3 of *Main Currents in American Thought: An Interpretation of American Literature from the Beginnings to 1920*. New York: Harcourt Brace, 1927.

———. *The Colonial Mind: 1620–1800*. Volume 1 of *Main Currents in American Thought: An Interpretation of American Literature from the Beginnings to 1920*. New York: Harcourt Brace, 1927.

———. *The Romantic Revolution in America: 1800–1860*. Volume 2 of *Main Currents in American Thought: An Interpretation of American Literature from the Beginnings to 1920*. New York: Harcourt Brace, 1927.

Pattee, Fred Lewis. *The First Century of American Literature: 1770–1870*. New York: D. Appleton-Century Company, 1935.

Peabody, Elizabeth Palmer, "Epistolary Thoughts on Hawthorne, 1838–1886" in *Letters of Elizabeth Palmer Peabody: American Renaissance Woman*, ed. Bruce A. Ronda, 199–201, 223–24, 417–21, 424–27, 430–32. Middletown, CT: Wesleyan UP, 1984. In Bosco/Murphy, 20–29.

———. "*Twice-told Tales.*" *New-Yorker* 5, no. 1/105 (24 March 1838): 1–2. In Idol/Jones, 29–34.

Pearce, Roy Harvey, ed. *Hawthorne Centenary Essays*. Columbus: Ohio State UP, 1964.

Pease, Donald E. *Visionary Compacts: American Renaissance Writings in Cultural Context*. Madison: The U of Wisconsin P, 1987.

Person, Leland S. *Aesthetic Headaches: Women and a Masculine Poetics in Poe, Melville, and Hawthorne*. Athens: U of Georgia P, 1988.

———, ed. *The Cambridge Introduction to Nathaniel Hawthorne*. New York: Cambridge UP, 2007.

———. "Nathaniel Hawthorne." *Prospects for the Study of American Literature (II)*, ed. Richard Kopley and Barbara Cantalupo, 26–49. New York: AMS Press, 2009.

———. Notes. *Time*, 22 February 1999 and 16 February 1998.

———, ed. *The Scarlet Letter and Other Writings*. New York: Norton, 2005.

Pfister, Joel. *The Production of Personal Life: Class, Gender, & the Psychological in Hawthorne's Fiction*. Stanford: Stanford UP, 1991.

Poe, Edgar Allan. "Tale-Writing — Nathaniel Hawthorne." *Godey's Magazine and Lady's Book* 35 (November 1847): 252–56. In Idol/Jones, 98–104.

———. "*Twice-told Tales*," *Graham's Magazine* 20, no. 5 (May 1842): 298–300. In Idol/Jones, 63–68.

Rands, William Brighty. "The problem of Hawthorne's ambivalence, from 'Nathaniel Hawthorne.'" *St. Paul's Magazine*, May 1871, viii, 150–61. In Crowley, 476–86.

Reed, Edward S. *From Soul to Mind: The Emergence of Psychology from Erasmus Darwin to William James*. New Haven: Yale UP, 1997.

Reynolds, David S. *Beneath the American Renaissance: The Subversive Imagination in the Age of Emerson and Melville*. New York: Knopf, 1988.

Reynolds, Larry J. *Devils and Rebels: The Making of Hawthorne's Damned Politics*. Ann Arbor: The U of Michigan P, 2008.

———. *European Revolutions and the American Literary Renaissance*. New Haven: Yale UP, 1988.

———, ed. *A Historical Guide to Nathaniel Hawthorne*. New York: Oxford UP, 2001.

Riley, Katherine. Book Group Coordinator, The Bay School of San Francisco. Letter to the author, 28 February 2006.

Riss, Arthur. *Race, Slavery, and Liberalism in Nineteenth-Century American Literature*. Cambridge: Cambridge UP, 2006.

Rosen, David. "The Scarlet Hypocrites: Republicans, Christians and the All-American Politics of Adultery." Accessed 25 April 2008. *Counterpunch*, 17 November 2007. http://counterpunch.org.

Roth, Philip. *The Human Stain*. Boston: Houghton Mifflin, 2000.

Rourke, Bryan. "*Scarlet Letter* Reminds that Times Haven't Really Changed That Much." *The Providence Journal*, 7 May 2009, D5.

Rowe, John Carlos. *Through the Custom-House: Nineteenth-Century American Fiction and Modern Theory*. Baltimore: The Johns Hopkins UP, 1982.

Roy, Ayon. "Hegel contra Schlegel: Kierkegaard contra deMan." *PMLA* 124, no. 1 (January 2009): 107–26.

Sanborn, Franklin B. "Nathaniel Hawthorne. Conversation about the Author of 'The Scarlet Letter'. His Friends Tell the Story of His Life Anew. Fresh

Facts about the Great Romancer." *Boston Herald* 5, 1 August 1880, 1–3. In Bosco/Murphy, 196–206.

Schiff, James. *Updike's Version: Rewriting* The Scarlet Letter. Columbia: U of Missouri P, 1992.

"'Sir Nathaniel': Hawthorne and the Delineation of the Abnormal, from 'American Authorship.'" *The New Monthly Magazine*, June 1853, xcviii, 202–12. In Crowley, 292–98.

Smith, Henry Nash. *Virgin Land: The American West as Symbol and Myth.* Cambridge, MA: Harvard UP, 1950.

Stanton, Theodore, ed. *A Manual of American Literature.* Leipzig: Bernhard Tauchnitz, 1909.

Stern, Milton R. *Contexts for Hawthorne: The Marble Faun and the Politics of Openness and Closure in American Literature.* Urbana: U of Illinois P, 1991.

Stearns, Frank Preston. *The Life and Genius of Nathaniel Hawthorne.* Boston: Houghton Mifflin, 1906. Google Books. Accessed 23 February 2011.

Stewart, Randall. *Nathaniel Hawthorne.* New Haven: Yale UP, 1948.

Stoddard, Richard Henry. "The biographical interest, from an unsigned essay, 'Nathaniel Hawthorne.'" *The National Magazine*, January 1853, ii, 17–24. In Crowley, 286–91.

Stoehr, Taylor. *Hawthorne's Mad Scientists: Pseudoscience and Social Science in Nineteenth-Century Life and Letters.* Hamden, CT: Archon Books, 1978.

Stokes, Claudia. *Writers in Retrospect: The Rise of American Literary History, 1875–1910.* Chapel Hill: The U of North Carolina P, 2006.

Stubbs, John Caldwell. *The Pursuit of Form: A Study of Hawthorne and the Romance.* Urbana: U of Illinois P, 1970.

Sutherland, Judith L. *The Problematic Fictions of Poe, James & Hawthorne.* Columbia: U of Missouri P, 1984.

Swann, Charles. *Nathaniel Hawthorne: Tradition and Revolution.* New York: Cambridge UP, 1991.

Swisshelm, Jane. "The Scarlet Letter." *The Saturday Visitor*, 24 November 1849, 2.

Talese, Gay. "A Life in Books: My Five Most Important Books." *Newsweek*, 29, January 2007, 16.

Tanner, Laura E. "Speaking with 'Hands at Our Throats': The Struggle for Artistic Voice in *The Blithedale Romance.*" *Studies in American Fiction 21* (1993): 1–19.

Thompson, G. R., and Eric Carl Link. *Neutral Ground: New Traditionalism and the American Romance Controversy.* Baton Rouge: Louisiana State UP, 1999.

Thompson, G. R., and Virgil L. Lokke, eds. *Ruined Eden of the Present: Hawthorne, Melville, Poe.* West Lafayette: Purdue UP, 1981.

Tompkins, Jane. *Sensational Designs: The Cultural Work of American Fiction: 1790–1860.* New York: Oxford UP, 1985.

Trilling, Lionel. *The Liberal Imagination: Essays on Literature and Society.* New York: Doubleday Anchor, 1950.

———. "Our Hawthorne." In *Hawthorne Centenary Essays,* ed. Roy Harvey Pearce, 429–58.

Trollope, Anthony. "The Genius of Nathaniel Hawthorne." *North American Review* 129, no. 274 (September 1879): 203–23. In Idol/Jones, 499–513.

Tuckerman, Henry T. Hawthorne as a psychological novelist from "Nathaniel Hawthorne." *Southern Literary Messenger,* xvii, June 1851, 344–49. In Crowley, 210–18.

Turner, Arlin. *Nathaniel Hawthorne: A Biography.* New York: Oxford UP, 1980.

Tyler, Moses Coit. *A History of American Literature.* New York: G. P. Putnam's Sons, 1878.

Ullen, Magnus. *The Half-Vanished Structure: Hawthorne's Allegorical Dialectics.* Uppsala University, Sweden, 2001.

Updike, John. *A Month of Sundays.* New York: Knopf, 1975.

———. *Roger's Version.* New York: Knopf, 1986.

———. *S.* New York: Knopf, 1988.

Valenti, Patricia Dunlavy. *Sophia Peabody Hawthorne: A Life, vol. 1, 1809–1847.* Columbia, MO: The U of Missouri P, 2004.

———. *To Myself a Stranger: A Biography of Rose Hawthorne Lathrop.* Baton Rouge: Louisiana UP, 1991.

Van Doren, Carl. "Nathaniel Hawthorne: Chapter Four." In *The American Novel.* New York: Macmillan, 1921.

Van Doren, Mark. *Nathaniel Hawthorne.* Westport, CT: Greenwood Press, 1949.

Wagenknecht, Edward. *Nathaniel Hawthorne Man and Writer.* New York: Oxford UP, 1961.

Waggoner, Hyatt H. *Hawthorne: A Critical Study.* 1953; rpt., Cambridge: Belknap Press, 1963.

———. *The Presence of Hawthorne.* Baton Rouge: Louisiana State UP, 1979.

Walker, Pierre A. "Why We Still Read Hawthorne 150 Years Later." February 2010. Accessed 23 February 2011. http://www.hawthorneinsalem.org/ScholarsForum/MMD2004.html.

"Web English Teacher: Nathaniel Hawthorne: Lesson Plans for *The Scarlet Letter* and Other Works." Accessed 23 February 2011. http://www.webenglishteacher.com/hawthorne.html.

Webber, Charles Wilkins. "Hawthorne." *American Whig Review* 4 (September 1846): 296–316. In Idol/Jones, 79–93.

Weinauer, Ellen. "Considering Possession in *The Scarlet Letter.*" *Studies in American Fiction* 29 (2001): 93–112.

Weinstein, Arnold. *Nobody's Home: Speech, Self, and Place in American Fiction from Hawthorne to DeLillo.* New York: Oxford UP, 1993.

Weinstein, Philip M. *Faulkner's Subject: A Cosmos No One Owns.* Cambridge: Cambridge UP, 1992.

Weldon, Roberta. *Hawthorne, Gender, and Death: Christianity and Its Discontents.* New York: Palgrave Macmillan, 2008.

Wendell, Barrett. *The Mystery of Education and Other Academic Performances.* New York: C. Scribner's Sons, 1909.

West, Peter. *The Arbiters of Reality: Hawthorne, Melville, and the Rise of Mass Information Culture.* Columbus: The Ohio State UP, 2008.

Whipple, E. P. From an unsigned review in the *American Whig Review*, xvi, November 1852. In Crowley, 267.

———. "His Final Assessment of Hawthorne, from an unsigned essay, 'Nathaniel Hawthorne.'" *The Atlantic Monthly*, May 1860, v, 641–22. In Crowley, 340–51.

———. "Review of New Books," *Graham's Magazine* 36, no. 5 (May 1850): 345–46. In Idol/Jones, 124.

Whitaker, Sandra. "Engaging Urban Learners in Reading *The Scarlet Letter.*" *The English Journal* 96, no. 6 (July 2007).

Whitcomb, Selden L. *Chronological Outline of American Literature.* New York: Macmilan, 1894.

Wineapple, Brenda. *Hawthorne: A Life.* New York: Knopf, 2003.

———. "Nathaniel Hawthorne, Writer; or The Fleeing of the Biographied." In *Hawthorne and the Real: Bicentennial Essays,* ed. Millicent Bell, 181–98. Columbus: Ohio State UP, 2005.

———. "*The Scarlet Letter* and Nathaniel Hawthorne's America." *History Now* 16 (June 2008). Accessed 23 February 2011. http://www.gilderlehrman.org/historynow/06_2008/historian.php.

Winters, Yvor. *In Defense of Reason.* Athens, OH: Swallow Press, 1987.

Woodberry, George E. *Nathaniel Hawthorne.* American Men of Letters. Boston: Houghton Mifflin, 1902.

"Writings of Nathaniel Hawthorne." *Southern Review*, n.s. 7 (April 1870): 328–54. In Idol/Jones, 470–82.

Yellin, Jean Fagan. "Hawthorne and the American National Sin." In *The Green American Tradition*, ed. H. Daniel Peck, 75–97. Baton Rouge: Louisiana State UP, 1989.

Young, Philip. *Hawthorne's Secret: An Un-Told Tale*. Boston: David R. Godine, 1984.

Zezima, Katie. "Historic Literary Couple are Reunited After 142-Year Separation." *The New York Times*, 27 June 2006. Accessed 23 February 2011. http://www.nytimes.com/2006/06/27/us/27hawthorne.html?_r=1&ref=nathanielhawthorne.

Ziff, Larzer. *Literary Democracy: The Declaration of Cultural Independence in America*. New York: The Viking Press, 1981.

Index